QUIET FLOWS THE RHINE

GERMAN GENERAL OFFICER CASUALTIES IN WORLD WAR II

By French L. MacLean

J.J. Fedorowicz Publishing

i

QUIET FLOWS THE RHINE
GERMAN GENERAL OFFICER CASUALTIES IN WORLD WAR II

By French L. MacLean

Copyright 1996 by
J.J. Fedorowicz Publishing

Published by
J.J. Fedorowicz Publishing Inc.
106 Browning Blvd.
Winnipeg, Manitoba
Canada R3K 0L7
(204) 837-6080

Printed in the USA
ISBN 0-921991-32-0

Typesetting by George R. Bradford
Printed by Publishers Press

PUBLISHER'S ACKNOWLEDGEMENTS

We wish to thank everyone who has contributed to the publishing of this book.

Signing Box by George Bradford

We also wish to thank you the reader for purchasing this book, and all those of you who have purchased our other books, and have written us with your kind words of praise and encouragement. It gives us impetus to continue to publish translations of the best German books and specially commissioned books, as you can see by the additional books which are in preparation for publication in the near future. Other titles are either being negotiated or seriously contemplated, many as a result of your helpful proposals.

John Fedorowicz & Michael Olive

Books published by J.J. Fedorowicz Publishing
THE LEIBSTANDARTE (1 SS Panzer Division) volumes I, II, III and IV/1
EUROPEAN VOLUNTEERS (5 SS Panzer Division)
DAS REICH I (2 SS Panzer Division) volumes I and II
THE HISTORY OF PANZERKORPS GROSSDEUTSCHLAND, volumes 1 and 2
OTTO WEIDINGER
OTTO KUMM
MANHAY, THE ARDENNES; CHRISTMAS 1944
ARMOR BATTLES OF THE WAFFEN-SS 1943-45
TIGER: THE HISTORY OF A LEGENDARY WEAPON 1942-45
HITLER MOVES EAST
TIGERS IN THE MUD
PANZER ACES
FOOTSTEPS OF THE HUNTER
HISTORY OF THE 12 SS PANZERDIVISION HITLERJUGEND
GRENADIERS (Kurt Meyer)
FIELD UNIFORMS OF THE GERMAN ARMY PANZER FORCES IN WW2
TIGERS IN COMBAT I
INFANTERIE ACES
FREINEUX AND LAMORMENIL – THE ARDENNES
THE CAUCASUS AND THE OIL
EAST FRONT DRAMA – 1944
HISTORY OF THE PANZERKORPS HERMANN GÖRING
MICHAEL WITTMANN AND THE TIGER COMMANDERS OF THE LEIBSTANDARTE
THE WESTERN FRONT 1944: MEMOIRS OF A PANZER LEHR OFFICER
LUFTWAFFE ACES
QUIET FLOWS THE RHINE

In preparation for publication
THE BRANDENBURGERS – GLOBAL MISSION
LEIBSTANDARTE IV/2
SS-POLIZEI: HISTORY OF THE 4SS PANZERGRENADIER DIVISION, Vols. 1 & 2

J.J. Fedorowicz Publishing Inc.

TABLE OF CONTENTS

DEDICATION

I would like to take this opportunity to thank the archivists at the Bundesarchiv Militärarchiv at both Freiburg and Koblenz of the Federal Republic of Germany, the Combined Arms Research Library and many of the professors at the Combat Studies Institute, Fort Leavenworth, to include Dr. Robert Baumann, Dr. Sam Lewis, Mr. John Reichley, and Dr. Roger Spiller. At Fort Benning, Georgia Sergeant Major Nicklaus provided expert assistance whenever a translation proved too difficult.

From Germany, Dr. Dermot Bradley and Oberst i.G. von Recum provided many valuable insights from their own massive research endeavors. Oberst a.D. Martin Steglich, Generalleutnant a.D. Heinz-Georg Lemm and the Association of Knight's Cross winners provided many first person observations concerning many general officers that have never before been published. Through both of these excellent soldiers and fine gentlemen history came alive for me.

Dr. Thomas Veve, one of my oldest friends, played a major role, nurturing my interest in history when we were lieutenants together in Germany, and providing a critical eye during the final stages of writing this manuscript. Finally, I would particularly like to thank my wife Olga, for seven years of patience and understanding, and our dog Max for not eating any of my research.

Author (right) with Martin Steglich.
(Author photo)

This work does not seek to glorify the German generals, their deaths or the system they fought for; it merely attempts to describe the events as they happened. For if war is perceived to be personally hazardous, and even lethal, for the military and political leaders themselves, as well as for the common foot soldier, perhaps we will all think before we choose to begin one.

CREDITS

All photographs shown in this work, unless otherwise specified, are from the Bundesarchive-Militärarchiv at Koblenz, the Federal Republic of Germany. Some of the photographs may be disturbing – war usually is. Maps in the book were created using the Broderbund Company's *PC Globe: Maps 'N' Facts* computer program.

"The cover of the tomb is closing upon us."
(German officer at Stalingrad)

PREFACE

I wrote this book because no one else did. For the last thirty years I have been fascinated by World War II; and if the truth were known perhaps nine of every ten books I read are on some aspect of that conflict – and I read a lot.

My father, as did the fathers of my boyhood friends, fought in the war; in his case against the German Army as an infantryman with the 9th Infantry Division. He was wounded three times and fought in such monumental struggles as the Hürtgen Forest and the Battle of the Bulge. It seemed quite natural then to read about his wartime enemy; and I quickly became hooked on the exploits of Field Marshal Rommel in North Africa and Colonel General Guderian in his work with Germany's panzer forces.

Reading led to visiting Germany and the European battlefields to see the remnants of history – and during my service in the U.S. Army my wife and I spent three tours of duty, almost eleven years, in the Federal Republic. My interest continued and I met numerous German Army veterans and gained their insights into the war. During our discussions, and my continued studies, I became amazed at the number of German general officer casualties during the war. Equally as interesting was the paucity of details concerning the demise of many of these men. Extensive searches at the German Army Archives and at the U.S. Army Combined Arms Center at Fort Leavenworth uncovered more information.

After several years, I feel the hunt has finally progressed to the stage that enables the writing of this book. As the reader will notice, some details concerning the deaths of several of these men still remain hidden. Part of this stems from the separation of official German records after the war between the victorious Allies. It is my opinion that we really don't know what historical documentation we have in total because much remains buried in different state archives. Additionally, and unfortunately, veteran eyewitnesses get fewer with each passing year, hindering first person accounts. Finally, the defeat of Germany was total, and many units simply lost the capability to record events for posterity as the war drew to a close. The alternative though would be to never write the book until one hundred percent of the information was known – and that might take decades, or more likely never be completed. War is a confusing affair and perhaps the best historians can do is to get the general flavor of the events rather then actually taste each and every course, not to mention ingredient.

✠ CHAPTER 1 ✠

You are talking to dead men.

(General Friedrich Paulus, commander of the surrounded German 6th Army) [1]

World War II was the most devastating war in all of history. Millions of soldiers of both sides were killed in action; tens of millions of civilians were also either deliberately or inadvertently killed as well. Most military casualties were suffered by lower ranking enlisted personnel, frequently simple, but courageous infantry soldiers.

However, many general officers died as well. Direct combat, illness, suicide, executions and accidents claimed leaders from every combatant nation. But in no country were these losses as large, or their impact severe as in Germany where over 600 died. This work will primarily examine the approximately 150 division, corps and army commanders who were killed in action or died of wounds received in action. Some, who died in front-line related accidents will also be examined as will some general officer suicides that occurred at the front as well.

Hitler proved almost as lethal an employer as the Allies were an enemy – twenty German generals were executed by the Nazi regime for real or perceived threats, while many more committed suicide in Germany, such as Erwin Rommel. Their demise is well covered in numerous works, and are not a major portion of this book. Neither are most of the deaths by "natural causes". Many German generals were no longer young men and thus were susceptible to the illnesses and ultimate deaths that we all are. To be sure, the harsh environmental conditions in many theaters, primarily the Eastern Front, aggravated health problems to often fatal levels. But weather was a product of nature, and not even the centralized state of Josef Stalin could control it as a weapon.

Many aspects of the German war machine were revolutionary in concept, equipment and scope – and were truly 20th century in characteristics. However, German general officer casualties seemed almost a throwback to earlier warfare; where combat commanders led and often died in the most forward of battle formations. And equally as often it seems as if these significant losses were almost self-inflicted – German Army doctrine demanded that senior leaders be forward with the troops; many general officers were in actuality products of the First World War, and the officer rotation system frequently sent general officer replacements into action with inadequate survival training.

World War I - Harbinger of Danger

During the Great War overall German military losses were calculated at 1,808,546 dead and 4,247,143 wounded. Sixty-three German general officers during the Great War either died on the field of battle or succumbed later to the effects of their wounds. Considering the duration of over four years and the immense scope of the conflict, these numbers of themselves should have signaled no great alarm as the German Army prepared for the next war. However, twenty-nine of these fatalities occurred during the first six months of the conflict – that period of relatively mobile warfare before the hostilities stalemated into stagnant trench warfare. This was a period when general officers were constantly moving; visiting the advancing units at the front and conducting personal reconnaissance. Additionally, this was the "break-in" period for officers transitioning from a peacetime mentality to that of wartime. Tactics and leadership techniques that were felt to be successful before the war were often less than perfect once the shooting started – and often a single leadership miscalculation on the part of a general officer could result in his death or serious injury.

This perhaps should have indicated to the Germans that the warfare they were planning for World War II, the *blitzkrieg*, would also place general officers at greater risk during even more mobile battles than in World War I. It did, and more than twice as many generals died as a result; but the German general officer assignment and education systems never adequately adapted.

World War II – The Firestorm

German general officer casualties in World War II were truly staggering and adversely affected unit proficiency. Due to these losses, divisions were often commanded by colonels, which forced regiments to be commanded by majors, and battalions by captains. This, in turn, caused a severe loss in the constancy of command and control of many ground formations – which ultimately resulted in many lost opportunities at the tactical-level . Officer losses also significantly degraded morale, both at the front and back in the Fatherland. Retired General Josef Folttmann, a former World War II division commander and leading expert on German officer fatalities, presents the following summary of these losses for Army leaders:

Army General Officer Casualties		
(by type)		
Killed in Action/Died of Wounds		223
Accidental Deaths		30
Suicides		64
Executed	(By Germany during WWII)	20
	(By Allies after WWII)	33
Died	(In Prisoner of War Camps)	128
	(Of Health Problems)	145
Missing in Action		32
Total Losses		**675**

The Germans themselves realized the enormity of these losses but seemed powerless to remedy the situation. The devastating effects can best be seen in the words of the senior German leaders themselves. The following is an extract from a situation report written by the chief of staff for the 4th Army during the Battle for White Russia, June 1944:

> *The large gap on 3 Pz Army's right leads one to suppose that there is no way of stopping an advance on Minsk by strong enemy forces ... Losses among commanders are horrifying. XXXIX Panzer Corps, for instance, lost three corps commanders within 24 hours. Only a few formations are still firmly under their commanders' control.* [3]

Peak unit proficiency simply could not be maintained with these losses. Over the course of the war this drain on leadership averaged a corps commander killed every three months and a division commander killed in action every three weeks! Although World War II was a very lethal war, could this problem have been minimized? An examination of German doctrine, general officer training, battlefield experience, and command rotation suggest it could have been.

This work will focus on those general officers who were in command of divisions, corps or armies, and who were killed in action (KIA), died of wounds (DOW) or committed suicide (S) in the face of the enemy. Some 148 of these officers from the Army fall into this category. A further sixteen Waffen-SS senior commanders were also killed in action, as were three Luftwaffe commanders.

Additionally, several colonels, who were killed while in temporary command of divisions, were posthumously promoted to the general ranks and are mentioned as well in this history, as are several general officers who committed suicide in combat situations. The extent of damage to the German command and control system by these losses is reflected in the following two tables:

General Officer Commander Casualties
(by grade)

GRADE	KILLED
Field Marshal	1
Colonel General	1
Lieutenant General	25
Major General	67
Brigadier General	74
Total Losses	**168**

General Officer Commander Casualties
(by position)

GRADE	KILLED
Army Group Commanders	1
Army Commanders	3
Corps Commanders	30
Division Commanders	134
Total Losses	**168**

Central to a thorough understanding of these factors is a review of the system of general officer ranks and their equivalent American counterparts, as the German ranks will be used throughout the book. The basic rank system is shown below. Waffen-SS ranks will be discussed later: [5]

General Officer Grades

German Grade	Abbreviation	English Translation
Generalfeldmarschall	GFM	Field Marshal
Generaloberst	GO	Colonel General
General der Infanterie	GdI	General of Infantry
General der Artillerie	GdA	General of Artillery
General der Panzer	GdPz	General of Panzers
General der Pionier	GdPi	General of Engineers
General der Gebirgstruppe	GdGebTr	General of Mountain Troops
General der Kavallerie	GdKav	General of Cavalry
Generalleutnant	GL	Lieutenant General
Generalmajor	GM	Major General

A German *generalmajor* was equivalent to an American brigadier general ⋆, a *generalleutnant* was equal to a U.S. major general ⋆⋆, and a *general der infanterie*, etc., was the same as an American lieutenant general ⋆⋆⋆. The German ranks of *generaloberst* was roughly equivalent to an American general ⋆⋆⋆⋆, while a *generalfeldmarschall* could be equated to a general of the army ⋆⋆⋆⋆⋆.

The German officer rank system was a well-organized hierarchy of command – it had to be, for it controlled an extremely large and lethal organization. [6]

CHAPTER NOTES

[1] Walter Görlitz, *Paulus and Stalingrad*, New York: The Citadel Press, 1963, p. 264.

[2] Josef Foltmann and Hanns Möller, *Opfergang der Generale*, Berlin: Berard & Gräfe, 1959, p. 85. Foltmann served as the division commander for the 164th Light Division, the 338th Infantry Division, and Fortress Division Crete. He finished the war on the Army High Command Staff in Berlin. Their work has been a standard starting point for any discussion on German general officer fatalities during the war – from those killed in action to those executed for anti-Nazi activities. As the work attempts to cover all deaths in all services, details are generally few and most often kimited to date of death and location. Additionally, much information concerning those generals killed in action was not available to scholars in the 1950s when the book was written; consequently, many generals listed as missing in action in the book were in fact still prisoners of war at the time in Russia.

[3] Gerd Niepold, *The Battle for White Russia: The Destruction of Army Group Center, June 1944*, London: Brassey's Defense Publishers, 1987, pp. 167-168.

[4] Wolf Keilig, *Die Generale des Heeres*, Friedberg, FRG: Podzun-Pallas-Verlag, 1983. This work contains short biographical sketches for all general officers in the German Army (but not Luftwaffe or Waffen-SS). Although date and general location of fate are given, no information is provided as to cause of death. Printed in 1983, the book is basically a reprint of Volume 3 of Keilig's earlier work *Das Deutsche Heer* – printed in 1953 before many archives were open to the public.

[5] Brigadier General statistics for the chart include colonels who were in command.

[6] In comparison to Germany, Amercan losses in World War II, although significant, were far less. Approximately 210,300 U.S. soldiers were killed in action (including deaths among prisoners of war), 26,700 personnel died of wounds, 21,800 were killed in aircraft accidents, 22,000 died in other accidents, 14,200 succumbed to disease and 7,100 were classified as homicides, suicides, executions and drownings. This compares to previous U.S. losses in World War I of 37,500 killed in action, 13,600 died of wounds, 51,400 falling to disease, and 4,400 dying of other injuries. Source: Gilbert W. Beebe and Michael E. De Bakey, *Battle Casualties: Incidence, Mortality and Logistic Considerations*, Springfield, IL: Charles C. Thomas, 1952.

✠ CHAPTER 2 ✠
THE GERMAN ARMY
ORGANIZATION AND COMMAND STRUCTURE

The German Army in World War II was an extremely large, multifaceted organization which conducted operations on two continents. Personnel strength numbered in the millions. The Army was divided into two major sub organizations, the Field Army and the Replacement Army. The Field Army conducted actual combat operations and foreign garrison missions while the Replacement Army provided individual and unit replacements to the Field Army, and assisted in routine military functions back in Germany. Soldiers could rotate between the two – trained in Germany with the Replacement Army – sent to the front to fight in the Field Army – and perhaps wounded to such a degree which required evacuation to less strenuous duties in Germany, again as part of the Replacement Army. Personnel figures through the war for both are shown on the following chart:

	Army Strength (in millions)					
	June 1940	**June 1941**	**June 1941**	**June 1943**	**June 1944**	**December 1944**
Field Army	3.7	3.8	4.1	4.5	4.0	3.8
Replacement Army	.9	1.2	1.9	1.8	2.3	2.6
TOTAL	**4.8**	**5.0**	**6.0**	**6.3**	**6.3**	**6.4**

To control this large force the Germans developed several echelons of command. The highest field command was the army group. Eighteen army groups were created during the war with the mission to control two to four armies in a single theater of operations for a single campaign. Most army groups were designated by letter or name (Army Group A or Army Group South) and were commanded by a *generalfeldmarschall*. [2]

Immediately subordinate to the army groups were the armies. An army was a more permanent command and was not formed for just a specific campaign. Twenty-seven armies were established between 1939 and 1945, with each army directing two to six corps. Armies were numbered (1st Army, 2nd Panzer Army, etc.) An army could be commanded by a *generalfeldmarschall,* a *generaloberst*, or a *general der infanterie, panzer, artillerie*, etc. [3]

The ninety-three corps directed the activities of between two and six divisions and could be commanded by a *general der infanterie*, etc., *generalleutnant,* or *generalmajor.* Corps were designated by Roman numeral (II Army Corps, XXIV Panzer Corps). It may be useful here to explain the origins of the branch grades, as these are somewhat unique to the German military system.

The grade *General der Infanterie* started during the Thirty Years War as the term *"General uber das Fussvolck"* or General of the Foot People, and continued throughout Prussian military history. During the Third Reich, 174 generals (52.1%) of the overall *Generäle* grade were of the Infantry.[4] Also started at this period was the grade of *General der Kavallerie*, known then as *"General uber die Reuterey"* or General of the Riders. It too continued to the twentieth century with 18 generals (5.3%) during the 1933-1945 period. With the advent of the panzer forces, the cavalry initially fell under the purview of Mobile Troops with the Panzer branch. Strangely enough, in 1943 this affiliation was switched to the Infantry![4]

The last of the traditional grades was that of *General der Artillerie*. Although this grade also sprang from the Thirty Years War, prior to 1889 the grade was closely associated with the Cavalry, divided into fortress artillery and foot artillery. That year the branch totally separated and quickly rose in prominence. In World War I three artillerymen commanded armies while in WWII fully 6 of 19 *Generalfeldmarschall* were of this branch. Within the Generäle rank, 71 (21.3%) were of the Artillery.[6] The grade of *General der Panzertruppen* was created October 29, 1935. Forty-seven (14.1%) general officers held this grade, 23 drawn from the Cavalry, 14 from the Artillery and 6 from the Infantry. Four generals "home grown" during the war from the Panzer branch itself.[7] The grade of *General der Gebirgstruppe* was first used in 1941. This grade was not part of a separate branch but rather a form of specialized infantry. Seventeen officers (5.1%) achieved this grade with 12 being from the Infantry, 2 from Artillery, 2 from Engineer, and 1 from the Signal branch.[8] Five officers (1.5%) held the grade of *General der Pionier*. This grade also was created in October 1935 and was known as one of the technical branch grades, that of Engineer. The first officer to achieve this grade did so in 1938.[9]

In examining the three hundred men who ultimately served as corps commanders in more detail, we find them to generally be experienced officers of approximately 50-57 years of age. About twenty-three percent were members of the nobility, and most were career soldiers with uninterrupted service from World War I. Concerning branch affiliation, 52% were infantry officers, 19% artillery and 16% panzer. Almost 50% of corps commanders were General Staff officers with many having staff experience as division operations officers and corps chiefs of staff. Over 89% had been previous division commanders, mostly of infantry divisions. Fifty-one corps commanders previously commanded panzer divisions. In examining the panzer corps, thirty-six (40.9% of the total) had previously commanded panzer divisions. Of every three panzer division commanders who later commanded at the corps level, two wound up commanding panzer corps while one would command a corps of a different type. When an individual proved he could successfully command division-size mobile forces, he was quite likely to be retained by GO Guderian and the panzer branch of service for further panzer corps command, rather than be transferred to other types of formations.

The lowest general officer commands were the divisions, and there were a lot of them. Within the Army, division strength peaked in June 1944 at 283. These divisions were of several types and included *infanterie* (infantry), *jäger* (light infantry), *gebirgs* (mountain), *panzer* (armored), *panzergrenadier* (armored infantry), *festung* (fortress or static infantry), and *kavallerie* (cavalry).[10] In addition, the Waffen-SS and Luftwaffe provided ground divisions for combat. The Waffen-SS fielded the same types of divisions as the army. The Luftwaffe featured *fallschirmjäger* (parachute or airborne), *feld* (field or infantry), *flak* (anti-aircraft), and panzer divisions. Divisions were commanded by a *generalleutnant* or *generalmajor*. When casualties or other wartime emergencies occurred, divisions could often be commanded by an *oberst* (colonel).[11] All divisions used Arabic numeral designations (i.e., 1st Infantry Division) and sometimes a name (i.e., *"Das Reich"*).

Over two thousand German officers achieved general officer grade from 1933-1945. Nineteen officers served in the rank of *generalfeldmarschall*, 38 as *generaloberst*, 334 as *generale* (all types), 795 as *generalleutnant* and 1158 as *generalmajor*. These men served at the pinnacle of an officer corps unique in military history. One of the "patron saints" of the 20th Century German Army was former Chief of Staff Helmut von Moltke.[12] Von Moltke considered officership an elite function derived more from an individual's character rather than intellect. This trait of character was seen as the ability for an individual to make a difficult decision, often under pressure, and then stick with this decision and follow through with its execution. Such character could not truly be developed in an individual. Rather, the officer possessing such character would be recognized and hopefully be pushed upward to positions of greater responsibility.[13]

OFFICER SELECTION

Many of the general officers killed in action in World War II entered the service before 1914. Prior to World War I an individual could become an officer by attending one of the ten cadet schools or by applying directly to a regimental commander. The highest graduates of these schools received "automatic" commissions; the remainder took a recommissioning examination to validate their performance. Applicants were evaluated for responsibility, willpower, and character. Education factors were considered secondary, with the most significant element of education being the *Abitur*, a diploma recognizing nine years of primary and secondary education, granting the recipient the right to enter a university. The important education of the potential officer would actually occur during extensive training within the regiment. After some one and one-half to two years of this enlisted service, the regimental candidate received his long awaited commission within the regiment. The state of Bavaria demanded the candidate possess the *Abitur* while by 1910 some 6% of all Prussian cadets had earned one. Long-term implications for the Abitur were even more significant as acceptance for General Staff training depended on it.[14]

During World War I the huge demands for officers caused a dilution in the character and educational standards of officer candidates. Casualties increased while replacements were drawn from older reservists and inexperienced young officers. Beginning in 1916 the Supreme Headquarters began to withdraw members of the "old officer corps" from the front lines to General Staff service in an attempt to prevent the total destruction of the traditional officer corps.[15]

After the conflict, selection again became difficult. Under the provisions of the Treaty of Versailles, the post war Reichswehr was reduced to 4,000 officers of whom 3,000 were wartime officers and 1,000 were promoted non commissioned officers. Outside candidates were expected to have an extensive pre university education level. The Abitur was desired but not required. In its place, the candidate could take special equivalent examinations, a system which assisted enlisted candidates lacking in formal education.[16]

The selection process for Eduard Zorn, later killed in action in World War II while commanding the 189th Infantry Division as an *oberst*, was a typical one and worthy of review. Late in 1920 Zorn applied in writing to the commander of Infantry Regiment 19, *Oberst* Ritter von Haack, for admission for officer training. In his application Zorn included information on: date of birth, state affiliation, religion, level of education, profession of father and personal history. In addition, he furnished two letters of recommendation from prominent citizens in his community. During the ensuing background investigation, Zorn underwent a physical aptitude and medical test. With these complete, he participated in a three day personal interview with *Oberst* von Haack and selected members of the regimental staff. The results of this process reflect Zorn's aptitude for service. He was a candidate for the *Abitur* which fulfilled educational requirements. His character was exemplary as he was the son of an officer killed in action during World War I. Additionally, his brother Hans (who also was later killed in action as a general in WWII) was already a junior officer in the regiment and had an excellent service record himself. In sum, Eduard Zorn was intelligent, physically fit, motivated and apolitical.[17]

It can be seen that the environment through which the future division, corps and army commanders entered service fostered candidates with all around excellent character rather than more educated technically oriented individuals. Character was often additionally judged by the status of family influence and wealth, but this was about to dramatically change.

During the 1930s the German Army dramatically increased in size during remilitarization. Prior to 1933, German rearmament was limited by the provisions of the Treaty of Versailles. After Hitler assumed power in January 1933, military expansion plans were begun in secret. The initial plan, drawn up by the *Truppenamt* – the ghost General Staff, called for a 500,000 man force manning 21 divisions. In 1935 secrecy was dropped and an even more ambitious target was envisioned, 36 divisions and the reinstitution of military conscription. The High Command was not completely comfortable with these plans as they felt such a rapid increase might dilute the quality of officer and non commissioned officer ranks. This uneasiness was compounded by what actually transpired which was an increase from 31 divisions to 103 divisions from 1935 to 1939.

This expansion directly effected the Officer Corps – many members of which thought the "old officer corps" was so diluted it had almost ceased to exist, and would be unready for impending war. There is some validity to this belief. In 1938 for example, the Army expanded by 7,600 officers: 2,000 recruits, 2,500 lateral transfers from the police, 1,500 Non-Commissioned Officer promotions, 1,800 reactivations from inactive service, and 1,600 Austrian officers incorporated into the Wehrmacht.[18]

During the mid 1930s many officers rejoined the *Reichswehr* from the *Polizei* (Police). As an inducement, these men retained their former Police rank ranging from *hauptmann* (captain) to generalmajor. Professional competence of most officers who did not remain in the Army after World War I was often not held in high regard. Günther Blumentritt, a former army group chief of staff and commander of the 1st Parachute Army in 1945, stated that the performances of officers who retired in 1919 and rejoined during the mid 1930s, as was the case for many officers transferring from the Police, was lower as these officers still believed in obsolete First World War experiences.[19] Despite Blumentritt's comments, twenty eight generals who returned to the Army in the mid-1930s from the Police achieved corps command, while numerous others commanded divisions. Most were absorbed in the infantry. Five later commanded at the army or army group level, representing 18% of all corps commanders with Police backgrounds. Many were excellent officers as evidenced by their Officer Efficiency Reports.

After the annexation of Austria in 1938, three Austrian corps composed of six divisions were incorporated into the German Army, with a corresponding number of senior officers.[20] It cannot be said that the Austrian officers were lacking in competency or leadership from their German brethren. Twelve Austrian officers achieved at least army command.

OFFICER PROMOTIONS

The basis for officer promotions in the German Army was the officer efficiency reporting system. This program had a time honored tradition, initially established in the Prussian Army by King Frederick Wilhelm I in 1725.[21] Prior to World War II the system called for an annual report for each officer. Based on these reports seven categories of proficiency were established into which an officer could be classified. The two highest classifications (1) Officers suitable for service at the High Command, and (2) Officers suitable for General Staff duty.[22] General officers were arranged on lists submitted every three months to the Army Personnel Office. The top three categories were: (1) "Born Leaders", (2) Officers who would perform well in the next higher command and (3) Officers who should be placed temporarily in the next higher command to prove their abilities.[23]

The narrative comments on the report furnished valuable insights into the potential of each officer. GL Källner, who was a former Police officer and later the commander of the XXIV Panzer Corps, who was killed in April

1945, provides an excellent example of a courageous and proficient officer, as evidenced by several of his own efficiency reports.

In the past six months, he has proven himself in an outstanding manner as brigade commander and deputy division commander, just as he did in his former assignment as regimental commander. He shows active leadership and has a sure instinct for what is necessary. His unfailing verve and optimism carries troops forward to maximum performance. While unsparing towards himself, he is a considerate and comradely leader. Undoubtedly, he is qualified for higher positions, and is therefore once more recommended that his eligibility for promotion be reviewed. He accomplishes his tasks exceptionally well.

(Comments by GM Schmidt, commander of the 19th Panzer Division, on *Oberst* Källner in November 1942.)

Particularly straightforward character. A very firm, strict and goal-oriented leader of his division. Prevails despite all difficulties. Particularly stable during crises. Untiringly dedicates himself to serving his division. Decidedly energetic and goal-oriented. Untiring commitment to serve.

Has proven himself as an especially resourceful and crisis-proof division commander during the heavy fighting east of Zhitomir in late December 1943.

(Comments by GdPz Balck, commander of the XXXXVIII Panzer Corps and GdPz Raus, commander of the 4th Panzer Army, on GM Källner then the commander of the 19th Panzer Division.)

These reports were prepared in secret and not seen by the rated officer, which resulted in a degree of honest reporting in that the rating officers were not forced to confront their subordinates with their ratings should these comments be less than favorable. In the case of Hans Källner, this would have posed no major problem as this report is highly favorable; but many other ratings were brutally harsh.[24]

Until 1942 the promotion system was oriented on seniority. However, after this time, under pressure from Hitler and growing officer losses, the system reoriented from seniority to front-line service. In practical terms this meant that General Staff officers could not qualify for promotion by staying in Berlin and not doing a front-line tour.[25] With this in mind Kurt Zeitzler, the former Chief of Staff of the Army, stated after the war that promotions were handed out too quickly and lavishly during the war.[26] The result was the rapid elevation of many officers to general officer rank who did not have a great deal of experience in dealing with matters of general officer responsibility – they were often well-versed in the branch of arms they grew up with (infantry, etc.) but were not well-grounded in combined arms. The following table shows this quite rapid expansion of general officer ranks from 1938 to 1944:[27]

Army General Officers in Service

Grade	1938	1942	1943	1944
Generalfeldmarschall	0	8	15	16
Generaloberst	3	19	18	26
General der Infanterie, etc.	31	99	141	170
Generalleutnant	87	223	369	473
Generalmajor	154	465	501	565
Total	**275**	**814**	**1,044**	**1,250**

This trend mirrors Hitler's increasing intervention in the officer corps as Germany continued to field new formations, often at the expense of understrength existing formations. Additionally, by January 1943 he ordered the reintegration of the General Staff into the regular officer corps and established performance as the primary criteria for promotion, not General Staff membership. This decree was the death knell of the General Staff's relative importance in the Army hierarchy which had begun to decrease beginning in 1941.[28] After the failure to take Moscow in December 1941, Hitler blamed not only several high-ranking commanders, but also the General Staff for the lack of adequate winter preparations – even though it was he who had predicted that the war would be successfully concluded by them. In September 1942, as the Stalingrad fiasco was starting to take shape, Hitler accused the General Staff of "cowardice" and berated GO Franz Halder, Chief of the Army General Staff. This led to Halder's dismissal and marked the end of the period when the General Staff truly conducted operations.[29] Concurrently, a new military force started rapid expansion in both numbers and importance – the Waffen-SS.

WAFFEN-SS

In June 1941 the Waffen-SS numbered only 165,000 men – some three percent of the whole Army. By the end of the war this figure had risen to 700,000; more than ten percent. While many formations later in the war were comprised of foreign, and even sometimes non-Germanic volunteers, these units often had German SS officers; as did the true German Waffen-SS formations.

The Waffen-SS correspondingly had a somewhat different type of officer corps then did the more established Army. The pre- and early-war Waffen-SS officer often had transferred from the Army or entered through the Police. Many joined the SS from blue collar jobs in search of a better standard of living. Unlike their Army brethren, many officers in the Waffen-SS did not come from long lines of traditional military families, and almost none came from the nobility. At the start of the war most Waffen-SS officers had less than ten years of military experience which was felt almost immediately. As the war progressed, SS casualties soared; and non-commissioned officers were sent to the *Junkerschulen* (Officer Candidate Schools) to receive officer training. Waffen-SS officers originally had only SS ranks such as *SS-Brigadeführer* (brigadier general). However, in 1940 *SS-Reichsführer* Heinrich Himmler instituted combined titles through the equivalent Army rank of *general der infanterie* in an effort to further assimilate the SS with its Army comrades in arms, and give senior Waffen-SS officers some interservice credibility – *SS-Brigadeführer* now became *SS-Brigadeführer und Generalmajor der Waffen-SS*. Waffen-SS officers progressed from commanding regimental-size formations to division and corps command. On April 2, 1942 Himmler added a new rank that of *SS-Oberstgruppenführer und Generaloberst der Waffen-SS* – equivalent to *generaloberst*, as Sepp Dietrich kept rising through higher command positions. By the end of the war, Waffen-SS officers were in command of armies, and commanded Army subordinate elements. The Waffen-SS had two ranks equivalent to an Army *oberst*, colonel and senior colonel. The following chart shows the general officer ranks of the Waffen-SS, to include the two grades of colonel, with respect to their German Army equivalent ranks:

Waffen-SS General Officer Grades

Waffen-SS Grade	Abbreviation	German Army Equivalent
SS-Oberstgruppenführer und Generaloberst der Waffen-SS	GOdSS	Generaloberst
SS-Obergruppenführer und General der Waffen-SS	GdSS	General der Infanterie, etc.
SS-Gruppenführer und Generalleutnant der Waffen-SS	GLdSS	Generalleutnant
SS-Brigadeführer und Generalmajor der Waffen-SS	GMdSS	Generalmajor
SS-Oberführer	OFdSS	Oberst (Senior)
SS-Standartenführer	SFdSS	Oberst

Senior Waffen-SS officers were somewhat younger than their Army counterparts and were often, but not always, members of the Nazi Party. Waffen-SS officers had a reputation for fighting hard – which further gave an even larger reputation to the Waffen-SS as being a "Fire Brigade"; sent at a moment's notice to threatened sectors of the front. Waffen-SS generals had less than their share of turncoats in adversity; but also had more "last ditchers" – those who would lead their men to useless death in hopeless situations. Sixteen Waffen-SS commanders, four corps and twelve division, were killed during the war. The following table lists the fates of these Waffen-SS commanders:

Waffen-SS Generals Killed in Action

Name		Unit	Date	Fate
GLdSS	Mülverstedt	4th SS Division "Polizei"	10.8.41	DOW
GdSS	Eicke	3rd SS Division "Totenkopf"	26.2.43	KIA
OFdSS	Schuldt	19th SS Division	15.3.44	KIA
GMdSS	Witt	12th SS Division "Hitlerjugend"	14.6.44	KIA
GLdSS	von Scholz	11th SS Division "Nordland"	28.7.44	DOW
GdSS	Phleps	V SS Corps	21.9.44	KIA
GMdSS	Rumohr	8th SS Division "Florian Geyer"	11.2.45	S
GMdSS	Zehender	22nd SS Division "Maria Theresa"	11.2.45	S
GMdSS	Augsberger	20th SS Division	17.3.45	S
SFdSS	Klingenberg	17th SS Division "Goetz von Berlichingen"	22.3.45	KIA
GLdSS	Ostendorff	2nd SS Division "Das Reich"	4.5.45	DOW
GdSS	Krüger, W.	VI SS Corps	8.5.45	S
GdSS	Kleinheisterkamp	XI SS Corps	9.5.45	S
SFdSS	Petersen	18th SS Division "Horst Wessel"	9.5.45	S
GdSS	Krüger, F.W.	V SS Corps	10.5.45	S
GMdSS	Freitag	14th SS Division	20.5.45	S

As later accounts will show, senior Waffen-SS commanders often led by example and did, in fact, fight viciously in hopeless combat situations.

LUFTWAFFE

As previously discussed, the German Luftwaffe deployed several ground combat divisions in addition to its more traditional flying organizations. Eleven German airborne divisions existed during the war as well as twenty-one field divisions. These field divisions were formed in 1942 from Luftwaffe personnel not required to man or support traditional bomber or fighter squadrons to respond to Hitler's demand for personnel for ground fighting. Luftwaffe general officers commanded airborne divisions with great success and initially commanded the field divisions. However the fighting performance of the field divisions was less satisfactory and in 1943 the army began to fill the senior leadership positions in these units. One Luftwaffe general was killed in action in command of an airborne division and two died while in command of flak divisions; while four army generals died commanding Luftwaffe field divisions.

Luftwaffe Division Commander Casualties

Name	Unit	Date Killed
GL Süssmann	7th Airborne	20.5.41
GM von Wedel	10th Field	5.2.44
GL Pistorious	4th Field	27.6.44
GL Peschel	6th Field	30.6.44
GM Crisolli	20th Field	12.9.44
GM Erhard	7th Flak	17.4.45
GM Krämer	11th Flak	11.5.45

It might initially be assumed that Luftwaffe generals were ill prepared for ground combat in that they might have spent much of their time planning and preparing for aerial operations. This was not the case; most senior Luftwaffe officers transferred from the Army to the new service in the mid-1930s. GL Robert Pistorius for example served in World War I in the 2nd Engineer Battalion and during the 1920s served in numerous capacities to include that of a platoon leader in the 8th Infantry Regiment. He transferred to the Luftwaffe on October 1, 1934. GL Wilhelm Süssmann entered the Army in 1909, served initially in World War I as a battalion adjutant in the 22nd Infantry Regiment, and spent a decade in the Police before joining the Luftwaffe on August 1, 1935.

Despite their varied backgrounds and social status, the German Army, Waffen-SS and Luftwaffe officer corps were highly professional organizations – steeped in tradition and willing to follow established procedures and doctrine – even if that doctrine placed them in harm's way.

CHAPTER NOTES

[1] W. Victor Madej, *German Army Order of Battle 1939-1945*, Allentown, Pennsylvania: Game Marketing Company, 1981, Vol. 1, p. 4.

[2] *Ibid.*, p. 37.

[3] *Ibid.*, p. 38.

[4] Reinhard Stumpf, *Die Wehrmacht-Elite*, Boppard am Rhein, FRG: Harald Boldt Verlag, 1982, p. 166.

[5] *Ibid.*, pp. 166, 170.

[6] *Ibid.*, pp. 166-168.

[7] *Ibid.*, p. 169.

[8] *Ibid.*, p. 170.

[9] *Ibid.*, pp. 169, 171.

[10] Later in the war the Germans created the Volks-Grenadier Division which was basically an infantry division for the purposes of this study.

[11] Ibid., p. 15.

[12] Born in 1800, the son of a Prussian Army Officer, von Miltke began military service in the Danish Royal Cadet Corps before entering the Prussian Army in 1823. He was accepted to the General Staff and served as a young officer both in Prussia and on two foreign tours to Turkey and Rome. A highly talented officer, he was made acting Chief of the General Staff in 1857. He held this position until 1883 and was instrumental in the Prussian victories over Austria in 1866 and France in 1870. (T.N. Dupuy, *A Genius for War – the German Army and General Staff, 1807-1945*, Englewood Cliffs, New Jersey: Prentice Hall, 1977, pp. 61-65, 124.)

[13] Dr. Dan Hughes, Historian to the United States Army Command and General Staff College, lecture – "The German Officer Corps", Fort Leavenworth, Kansas, November 22, 1988.

[14] Martin van Creveld, *Fighting Power: German and U.S. Army Performance, 1939-1945.*, London: Arms and Armour Press, 1983, pp. 150-152.

[15] *Ibid.*

[16] *Ibid.*

[17] David Nelson Spires, "The Career of the Reichswehr Officer", (Doctor of Philosophy Dissertation: University of Washington), 1979, pp. 9-12.

[18] Michael Geyer, "The Transformation of the German Officer Corps", Ann Arbor, MI: University of Michigan, p. 44.

[19] Günther Blumenritt, "The German Armies of 1914 and 1939", U.S. Army Historical Division Study MS# B-292, Washington, D.C.: Office of the Chief of Military History, 1947, p. 46.

[20] Friedrich Stahl, *Heereseinteilung 1939*, Friedberg, FRG: Podzun-Pallas-Verlag, 1953, p. 145.

[21] Rudolf Hofmann, "German Efficiency Report System", U.S. Army Historical Division Study MS# P-134, Washington, D.C.: Office of the Chief of Military

History, 1952, p. 3.

[22] Martin van Creveld, *Fighting Power*, p. 166.

[23] Helmet Kleikamp, "German Army High Command, The Personnel Office", U.S. Army Historical Division Study MS# P-041hh, Washington, D.C.: Office of the Chief of Military History, 1952, p. 21.

[24] An officer efficiency report on Franz Böhme, then commander of the XVIII Mountain Corps, written by GO Eduard Dietl, stated that Böhme was sometimes indecisive and nervous and needed to overcome these tendencies before he should be elevated to army command.

[25] Martin van Creveld, *Fighting Power*, p. 167.

[26] Heinz Guderian and Kurt Zeitzler, "Comments on P-41s - P-41hh", U.S. Army Historical Division Study MS# P-041, Washington, D.C.: Office of the Chief of Military History, 1953, p. 34.

[27] Wolf Keilig, *Das Deutsche Heer, 1939-1945, Band I-III*, Bad Nauheim, FRG: Podzun-Verlag, 1956, Vol. III, p. 203.

[28] Walter Görlitz, *History of the German General Staff, 1657-1945*, New York: Praeger, 1953.

[29] Hansgeorg Model, *Der Deutsche Generalstabsoffizier*, Frankfurt, FRG: Bernard & Gräfe Verlag, 1968, p. 127.

[30] Robert Lewis Köhl, *The Black Corps*, Madison, WI: University of Wisconsin Press, 1983, pp. 237-238. The National Committee for a Free Germany was formed in July 1943 from German emigres and prisoners of war held in the Soviet Union. Soviets encouraged higher ranking officers to join to legitimize the movement. No Waffen SS generals are known to have participated in this organization.

✠ CHAPTER 3 ✠
GERMAN DOCTRINE

The IVth Corps has been ordered by the Commander in Chief to hold the southern sector of Fortress Stalingrad. It goes without saying that in such a situation the Generals will fight beside their men.

(IV Corps message to GFM Paulus during the last days of Stalingrad) [1]

GdI Fretter-Pico visiting forward trenches in Russia.

German Army doctrine traditionally valued front-line leadership. Prior to World War I this doctrine was primarily verbal in nature; passed along from one generation of officers to another in professional discussions and by personal example in war games or actual combat. As time went by, these lessons became formalized in written documents. A portion of the January 1, 1918 training directive entitled "The Attack in the War of Position" commented on the role of senior leaders on the battlefield:

The greater the mobility of the attack the farther forward is the proper place of senior commanders, often on horseback. [2]

18

Later doctrine, refined in the 1930's, also stressed front-line leadership by senior level leaders. The German Army's views on war, which would be executed in World War II, were outlined in 1936, in the *Truppenführung* (The doctrinal manual concerning the Command of Troops). The following guidelines reflected the importance of front-line senior level leadership: [3]

GFM von Manstein visits the fighting troops, September 1943.

Personal influence by the commanding Officer on his troops is of the greatest importance. He must be located near the fighting troops.

A divisional commander's place is with his troops...During encounters with the enemy seeing for oneself is best.

Commanders are to live with the troops and share with them danger, deprivation, happiness, and suffering. Only then can they gain a real insight into their troops' combat power and requirements.

The example of officers and men in commanding positions has a crucial effect on the troops. The officer who demonstrates cold bloodedness, determination, and courage in front of the enemy pulls the troops along with himself.

The doctrine of personal leadership from the front laid the foundation for the *blitzkrieg* or "lightning war" which emphasized maneuver and deep attacks through the enemy's vulnerable rear area – with the intent of paralyz-

19

GL Zorn visits assault troops near Vitebsk, July 7, 1941 (KIA August 2, 1943)

ing his command and control. This type of warfare would eliminate the stagnation of trench warfare, or so hoped the German High Command, prevalent in the Great War, and allow the German Army to defeat almost every other army in Europe. This doctrine was taught in branch service schools and General Staff training, which many senior commanders had undergone as younger officers – who took this doctrine to heart, achieved spectacular tactical successes, and paid a high price in blood. There was nothing surprising in this, as their attitude to combat had already been strongly shaped during World War I.

CHAPTER NOTES

[1] Heinz Schröter, *Stalingrad*, New York: E.P. Hutton, 1958, p. 233.

[2] Martin van Creveld, *Command in War,* Cambridge, Massachusetts: Harvard University Press, 1985, pp. 174-175.

[3] *Truppenführung*, Berlin: E.S. Mittler @ Sohn, 1936, pp. 2, 3, 4, 33, 34.

✠ CHAPTER 4 ✠

GERMAN OFFICERS IN COMBAT
SERVICE AND BRAVERY

WORLD WAR I SERVICE

The World War I service of many German junior officers who later became generals in World War II was characterized by a high degree of front-line service and bravery. The early experience of these officers helped form their basic professional ethic concerning leadership, personal danger, and responsibility to their men. That ethic would be reflected in their wartime actions some twenty years later. By examining this early wartime service, we can better understand these officers frame of mind with respect to leadership and their concept of battlefield lethality; a concept that would be greatly outdated in the next war.

One measure of front-line service and bravery is awards. This section will use the awards and decorations received by the World War II German generals killed in action as a guide to the level of service and bravery they displayed in combat. During World War I the basic decorations for front-line bravery were the Iron Cross 1st Class and 2nd Class. The Iron Cross 2nd Class indicated a single act of bravery in combat, while the Iron Cross 1st Class was awarded for an additional acts of valor. It was only possible for an individual to win each of the classes once. Additionally, to measure wounds received in combat, Kaiser Wilhelm II instituted the Wound Badge on March 3, 1918. Different grades were awarded based on the cumulative number of incidents in which wounds were received. The wound badge in black designated one or two wounds, the badge in white for three to four wounds, and the badge in yellow-gold for five or more wounds.[1] World War I awards are known for ninety-seven of the German Army generals killed in action. While in every military awards system inequities sometimes exist – individuals deserving of an award but never receiving it and vice-versa, the German World War I system seems to have been as fair as most. As seen in the following table, ninety-six percent were awarded one of the grades of Iron Cross. Fifty-three percent were wounded in action at least once, while thirteen percent were wounded on three or more combat engagements. Repeated demonstrated bravery in action was expected of German junior officers during the war and this professional ethic is amply represented by the exploits of these individuals. Overall it is evident that these junior German officers, who were later killed in action as general officers during World War II, developed their concept of battlefield leadership and danger the hard way – they earned it.[2]

Army Recipients of World War I Decorations

Award	Number	Percentage (Based on 97 Officers)
Iron Cross 2nd Class	93	94
Iron Cross 1st Class	86	88
Wound Badge in Black	40	41
Wound Badge in White	12	12

WORLD WAR II SERVICE

As shown, a large number of German general officers killed in World War II had exceptional front-line service in World War I. The next step in this evaluation process is to determine whether these men continued to show front-line service and bravery as senior officers. Once again we will rely on the Germans' own system of awards and decorations, to determine the extent of this assertion.

At the outbreak of World War II the German Armed Forces re-instituted the Iron Cross 1st Class and 2nd Class. Hitler stated the Iron Cross 2nd Class would reward a single act of bravery in combat beyond the normal requirements of duty. It could be awarded to all members of the Armed Forces or to non-military individuals serving with the military. The Iron Cross 1st Class, also re-instituted on September 1, 1939, was usually awarded for an additional three to five significant acts of valor.[3] Recommendations for both awards went first from company to battalion to regiment, with the approving authority resting with the division commander. For non-divisional units assigned to a corps, the corps commander approved receipt of the award. Although the intent was to let an appropriate time pass between the award of the 2nd Class and the 1st Class, this could be compressed to one or two days.[4] General officers were usually awarded these decorations by their next higher commander, i.e. division commander by his corps commander, corps commander by his army commander. For soldiers who had already been awarded the Iron Cross in World War I, the actual World War II version of the decoration was not presented. Instead, they received a clasp denoting the achievement of winning the decoration again in this latest conflict.

In September 1, 1939 Hitler also instituted a new decoration, the *Ritterkreuz* (Knight's Cross of the Iron Cross) for continuous acts of exceptional bravery, or in the cases of higher ranks for successful execution of battle or for formulating outstanding battle plans.[5] Recommendation for the

World War II German postcard showing the Iron Cross 2nd Class and clasp. The Iron Cross 2nd Class was awarded to some 3,000,000 soldiers during the war. (Author photo)

Knight's Cross required the endorsement of the chain of command through army commander with the final decision resting with Hitler.[6] Prerequisites included previous award of both classes of the Iron Cross.

Enlisted personnel as well as officers were eligible for this award. In the course of the war some 7,300 Knight's Crosses were awarded.[8]

For commanding officers however, bravery alone was not justification for recommendation for the Knight's Cross. In addition, the officer had to demonstrate several instances of exercising independent decisions. This is best amplified by comments made by GFM Ferdinand Schörner concerning a recommendation for the award to a colonel. Schörner wrote that for a regimental commander to personally lead a counterattack with a machine-gun and hand grenades [which is what the officer recommended for the award had done] was not exceptional bravery but a "self evident duty".[9]

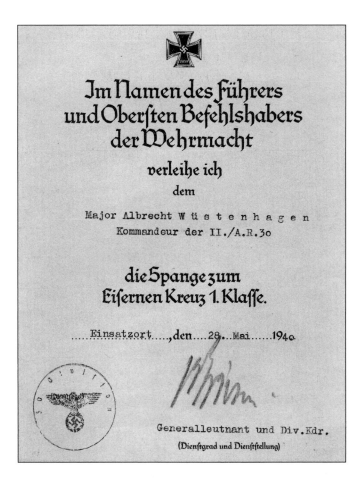

Im Namen des Führers und Obersten Befehlshabers der Wehrmacht

verleihe ich

dem

Major Albrecht W ü s t e n h a g e n
Kommandeur der II./A.R.30

die Spange zum Eisernen Kreuz 1. Klasse.

.....Einsatzort...., den ....28...Mai.....1940.

Generalleutnant und Div.Kdr.

(Dienstgrad und Dienststellung)

Iron Cross 1st Class certificate to then Major Wüstenhagen in 1940
(KIA June 26, 1944) [7] (Author photo)

One commanding officer who did demonstrate exceptional bravery was *Generalmajor* Gerhard Berthold, commander of the 31st Infantry Division. Berthold, who was killed in action in 1942, was awarded the Knight's Cross on December 4, 1941. The recommendation for his award reads as follows:[10]

> *During the offensive by Bryansk on October 6, 1941, at about 10:00 AM, the 17th Jäger Regiment reported to Generalmajor Berthold that Russian tanks were attacking a portion of the regiment. Enemy tanks had already reached the immediate vicinity of the forward positions. These tanks, according to captured prisoners of war and enemy documents showed that these 52, 25 and 32 ton heavy tanks were the remains of the 108th Russian Tank Division.*
>
> *The Division Commander, after a short discussion with the division*

operations officer, immediately drove through heavy artillery and machine-gun fire to the battlefield to take command of the battle into his own hands. Driving in an open command car through the Shiryatino battlefield, he hastily mobilized the division anti-tank detachment and set an 8.8 cm anti-aircraft gun into position. This action brought immediate and effective relief to the sorely distressed men.

Many of the Russian tanks retreated because of this calm and sure fire. The few Russian tanks that penetrated the lines were destroyed.

Thanks to the astonishing courageousness of the Division Commander, to his calm clear command, and to his personal action, the defense was successful.

His independent resolve, outstanding courage and ultimate success, distinguish the action of the Commander of the 31st Jäger Division.

Further evidence of his extraordinary leadership and singular acts of courage lie in the battles at the Bug River bridgehead and the bridgehead at Staryj-Buchov, and from the battles by Iskany and Wetj as well as at Rogatsch and Gomel.

GM Gerhard Berthold (KIA April 14, 1942)

Berthold continued to display immense courage until he fell in combat April 14, 1942 while leading his division.

On June 3, 1940 Hitler instituted the next higher grade of the Knight's Cross, the Knight's Cross of the Iron Cross with Oak Leaves *(Ritterkreuz mit Eichenlaub)*. This award recognized previous winners of the Knight's Cross for continued significant bravery and initiative. Enlisted personnel, officers and foreign military personnel were eligible to receive the Oak Leaves, and by war's end 910 had done so.[11] Awards of the Oak Leaves were spread among all of Germany's Armed Forces. Five hundred nineteen winners of this award were from the Army, 254 were from the *Luftwaffe*, 53 were assigned to the *Kriegsmarine* and 77 were soldiers from the Waffen-SS. The remainder were awarded to foreign personnel.

Another postcard depicting the Knight's Cross with Oak Leaves. This award was received by 46 general officer commanders later killed in action. (Author photo)

One year later Hitler again introduced another higher grade of award – the Knight's Cross of the Iron Cross with Oak Leaves and Swords *(Ritterkreuz mit Eichenlaub und Schwertern)*. This grade recognized previous recipients of the Oak Leaves who accomplished additional feats of military achievement. Although all German military personnel of all ranks theoretically were eligible to receive this award, only 159 officers actually did.[12] One senior commander who narrowly missed death, GdPz Friedrich Gräser, reflected great credit on the Army late in the war as reflected in his nomination for the Swords:

> *General der Panzer Gräser, Commander of the 4th Panzer Army, has once again proven himself a special caliber leader of troops, since the beginning of the great Soviet offensive on April 16, 1945.*
>
> *The 4th Panzer Army, though far outnumbered and despite limited ammunition stocks, caused severe losses to the enemy during the first three days of the offensive. Despite this example of troop perseverance and all their readiness, energy and leadership, the enemy, with their five rifle armies and eleven mechanized corps supported by superior artillery and concentrated air power finally succeeded in breaking through to Bautzen and the area south of Spremberg. In this crisis, by skillful strikes to the enemy's flanks, General Gräser caused significant losses to both men and material on the battlefield. He did this with little or no lines of communication, and often led from the forward lines. In the heat of battle, he commanded with talent and improvisation, taking appropriate counter-measures when necessary.*
>
> *Tried in action in command of motorized formations, he succeeded, during the period of 21-22 April, in defeating the numerically superior enemy with repeated assaults and well-planned counterattacks. He closed the southern hole of the front, and cut off the advancing Bolshevists from their rear lines of supply. This sharply concentrated attack turned the enemy around and resulted in the enemy withdrawing three mechanized corps that had already advanced beyond Bischofswerda, and forced the enemy to give up his plan to strike for Dresden and seize the Elbe River.*
>
> *The enemy's operational goal of outflanking of the Army Group was impaired. The personal involvement of the Commander of the 4th Panzer Army was evidenced in an exceptional way. Ignoring the strong anti-tank and mortar fire, he tore through the attack in his personal vehicle to the front lines of the infantry. He personally deployed an armored group from Barschuetz to the attack toward Bautzen. During this action General Gräser was wounded for the* **7th time** *[emphasis in the original]. On the evening of April 23rd Bautzen was again in German hands. Large portions of the 52nd Rifle Army, the 2nd Polish Army as well as significant forces from the VIIth Mechanized Corps and the 1st Polish Tank Corps were*

destroyed; and the 16th Polish Tank Brigade was severely damaged.

The Commander was personally involved in the extraordinary success of the 4th Panzer Army and its excellent troops and leadership. His swift decisiveness, clear and energetic command, personal engagement on the battlefield and exemplary courage in every situation, truly made a difference.

GdPz Gräser, although severely impaired by his leg prosthesis, has earned the Oak Leaves and Swords for his high personal worth and his continual demonstration of leadership in a crisis.

On July 15, 1941 Hitler introduced what was believed to be the final upgrade – the Knight's Cross of the Iron Cross with Oak Leaves, Swords and Diamonds *(Ritterkreuz mit Eichenlaub, Schwertern und Brillanten)*. Again it rewarded even further achievement. By the end of the war only 27 had been awarded.[14] By December 29, 1944, however, the German High Command and Hitler decided that one ultimate award be created for Germany's twelve bravest men – the Knight's Cross of the Iron Cross with Golden Oak Leaves, Swords and Diamonds. Three days later the first of these decorations was bestowed on Luftwaffe Stuka pilot Colonel Hans Rudel. No further presentations were made.[15]

The importance of the bestowal of the grades of the Knight's Cross cannot be overestimated. Rudolf Hofmann, a former department chief in the Army Personnel Office, in his description of the officer promotion system, stated that Knight's Cross winners "automatically" were given more generous, preferential promotions.[16] Recipients received favorable publicity including tours of civilian industry, postcards in their honor and free gifts. One of the clearest examples of this high regard the Services had for these awards is seen in an order of the day from GdPz Rommel to the Africa Corps:[17]

The Führer has invested me with the Oak Leaves and Swords to the Knight's Cross of the Iron Cross in recognition of the defensive victory gained, up to the present against superior enemy forces, by the heroic German-Italian troops. I am proud of this award in which we all share. Let it, henceforth, spur us on to inflict final defeat upon the enemy.

The awards were not for general officers only. Troops of all ranks were eligible and thousands of decorations were awarded. Of 910 awards of the Oak Leaves for example, 242 were awarded to general officers with the remainder going to more junior personnel. Within army units, the following numbers of awards for nine divisions are representative to the positive nature of the awards system and stand as testimony to the system's underlying purpose – to foster bravery and increased military efficiency.

Within the Waffen-SS there were 52 recipients of the Knight's Cross in the

Military Awards By Division

Division	Iron Cross 1st Class	Iron Cross 2nd Class	Knight's Cross
1st Infantry	2,324	15,512	43
1st Mountain	1,193	12,696	29
3rd Panzer	1,867	13,852	17
5th Jäger	2,365	17,777	34
96th Infantry	1,760	12,280	17
10th Infantry	1,389	12,021	25
110th Infantry	1,080	7,870	10
125th Infantry	907	7,652	6
134th Infantry	1,874	12,937	22

1st SS Division *"Leibstandarte Adolf Hitler"*, 73 in the 2nd SS Division *"Das Reich"*, 46 in the 3rd SS Division *"Totenkopf"*, 54 in the 5th SS Division "Wiking" and 30 in the 11th SS Division *"Nordland"*. All other SS divisions had recipients also.

Division, corps and army commanders killed in action, figured prominently as recipients of all of these awards. About seventy percent received at least the Knight's Cross of the Iron Cross; while many of the remainder won other decorations. The following is the distribution of these awards to those generals who were killed in action or who died of their wounds:[18]

Many general officers were awarded the World War II edition of the

Highest World War Two Decorations Received by General Officer Commanders Killed in Action

Award	Number	Percentage of Total
Knight's Cross	69	41.1
Oak Leaves	35	20.8
Swords	9	5.4
Diamonds	2	1.2
TOTAL	**115**	**68.5**

Wound Badge as well. GM Harald von Hirschfeld presents a dramatic example of the dangers of combat during the war. On June 22, 1941 he was wounded by infantry fire in the ankle. On August 1, 1941 he received wounds to his left eye. On September 15, 1941 artillery fire struck him in the lower leg. Just five days later on September 20 he was wounded in the left shoulder by infantry fire. On October 1, 1941 he was wounded by artillery fire to both the left ankle and left arm. On October 1, 1942 he was wounded again on the left ankle. He received his final, and mortal wound on January 18, 1945. No less incredible were the wounds received by GM Erich Bärenfänger the last commandant of Berlin. On June 6, 1940 he received shrapnel on his right forearm and left hand. On July 12, 1941 he was shot through the right hand. On August 5, 1941 he received almost a direct hit of artillery fire and was wounded in numerous locations by the shrapnel. Sixteen days later a mine exploded and threw his command car ten meters into the air injuring his knee. On November 21, 1941 he was hit by a piece of shrapnel on the left ankle; the next day both knees were hit by artillery shrapnel. On November 16, 1942 he was again hit by shrapnel in the back and both lower legs. His last, and finally fatal, wound was self inflicted in the basement of a destroyed house near the Prenzlauer U-Bahn station on May 1, 1945 during the battle for Berlin.

It is apparent from these results that the general officer commanders continued to display high degrees of bravery and independent action during the Second World War. Over two thirds received Germany's highest awards for valor and achievement. These are not characteristics the German High Command would have wanted changed in their combat leaders, bravery and independent action went hand in hand with their concept of *Auftragstaktik* – the ability of subordinate commanders to act independently within a general framework of commander's intent, but responding to specific conditions and exploiting specific opportunities without having to refer to higher headquarters. Moltke emphasized the concept.

> *A favorable situation will never be exploited if commanders wait for orders. The highest commander and the youngest soldier must always be conscious of the fact that omission and inactivity are worse than resorting to the wrong expedient.*[19]

If, however, doctrine and personal bravery caused leaders to command from the front, then command rotation and general officer training courses put them at a severe disadvantage when they got there – which was exacerbated by the German system of officer personnel management.

CHAPTER NOTES

[1] John R. Angolia, *For Führer and Fatherland; Military Awards of the Third Reich (Volume 1-2)*, San Jose, CA: R. James Bender, 1976, Vol. 1, pp. 256, 337 and 343.

[2] *Rangliste des Deutschen Reichsheers (nach dem Stande 1. Mai 1929)*, Berlin: Mittler & Sohn, 1929. This book is a rank listing for all officers of the *Reichswehr*. Included in it is a listing of all World War I awards for each individual. Those officers who were not on the *Reichswehr* roles, i.e. those who entered service at a later date or who transferred from the German Police ar Austrian Army in the mid-1930s are not listed. Several generals KIA in World War II won even higher decorations as junior officers in World War I. Captain Otto Lancelle received the Prussian *Pour le Merite* on October 9, 1918. Captain Ritter von Schobert won the Bavarian Military Order of Max Joseph on March 23, 1918. Lieutenant Ritter von Speck won this same award on September 7, 1914.

[3] John R. Angolia, *For Führer, Vol. 1*, pp. 337 and 343.

[4] Unpublished award documents, for example, show *Unteroffizier* Karl Binz, 25th Infantry Division, receiving the Iron Cross 2nd Class on June 5, 1940 and the Iron Cross First Class the following day. Of some of the generals mentioned in this work, Theodore Eicke received the Clasp to the Iron Cross 2nd Class on May 26, 1940 and the Clasp to the Iron Cross 1st Class five days later. Fritz Klingenberg received his Iron Cross 2nd Class on June 23, 1940 and his 1st Class a day later.

[5] John R. Angolia, *For Führer, Vol. 1*, pp. 356-357.

[6] Martin van Creveld, *Fighting Power*, p. 126.

[7] Award document denotes Wüstenhagen was awarded the Clasp to the Iron Cross 1st Class – he had won the Iron Cross 1st Class in WWI and now again in WWII. The document is signed by GL Kurt von Briesen who was killed in 1941.

[8] John R. Angolia, *On The Field of Honor, A History of the Knight's Cross Bearers (Volume 1-2)*, San Jose, CA: R. Bender, 1980, Vol. 1, pp. 14-22.

[9] Martin van Creveld, *Fighting Power*, p. 126.

[10] Award recommendation to *Generalmajor* Berthold, Bundesarchiv-Militärarchiv Freiburg.

[11] John R. Angolia, *On The Field, Vol. 2*, pp. 108 and 125.

[12] John R. Angolia, *For Führer, Vol. 1*, pp. 366-367.

[13] Award recommendation tp GdPz Gräser, Bundesarchiv-Militärarchiv Feiburg.

[14] John R. Angolia, *On The Field, Vol. 1*, p. 52.

[15] Ibid., pp. 46-50. Rudel was a legend in World War II Germany for his incedible feats of dive bombing efficiency in his Stuka. By war's end he had destroyed 1 battleship, 1 cruiser, numerous smaller ships and more than 519 armored vehicles. He was wounded five times, one resulting in the loss of a leg. He survived the war.

[16] Rudolf Hofmann, "German Efficiency Report System", p. 46.

[17] Richard D. Law & Craig W.H. Luther, *Rommel: A Narrative & Pictorial History*, San Jose, CA: R. James Bender Publishing, 1980, p. 123.

[18] Walter-Peer Fellgieble, *Die Träger des Ritterkreuzes des Eisernen Kreuzes, 1939-1945*, Friedberg, FRG: Podzun-Pallas Verlag, 1986. Multiple pages – each name was cross-referenced to determine if he won any of the grades of this award.

[19] T.N. Dupuy, *A Genius for War: The German Army and General Staff, 1807-1945*, Fairfax, VA: Hero Books, 1984, p. 116.

✠ CHAPTER 5 ✠
ROTATION OF GENERAL OFFICERS AND COMMAND DURATION

1926 war games in Bavaria – service in Germany was much different than front-line action (tall officer in center is Friedrich Paulus, later GFM)

The history of the German general officer replacement system in World War II is an interesting saga; one in which, the system attempted unsuccessfully to meet increasing officer needs with decreasing personnel assets. Initially efficient, it deteriorated during the war in part due to heavy officer casualties.

During preparation for mobilization in the late 1930s, the Central Branch of the Army General Staff filled general officer vacancies to brigade level and General Staff positions. When war began general officers were directly assigned by a different organization – the Army Personnel Office. After 1942, the procedure changed again. General officer unit commanders were assigned by the Personnel Office in accordance with instructions from the Commander in Chief of the Army but with input from the Chief of the Army General Staff.[1] Senior General Staff officers, on the other hand, scheduled for assignment as chiefs of staff for army groups, armies, and corps, were selected directly by the Chief of the Army General Staff. Many of these officers were also in demand for unit command.[2] This was quite a convoluted process even without serious personnel losses.

Beginning in the Fall of 1942, losses began to mount for both line and General Staff officers. At the same time the Personnel Office initiated increased requirements for more General Staff officers to be released for duty as unit commanders at the front.[3] Unfortunately, there were already too few General Staff officers for the necessary General Staff positions. This condition had existed since the beginning of the war. On September 1, 1939 there were only 508 General Staff officers to fill the 589 General Staff positions. To further compound this problem, some 93 of these officers were not in General Staff positions but were serving as commanding officers.[4]

Political infighting exacerbated the situation. Older army generals viewed infantry as the dominant branch and attempted to control the Army Personnel Branch to the detriment of other branch officers.[5] This was especially so with respect to the formation during the war of new panzer forces. Hasso von Manteuffel stated that the new Panzer Branch required special leaders and commanders, but the older arms displayed opposing views. To maintain stability within the armored force, GO Heinz Guderian, in his role as Inspector-General of Armored Troops, reported directly to Hitler and had full input concerning the appointments to the command of armored formations.[6] But still the bickering continued.

Further compounding the problem was the increasing number of units requiring general officer commanders. The strength of the German Army in December 1940 stood at 140 divisions. This total increased to 208 at the start of the Russian Campaign, to 226 in July 1942, and to 243 by July 1943. By the beginning of June 1944 the division total had reached 257.[7] The number of corps also increased during the war, peaking at seventy-seven in January 1945.[8] The Luftwaffe Field divisions, which were created in mid-war, required commanders as well. Initially led by Luftwaffe generals, their performance was so lackluster that Hitler ordered Army generals into these command positions – which stretched the system even further.

Many general officers transferred from more protected rear area staff assignments directly to the front with fatal results. GL Henning von Thadden, for example, remained in Germany from 1943 to 1945 as the Chief of Staff for the 1st Military District Corps. He then went to the Eastern Front to command the 1st Infantry Division and was killed within two months. GM Otto Beutler, commander of the 340th Infantry Division, served with the General Staff in the Organization for Total War office in Berlin for 11 months.[9] He was then accused of anti-Nazi beliefs and placed in temporary retirement three months before his military tribunal. Acquitted of all charges, he was assigned to Army Group North Ukraine for a month before assuming command.[10] He was killed in action just 35 days later.[11] Beutler had not served in combat in World War II below the division staff level – his previous front-line combat service was in 1915 as an infantry platoon leader! GM Werner Dürking served as the commander of the War School at Dresden for about two years before going to the Eastern Front as commander of the 96th Infantry Division. He died of wounds received in combat after only ten days in command.[12]

Command durations are known for every general officer commander who was killed during the war. These examples of lethality and command durations for general officers killed in action are shown in the following table:[13]

Command Durations for General Officer Commanders Killed in Action		
Duration	Number Killed	Percentage
One Month or Less	31	18.5
Two to Five Months	37	22.0
Six to Nine Months	38	22.6
Ten to Twelve Months	26	15.5
More than Twelve Months	36	21.4

It is evident that some type of maturation occurred the longer one stayed in command. Almost one in five commanders killed met their fate in the first month of command. Forty percent served for less than five months before being killed, while sixty-three percent fell before their tenth month in command. If an individual could learn quickly and survive the initial dangerous months of combat, he became more likely to safely complete his command. The distribution of command duration prior to being killed in action supports the danger to newer, less experienced general officer commanders in combat. This, in turn, is partly the result of increased battlefield mobility of general officers.

CHAPTER NOTES

[1] Helmut Kleikamp, "Personnel Office". pp. 8, 10. Kleikamp served in the Army Personnel Office before assuming command of the 36th Infantry Division.

[2] Franz Halder, "Control of the German Army General Staff", U.S. Army Historical Division Study MS# P-014d, Washington, D.C.: Office of the Chief of Military History, 1952, p. 6. Halder served as Chief of the Army General Staff from 1938 to 1942.

[3] Helmut Kliekamp, "Personnel Office", p. 12.

[4] Hansgeorg Model, *Der deutsche Generalstabsoffizier*, p. 111.

[5] Heinz Guderian and Kurt Zeitzler, "Comments on P-41a - P-41hh", U.S. Army

Historical Division Study MS# P-04ll, Washington, D.C.: Office of the Chief of Military History, 1953, p. 32.

[6] Hasso von Manteuffel, "Fast Mobile and Armored Troops", U.S. Army Historical Division Study MS# B-036, Washington, D.C.: Office of the Chief of Military History, 1945, pp. 3, 10, 19.

[7] Burkhart Müller-Hillebrand, *Das Heer 1933-1945, Band I-III*, Frankfurt, FRG: E. S. Mittler & Sohn, 1969, Vol. 2, pp. 110-111; Vol. 3, pp. 122, 155. Müller-Hillebrand served as the Chief of Staff for the XXXXVI Panzer Corps and the 3rd Panzer Army.

[8] Georg Tessin, *Verbände und Truppen de deutschen Wehrmacht und Waffen-SS in Zweiten Weltkrieg 1939-1945 (Band I-XIV)*, Osnabrück, FRG: Biblio Verlag, 1979, Vol. 1, pp. 17-19.

[9] Burkhart Müller-Hillebrand, *Das Heer, Vol. 3*, p. 211:337.

[10] Beutler was fortunate. The following generals were executed for anti-Nazi "crimes": GM Karl von Dewitz, GM Graf zu Dohna-Schlobitten, GdNT Erich Fellgiebel, GO Friedrich Fromm, GM Reinhard Githsche, GL Paul von Hase, GL Gustav Heisterman, GM Otto Herfurth, GO Erich Höpner, GdA Fritz Lindemann, GdI Friedrich Olbricht, GM Hans Oster, GdA Friedrich Rabenau, GL Graf von Sponeck, GM Helmuth Stieff, GdI Heinrich von Stulpnagel, GL Fritz Thiele, GL Karl von Thüngen and GFM Erwin Witzleben.

[11] *Ibid.*, p. 211:27.

[12] *Ibid.*, p. 211:70.

[13] Wolf Keilig, Die Generale des Heeres. Durations of command were determined after reviewing biographies of each general officer killed in action or died of wounds.

✠ CHAPTER 6 ✠

BATTLEFIELD MOBILITY

The German Army in World War II at one time stretched from the North Cape of Norway to the Sahara Desert, north to south; and from the Atlantic coast of France to the Volga River in Russia, east to west.

Given the enormity of the *Reich*, it was quite natural for German general officers to use a variety of transportation assets to conduct their military operations to achieve a level of operational mobility only dreamed about by the great von Moltke. But were these conveyances really deathtraps that actually compounded already dangerous situations?

TRAINS

The German Armed Forces made extensive use of Europe's railway systems during the war; German general officers utilized them as well. The *Reichsbahn* (State Railways) could create Special trains, composed of a specified kind and combination of Pullman cars, for Hitler, visiting heads of state, and high ranking German officials.

One of Hitler's trains, for example, had the following composition of cars: locomotive, armored anti-aircraft car with 20mm cannon, baggage and power-engine car, Hitler's private Pullman, conference car with communications center, escort car for Hitler's SS escort detachment, dining car, two sleeping cars for guests, bath car, dining car, two cars for secretaries and aides, press chief's car, baggage and power-engine car, and anti-aircraft car.

Hitler's Special train was initially codenamed *Amerika* which was later renamed *Brandenburg*. Göring had a train *Asien* later named *Pommern*, GFM Keitel had a Special train *Afrika*, later known as *Braunschweig*, and the OKW staff had two Specials – *Atlas*, later renamed *Franken I*, and *Franken II*.[1]

Security for these trains, and ones with more regular configurations, seems to have been good. Although there are numerous examples of regular troop and supply trains being ambushed, and sometimes destroyed, by partisans or Allied aircraft throughout Europe, there is no record of any attacks on these trains when generals (or for that matter Hitler and other high ranking Nazi officials) were on board. One general is believed to have been killed – by Soviet artillery fire, while riding aboard a train.

AIRPLANES

German general officers frequently used air assets for two purposes; long range transportation, often to Germany and back to their theater of operations; and short range aerial observation aircraft to gain a better appreciation of some aspect of front-line fighting.

For long range transportation, the generals primarily used two types of aircraft; the four-engine Focke-Wulf Condor (Fw 200) and the Junkers (Ju 52/3m). Hitler frequently flew in an Fw 200; it had originally been designed as a 26-passenger transport for Lufthansa, it was modified to seat 7, had a 2,212 mile range and was armed with three defensive machine guns and a 20mm cannon. Top speed for the Condor was 224 mph, while it generally cruised at 208 mph. No German general officers are known to have been killed in a Fw 200; either in shootdowns or in accidental crashes.[2]

For battlefield reconnaissance, most generals used the Fieseler *Storch* (Stork) 156. This two to three seat light plane was extremely light and could take off and land on a postage stamp; it needed only 230 feet to lift off and only 85 feet to land! The Stork could carry one light machine gun for rearward defense, but was at a severe disadvantage if attacked by either enemy aircraft or flak.Its maximum speed was only 109 mph.[3] Three general officers were killed while flying in the Stork, two by anti-aircraft fire and one in a landing in a minefield.

The tri-motor Junkers Ju 52 truly was the workhorse of the German armed forces. In its transport role, the Ju 52, nicknamed the *Tante Ju*, or Auntie Ju, could seat up to 17 passengers, and travel up to 683 miles. Unlike the Fw 200, it was lightly armed, generally carrying only one machine gun which provided rearward defense.[4] German generals used the numerous Ju 52s for most long range aerial travel.

The Ju 52 certainly could not outrun any attacking enemy fighters – its maximum speed was 178 mph, as compared to 365 mph for the Spitfire MK 1A, 342 mph for the Hurricane MK IIA, 429 mph for the P-47B Thunderbolt and 437 mph for the P-51D Mustang.

Given this disparity in speed from its pursuers, only one division commander was killed in an aircraft shootdown involving a Ju 52; however, several more were killed in accidental crashes of the usually reliable aircraft.

AIRCRAFT ACCIDENTS

German transportation aircraft generally were extremely reliable and provided a safe means of transportation for general officers for both long distances, such as visits back to Germany, and short trips around the battlefield. However, weather conditions were often marginal for flying, as well as periodic aircraft maintenance problems and pilot error – and aircraft accidents further robbed German leadership. GL Hermann Balck, the incoming commander of the XIV Panzer Corps in Italy, crashed in a light observation plane in September 1943, suffered multiple fractures and had to remain in a hospi-

GO Hans Hube (Author photo)

tal for several months recovering, before going on to higher command and further military achievements.[5]

Others were not so fortunate. On April 20, 1944, Hitler's birthday, GO Hans Hube the commander of the 1st Panzer Army visited the Führer at Obersalzberg to receive the Knight's Cross with Oak Leaves, Swords and Diamonds. Hube departed at about 5:00 AM the next morning to return to the front. About 250 feet in the air an engine on his aircraft caught fire and the craft plummeted to the ground killing Hube and the entire crew.

He was given a state funeral and laid to rest at the Invalids Cemetery in Berlin.[6] Hube was typical of many German generals in their disregard for danger. As a lieutenant in World War I, he was severely wounded in the left arm on September 14, 1914 near Fontenay France. His arm was so badly injured that it later was amputated, but this serious handicap did not prevent him from returning to front-line duty during the war, where he was gassed during an Allied attack.[7]

The single worst aircraft accident, in terms of general officer fatalities,

GO Dietl in his Ju 52

occurred June 23, 1944. GO Eduard Dietl, commander of the 20th Mountain Army in northern Finland, also was called to visit Hitler at Obersalzberg.

On his return flight, he stopped for a visit at Graz, Austria, and then continued his flight toward Vienna and ultimately Finland. Flying with the general in his Ju 52 were GdGebtr Karl Eglseer, the commander of the XVIII Mountain Corps, GL Franz Rossi, the commandant of Petsamo and GdI Thomas von Wickede, commander of the X Corps.

The pre-flight weather report at Graz predicted cloud cover between 500 and 2500 meters and the pilot was advised to therefore fly around the Alps to Vienna. Dietl, however, instructed the pilot to fly over the Alps instead, so the mountain general could see his beloved highlands once again. Dietl added that he knew the ranges well and would assist in the crossing.

The flight started smoothly, but at Mürzzuschlag the ground rose sharply and the pilot had to fly somewhat lower as the cloud cover began descending. This combination caused the pilot to fly blind and at Hartberg am Semmering, Austria the plane struck trees and crashed killing everyone on board.[8] Dietl was buried with full military honors in a state funeral at Munich several days later.

Thus, in one incident four general officers, including an army and two corps commanders, suddenly became fatalities.[9]

AUTOMOBILES

GO Heinrici's command car.

German generals rode in a variety of automobiles. Mercedes Benz, Horch, Kübelwagens and even motorcycles with sidecars, to name but a few, were all pressed into service for various commanding officers. Unlike Hitler's special touring cars, it is not believed that these vehicles had special armor plating or bullet resistant glass. Their function was purely transportation and not defense.[10]

GFM von Manstein's staff car. Note pennant and placard, lack of camouflage paint, absence of any armor plating and large flat glass windshield which easily reflects sunlight which can be seen by aircraft.

40

While wartime photos reveal some commanders employed effective camouflage paint schemes to make their vehicles less observable, other commanders sometimes personalized their vehicles with special flags and insignia, which, no doubt, made tracking the general's movement in occupied territories by underground or partisan members that much easier.

The following command pennants and tactical symbols were used to designate the various levels and sizes of units and their corresponding commanders.

The top left flag in the illustration (1) is for the commander of an army, the top right flag (2) is that of a panzer group commander, the lower left flag (3) is for a corps commander, while the lower right flag (4) is that displayed by a division commander. Army, corps and division car flags were the same for both armored and non-armored formations. These pennants were visible to the naked eye to about 50 yards; through field glasses or a sniper scope they could be seen at even greater distances.

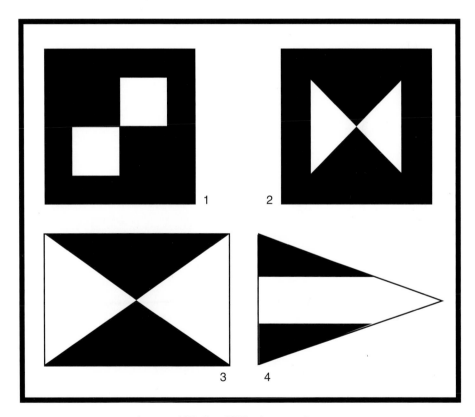

Army and Waffen-SS Headquarters Pennants

Overall, German staff cars provided convenient but vulnerable ground transportation for general officers. Best suited for transportation in low-threat areas, they were sadly lacking protection under any type of fire.

For actual combat, the battle-wise general was advised to ride in special command and control tactical vehicles. In addition to possessing radio communications, which most automobiles did not have, they were armored and afforded a marked increase in protection.

German commanders often rode in Sdkfz 251 halftracks, Sdkfz 251/6 medium command halftracks, and Sdkfz 251/3 radio equipped armored command vehicles. The armor thickness on these vehicles ranged from 14.5 mm on frontal portions to 8mm on the sides – some protection from small arms but almost none against tank or anti-tank fire. The tops of these vehicles were basically open and offered little protection from artillery fire exploding overhead or from attacking enemy aircraft. Maximum road speed was 33 mph; but the important item concerning mobility was that these vehicles could keep up with the mechanized infantry and tanks both on and off road, and thus would not be stranded on the battlefield where they would become easier targets.

At least two generals were killed in command halftracks and two more in command tanks, but this was far less lethal than riding in unarmored staff cars, or the even less-protected motorcycle sidecar – which some high risk-taking generals appeared to have used on occasion!

GdPz Fehn in motorcycle. (Executed in Yugoslavia, probably by partisans, June 5, 1945)

GdI Allmendinger's Kübelwagen.

GO Guderian's armored command vehicle.

AUTOMOBILE ACCIDENTS

Automobile accidents, the bane of 20th century Western societies, claimed several general officer lives. GdI Helmuth Volkmann, the commander of the 94th Infantry Division, died in an auto wreck on August 21, 1940. The following year on April 27, 1941 the commander of the 45th Infantry Division, GM Gerhard Körner, was killed in an automobile in Germany while visiting his family as his division was repositioning from France to Poland in preparation for the offensive against the Soviet Union. GM Joachim von Schleinitz, 96th Infantry Division, was the next to die in an automobile accident when he was killed October 5, 1942 in Russia during a night drive from corps headquarters back to his division.

In Italy GL Walter Wessel, the Inspector of the Panzer Forces, was killed in an auto wreck on a visit to an armored unit near Morano Italy, July 20, 1943. GMdSS Herbert Vahl, the incoming commander of the 4th SS Division *"Polizei"*, also fell victim to an accident. While on a visit to the 4th SS Panzer Battalion on anti-partisan duty near Larissa Greece, he was fatally injured on July 22, 1944 and died shortly thereafter.

On the Western Front GM Johannes Hintz of the Luftwaffe was killed in an auto wreck in Paris May 21, 1944, while back in the East, GM Oswin Grolig, commander of the 25th Panzer Division, was killed in his command car in Poland August 18, 1944. In Germany, GdI Walter Schroth, the commander of the XII Military District of the Replacement Army died in an accident on October 6, 1944.

A close call was experienced by GFM Albert Kesselring. On October 26, 1944, while traveling in his command car at night from Bologna to Forli, he ran into a German artillery piece as it was turning on a narrow Italian road. Kesselring's skull was fractured and he had to undergo emergency brain surgery to save his life; as a result, he was out of action for several months due to the mishap.[12]

All in all, German air and ground transportation was efficient, reliable, relatively safe from accidents and representative of 20th Century technology. On the other hand, the German Army medical system was a far more overtaxed organization, and contributed to the alarming number of general officers who died of their wounds.

CHAPTER NOTES

[1] Peter Hoffmann, *Hitler's Personal Security*, Cambridge, Massachusetts: The MIT Press, 1979, pp. 66-71.

[2] Kenneth Munson, *German Aircraft of World War 2*, Poole, England: Blandford Press, pp. 66-67.

[3] *Ibid.*, pp. 50-51

[4] *Ibid.*, pp. 99-101.

[5] Samuel Mitcham and Friedrich von Stauffenberg, *The Battle of Sicily*, New York: Orion Books, 1991, p. 304.

[6] Guenter Fraschka, *... mit Schwerten und Brillanten*, Rastatt, FRG: 1965, p. 164.

[7] "Der Landser" Magazin, Nummer 475, pp. 57-58.

[8] Ron Gamage, "The Death of Generaloberst Dietl", *After the Battle Magazine*, London: Plaistow Press, Number 72, pp. 32-34.

[9] Numerous other notable air accidents robbed German leadership. Air ace Werner Mölders was killed in an air crash. Vice Admiral Lothar von Arnauld de la Periere of the *Kriegsmarine* was killed at the Paris Le Bourget airport February 24, 1941 enroute to take command of German Naval Forces South. Luftwaffe *General der Flakartillerie* Ludwig von Schröder, Military Commander of Serbia died in an air-crash July 28, 1941. GM Julius von Bernuth, Chief of staff for the 4th Panzer Army was killed in an air crash July 12, 1942 near Ssochkranaja, USSR. Another aircraft accident killed Luftwaffe *General der Flieger* Otto Hoffmann von Waldau on May 17, 1943 near Petric, Macedonia in northern Greece. Von Waldau was serving as the commander of Luftwaffe Command Southeast at the time of the crash. GdGebT Franz Böhme, then commander of the 2nd Panzer Army, was seriously injured in a crash of a Fieseler Stork on July 15, 1944 and remained out of command until January 1945.

[10] Allied command cars were not designed for self defense either.

[11] Duncan Crow, ed, *Armored Fighting Vehicles of Germany, World War II*, New York: ARCO Publishing Company, pp. 166-169.

[12] Kenneth Macksey, *Kesselring: The Making of the Luftwaffe*, New York: David McKay Company, 1978, p. 226.

✛ CHAPTER 7 ✛

THE GERMAN ARMY MEDICAL SYSTEM

DEATHS AND SERIOUS WOUNDS

During World War Two, the German Central Archives for Military Medicine analyzed some 3,015,589 wounded soldiers with extremely detailed results. Overall, they found that of every 100 casualties, 24% were killed in action, 30% were seriously wounded and 46% were classified as lightly wounded. This compared to a casualty rate of 13.8% killed and 86.2% wounded in World War I. The archivists believed the increased death rate was due, in part, to an increase in weapons' lethality; additionally, the greater fluidity of the World War II battlefields made casualty evacuation more difficult than in the more static World War I battlefields.[1]

In 1942 the Archives did a study as to the location of war wounds on the human body. They found that of all wounds inflicted on German soldiers 5% were skull wounds, 8% facial wounds, 1.3% throat wounds, 6.3% shoulder wounds, 7.3% chest wounds, 6.3% upper arm wounds, 16.5% lower arm wounds, 3.5% stomach wounds, 10.1% upper leg wounds, 28.3% lower leg wounds and 3.4% back wounds.[2] By 1944 wounds were further categorized (shown below) as to location on the body (such as direct hit (massive simultaneous multiple wounds), head, chest, stomach, back, throat, legs and arms) with respect to casualties who were fatally wounded, seriously wounded (but survived) and lightly wounded.[3]

Wound Locations
(by percentage)

Site of Wound on Body	Fatally Wounded	Seriously Wounded	Lightly Wounded
Direct Hit	15.23	0.45	0.17
Head	42.61	16.66	16.49
Chest	22.11	11.28	3.00
Stomach	7.95	7.69	0.79
Back	4.11	10.45	9.06
Throat	3.36	2.92	2.82
Legs	3.04	28.02	29.90
Arms	0.64	22.53	37.77

Thus it was shown that of those patients who were fatally wounded, 42.61% had received head wounds while only 3.04% had been wounded in the legs. Leg wounds (28.02%), on the other hand, were the most frequent injury for seriously wounded patients, while arm injuries (37.77%) were the most frequent type of injury to those patients who were classified as lightly wounded.

Casualties who had serious wounds in their arms or legs had their damaged limbs amputated more frequently than in Western Allied armies. Amputations reduced the possibility of infections and actually allowed the soldier to sometimes return to limited duty. Several German generals, including GO Hans Hube (arm), GdA Erich Marcks (leg), GdPz Friedrich Gräser (leg) and GdA Walter Hartmann (arm and leg) had a limb amputated and still returned to command divisions, corps and even armies.

CASUALTY EVACUATION

The German system of evacuation of casualties was based on an immediate sorting of wounded so that less injured soldiers could be returned to their units as quickly as possible; while those more seriously wounded could receive advanced medical care quickly. Serious casualties – those unable to walk, were initially carried from the battlefield by battalion stretcher bearers to the battalion aid station. This aid station would give first aid in emergency cases; and as quickly as movement could be made, the patient would be transported to the regimental aid station. At this station, often only 200 to 500 yards to the rear of the front-lines, the wounded would receive more care while stretcher cases were carried to an ambulance loading post for continued rearward movement.

The patient was then transported to the main dressing station where more serious medical procedures could be performed such as amputations and blood transfusions.[4] After treatment at the main dressing station, casualties who could not be moved great distances without grave risk were moved to the nearest mobile field hospital, while those who could travel were moved to the rear to a base hospital or general hospital. Base hospitals were large, relatively permanent installations of upwards of 500 beds, established by an army or army group well to the rear of a combat zone. General hospitals were permanent installations inside Germany.[5]

General officer casualties often, but not always, received quicker, more efficient evacuation than the average line soldier, and often had specialist surgeons flown in to help. Even so, a surprisingly large number still died of their wounds while in hospital. GMdSS von Scholz, a division commander in the Waffen-SS, was a case in point of the often primitive conditions of combat versus the clean textbook theories of medical evacuation. He was wounded in the head by a Soviet artillery shell fragment and was carried on a wooden plank to the regimental aid station. A local supply truck was then pressed into service to transport von Scholz to a specialist surgery station, and the general was placed in the back of the vehicle on a straw mattress. A medical orderly tried to staunch the flow of blood and to keep the swarms of buzzing Russian flies off the wounded patient, but the rough ride caused von Scholz to bleed to death.[6]

A German field marshal also fell victim during medical transportation. GFM Walther von Reichenau, the commander of the 6th Army from 1939 to early 1942, was not a well man. During the Polish Campaign then GdA von Reichenau experienced a fainting spell while leading his troops. In early 1941 he suffered a slight stroke while in Berlin but appeared to have made a complete recovery. Several months later he was afflicted with phlebitis and severe thrombosis. Von Reichenau also experienced severe mental anxiety. When the *SS-Leibstandarte* massacred several hundred unarmed Jewish civilians near Radom, Poland in September 1939, von Reichenau wrote a letter to Hitler stating he no longer wished to have any SS units assigned to his army. He believed in 1940 that the planned invasion through Belgium (Plan Yellow) was "criminal" as it deployed into a neutral nation. During the 6th Army's advance through the Ukraine in the Autumn of 1941, von Reichenau berated the leader of an *SS-Einsatzgruppe* (mobile death squad) when he found out that the SS had murdered ninety Jews near Belaya Tserkov. All these complaints obviously fell on deaf ears.

Physical and mental afflictions culminated on January 15, 1942 when, after a usual morning jog through the brisk air at the headquarters of Army Group South at Poltava, the field marshal suffered a cerebral hemorrhage. On January 17, 1942 Hitler ordered that the unconscious von Reichenau be flown back to Germany for advanced medical treatment from some of the best medical specialists in the *Reich*. The evacuation flight left Poltava that day but later, due to fog, had to make an emergency landing in a ploughed field near Cracow, Poland – and the rough ride caused von Reichenau to go into terminal heart failure. The veteran troop commander was replaced by the relatively inexperienced Friedrich Paulus.

These often less-than-adequate evacuation conditions simply increased battlefield lethality which in itself had unfortunately heightened from previous conflicts.

CHAPTER NOTES

[1] Hubert Fischer, *Der deutsche Sanitätsdienst 1921-1945, Band 4*, Osnabrück, FRG: Biblio Verlag, 1985, pp. 3191-3193.

[2] *Ibid.*

[3] *Ibid.*, Cold Weather injuries also took their toll. Casualty returns for the German Army in front of Moscow, December 1941 show over 100,000 cases of frostbite. Over 14,000 were classified as "major" and required one or more amputations. About 62,000 were "moderate", resulting in total incapacity but not requiring amputation; 36,000 were classified as "light", with the patient able to return to duty in 10 days or less. To commemorate the campaign, Hitler instituted the Eastern Front Medal! The troops referred to the decoration as the *Gefrierfleisch Orden* – Order of the Frozen Meat!

[4] *Handbook on German Military Forces*, Gaithersburg, Maryland: The Military Press, 1970, pp. VI-23, VI-24.

[5] *Ibid.*

[6] Richard Landwehr, *Narva 1944: The Waffen-SS and the Battle for Europe*, Silver Spring, Maryland: Bibliophile Legion Books, 1981, pp. 88-89.

✠ CHAPTER 8 ✠
BATTLEFIELD LETHALITY

Battlefield lethality increased from World War I to World War II, multiplying the ways a general officer commander could be killed in action. It included enemy artillery, minefields, anti tank fire, small arms fire, grenades, air attacks, tank fire, snipers, aircraft shootdowns, naval gunfire and partisans. Many of these causes, such as air attacks and tank fire, were relatively infrequent occurrences in World War I. Others, like artillery fire directed by the results of radio direction finding, were quantum improvements over previously less accurate acquisition means.

The turbulent situation during the last years of the war limits our knowledge of the exact cause of death to only 101 of the general officer commander fatalities. Assuming the following table reflects a relative consistency in cause of death, the enemy attack means were quite varied:

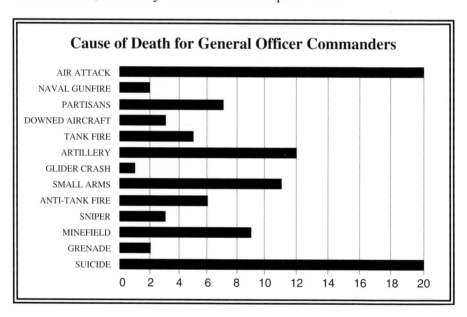

As was seen previously in the section concerning World War I awards, over two-thirds of the general officers killed in action in World War I had seen front-line service in the Great War. Serving in that earlier conflict as captains and lieutenants, their concept of personal danger was shaped by their first experiences in combat. This, coupled with command rotation policies caused many generals to be sadly ignorant of the multitude of ways in which they could be killed. In World War I personal danger for officers had been the great artillery barrages and heavy machine gun fire. Although these two weapons systems again accounted for many general officer deaths, a wide variety of other systems played an equally deadly role. The total number of causes of death, however, tell only part of the story. The following accounts of individual demises reflect this increased lethality, and better describe the significant dangers to these senior commanders.

AIR ATTACK

The enemy's air superiority has a very grave effect on our movements. There's simply no answer to it.

(GFM Erwin Rommel)[1]

Enemy air attack was the most overwhelming cause of German general officer fatalities in battle during the war; and the impact of enemy air attacks began to be felt early on. During the campaign for North Africa, GM Max Sümmermann, commander of the 90th Light Division, was killed by a strafing British aircraft at 7:00 PM, December 10, 1941. He was riding in his command vehicle when hit.[2] Erwin Rommel had lost a key division commander and the impact of the loss of command of the air was a lesson the field marshal never forget.

Later in the war, just as GFM Rommel had predicted, Allied air power played a decisive role during the invasion and campaign at Normandy. Three German generals during this campaign were killed in air attacks. One, GdA Erich Marcks, commander LXXIV Corps, was killed enroute to Carentan by a strafing fighter when his wooden leg prevented a quick escape from his automobile.[3]

GM Rudolf Stegmann, commander of the 77th Infantry Division, was struck in the head by 20 mm cannon fire from a strafing Allied fighter plane while driving in his command car near Briebeque France, June 18, 1944. The day before GL Heinz Hellmich, commander 243rd Infantry Division, was killed by another strafing fighter near Cherbourg.[4]

Rommel himself was severely wounded in perhaps the most well-known strafing incident of the war. On July 17, 1944 he spent the day visiting combat units to include the 277th Infantry and 276th Infantry Divisions who were trying to hold the line against mounting Allied pressure in Normandy. He finished his tour by visiting GdSS Dietrich at his I SS Panzer Corps headquarters in St. Pierre-sur-Dives. As Rommel prepared to depart and make the return drive to his own headquarters in La Roche-Guyon, Allied air activity was high, but he decided to make the journey anyway.

The Horch staff car with Rommel, Captain Lang his aide-de-camp, Major Neuhaus, Sergeant Daniel his driver and Holke began the return trip at approximately 4:00 PM. During the trip Captain Lang recalled seeing "eight enemy Jabos (fighter bombers) over Livarot, which, as was determined later, had been watching and strafing traffic on the roads leading to Livarot for

Generals Marcks and Falley – both KIA in Normandy. Note awkward movement by Marcks as he attempts to sit, caused by the loss of his leg.

about four hours. Since we believed that we had not been spotted by the enemy planes the trip was continued on the direct route from Livarot to Vimoutiers." [5] As the car continued, approaching a small rise, Holke, who was acting as an aircraft lookout, spotted two aircraft turning toward their direction. Rommel ordered his driver to accelerate in an attempt to reach a wooded area some 300 yards away, but the Allied planes were too quick and closed to firing positions.

Lang continued: "At this moment GFM Rommel looked back. The strafing plane unloosed high-explosive shells. Rommel was hit in the face by glass splinters and received a blow against the left temple and cheekbone, which resulted in a triple fracture of the skull (probably from striking the pillar of the windshield) and immediate unconsciousness.[6] Neuhaus was seriously injured as was Daniel who lost control of the vehicle causing it to plunge into a ditch. Rommel was thrown 20 yards from the vehicle onto the road. Rommel was taken first to a pharmacy and then to a hospital, but his commanding days were over and he never saw action again.

The aerial advantage enjoyed by the Allies, and it's potential for danger to German general officers perhaps can best be explained by an Allied pilot flying over Normandy one morning in a Typhoon ground attack plane.

Swirling clouds of yellow dust hung over the busy roads beneath us, and further to the southeast the battered city of Caen flickered and smoldered under a huge mushroom of pink and black smoke. Southward, in the region of Villers-Bocage, a furious gun battle was taking place, and to the west, thin streams of coloured tracer spouted into the morning sky before falling away in chains of red-hot clusters. In the more open country the field were strewn with the bloated carcasses of hundreds of tan and white cattle. Shell craters, bomb holes and burnt-out tanks littered the tortured countryside.

To the south of Potigny we began climbing but streams of light flak came racing up towards us. So I hastily sank down again to the comparative safety of the taller trees and hedgerows. I caught sight of the object of our early morning mission. The road was crammed with enemy vehicles – tanks, trucks, half-tracks, even horse-drawn wagons and ambulances, nose to tail, all pressing forward in a frantic bid to reach cover before the skies once more became alive with the winged death of the 2nd Tactical Air Force. As I sped to the head of this mile-long column, hundreds of German troops began spilling out into the road to sprint for the open fields and hedgerows.

I zoomed up sharply over a ploughed field where 20 or 30 Germans in close array were running for a clump of trees. They were promptly scythed down by a lone Mustang which appeared from nowhere. The convoy's lead vehicle was a large half-track. In my haste to cripple it and seal the road, I let fly with all eight rockets in a single salvo; I missed but hit the truck that was following it. It was thrown into the air along with several bodies, and fell back on its side. Two other trucks in close attendance piled into it.

Within seconds the whole stretch of road was bursting and blazing under streams of rocket and cannon fire. Ammunition wagons exploded like multi-coloured volcanoes. Several teams of horses stampeded and careered wildly across the fields, dragging their broken wagons behind them. Others fell in tangled, kicking heaps, or were caught up in the fences and hedges. It was an awesome sight: Flames, smoke, bursting rockets and showers of coloured tracer – an army in retreat, trapped and without air protection. [7]

The eyes of the eagles were indeed sharp; and ever vigilant for the moving target be it tank, truck or even command car of a German general.

Twelve general officers are known to have died by Red Air Force attacks on the Eastern Front. During the first part of the war, when the German Luftwaffe enjoyed general air superiority, Soviet ground attack aircraft concentrated on German motorized columns, with attacking units often consisting of two pair of aircraft. At this time Soviet fighter planes were mainly involved against the German Luftwaffe.

Attacks were initially carried out from altitudes of 150-300 meters, but this was increased in 1942 to 800-1200 meters which improved accuracy. During the mid-war period Soviet ground attack techniques evolved further as the Red Air Force began to achieve air parity over sections of the front. Targets were expanded from the earlier emphasis on enemy tactical columns to now include disruption of rail and highway communications. Additionally, ground-attack aircraft were given "free hunting" missions based on defined geographic regions.

One pair of aircraft would be given an assigned area but allowed to select their own targets and methods of attack. A final method of attack was the "circle of death" in which Soviet aircraft would initially approach line astern of a German target. Then, the first aircraft would dive, circle and attack the target. It would be followed in turn by each aircraft, the circle being maintained until the target was destroyed or all attacking aircraft had run out of ammunition. These Soviet ground attack aircraft, the most famous and effective was the IL-2 *Sturmovik*, were indeed effective – the Germans referred to the *Sturmovik* as the "Black Death".[8]

The official history of the Soviet Air Force in World War II makes no claim that Soviet air units killed any German general officers in their attacks. This would seem to indicate that none of the attacks which occurred were specifically planned or the results of enemy generals killed from the air known to the Soviet command.[9] Instead, the Soviet Air Force had as its objective the destruction of enemy troops and equipment on the battlefield and in the operational rear. As many as 1,500-2,000 aircraft were often employed over relatively small sectors of the front to ensure the success of breakthrough operations; and this number of aircraft made life for German generals hazardous indeed – even if the generals were not knowingly attacked by Soviet ground attack pilots.

Whatever the techniques used, or the plans behind them, one German army commander, GdI Ernst von Krosigk, 16th Army, was killed at his headquarters at Zabeln, in the Courland region of Latvia, by a Soviet fighter bomber attack March 16, 1945.[10]

Five corps commanders also died from Soviet air attacks on the Eastern Front. GdI Kurt von Briesen, LII Corps, was killed at 12:30 PM, November 20, 1941 southeast of Andrejewka by attacking Soviet aircraft. Making a visit to his forward infantry regiments, his moving car was strafed from the right rear by two Soviet fighters boring in at an altitude of only 150 feet. Several other occupants jumped from the vehicle and made their escape, but the general was not so fortunate. His body was found – still in the wrecked, smoldering automobile, riddled with twelve machine-gun bullets.[11]

GdI von Briesen (KIA November 20, 1941) – did he understand the military use of the horse better than he did the lethality of the airplane?

GdI Hans Zorn, commander XXXXVI Panzer Corps, was killed from the air enroute to a front-line unit on August 2, 1943.[12] GdA Robert Martinek was killed by a bomb splinter, June 28, 1944 east of the Beresina River while commander of the XXXIX Panzer Corps.[13] Leading a column of corps vehicles from Belenitschi toward the Beresina River at about 5:00 PM, the general and his unit were blocked on the road by a huge traffic jam caused by fleeing German units. At that instant several Soviet fighter bombers pounced on the Germans and the general was killed.[14] That same day at about 8:00 PM, GdA Georg Pfeiffer, commander VI Corps, was killed from the air in the vicinity of Mogilev.[15] Finally, Soviet air attacks killed GdI Wilhelm Wegener, commander L Corps, on September 24, 1944 as he was enroute to visit a subordinate infantry division in Courland.[16]

German division commanders did not escape Soviet air attacks either. GL Otto Gabcke, commander of the 294th Infantry Division was killed, along with his operations officer and seven soldiers, when two Rata aircraft bombed a school in Michailowka, which was serving at the time as the headquarters for the division, on March 22, 1942. GL Ernst Haccius of the 46th Infantry Division was killed February 14, 1943 by an air attack near Taman as Soviet commanders attempted to exploit the recent defeat of the German 6th Army with further offensives.[18]

GL Ernst Haccius (KIA February 14, 1943)

In the Kuban area of southern Russia, Soviet aircraft, dropping bombs and strafing with machine guns, attacked the headquarters of the 97th Jäger Division approximately 4:00 PM, May 30, 1943. GL Ernst Rupp, the division commander, was killed by a bomb fragment during the incident.[19]

By the fall of 1943 Soviet attack aircraft became even bolder. Reports from the German 137th Infantry Division state that enemy attack aircraft now were striking not only the German front lines, but also supporting artillery positions and throughout the depth of the division sector. GL Hans Kamecke, the division commander, was a victim of one such attack. In the early morning hours of October 15, 1943, he drove to the forward command post of the 447th Infantry Regiment for an orientation of the current battle situation. On his return trip to division headquarters near Kolpen, he was suddenly strafed by Soviet fighters and was mortally wounded. He died the next day. Two days later the division published a special order of the day which read:[20]

GL Kamecke consulting a battle map (KIA October 16, 1943).

Generalleutnant Kamecke died on the morning of 16 October 1943 from serious wounds received the day before south of Kolpen. After the heroic death of the first commander of the division, Generalleutnant Bergmann, he (Kamecke) has led the division with the exception of one month when he was wounded, through two heavy defense campaigns in both Winter and Summer. We lower our colors to this valiant and renowned general in mourning and respect.

GM Friedrich Blümke, the commander of the 257th Infantry Division was severely wounded in a Soviet air attack near Tighina by Tirasopol on August 24, 1944. Struck in the chest by a large piece of shrapnel, he died of his wounds on September 4.

GM Harald von Hirschfeld of the 78th Volks-Grenadier Division was mortally wounded by a bomb fragment January 18, 1945 at the Dunajec Bridge near Tarnow, Poland.[21] His adjutant made a desperate attempt to get the general to a field hospital, but von Hirschfeld died in his arms. In the desperate final days of fighting on the Eastern Front, GM Maximilian Wengler and his 83rd Infantry Division made a last ditch stand at the citadel at Pillau along the Baltic coast. As resistance crumbled on April 25, 1945, Wengler ordered the division to flee from the city, south across the Pillau Canal to safety. Waiting for the last boat, he was killed by a Soviet air attack along with members of his staff.[22] The following chart summarizes these fatalities and shows the rise of Soviet airpower:

Eastern Front Air Attacks

Name	Unit	Date of Death
GdI von Briesen	LII Army Corps	November 20, 1941
GL Gabcke	294 Onfantry Division	March 22, 1942
GL Haccius	46 Infantry Division	February 14, 1943
GL Rupp	97 Jäger Division	May 30, 1943
GdI Zorn	XXXXVI Panzer Corps	August 2, 1943
GL Kamecke	137 Infantry Division	October 16, 1943
GdA Pfeiffer	VI Army Corps	June 26, 1944
GdA Martinek	XXXIX Army Corps	June 28, 1944
GL Schünemann	XXXIX Army Corps	June 29, 1944
GM Blümke	257 Infantry Division	September 2, 1944
GdI Wegener	L Army Corps	September 24, 1944
GM von Hirschfeld	78 Infantry Division	January 18, 1945
GdI von Krosigk	16 Army	March 16, 1945
GM Wengler	83 Infantry Division	April 25, 1945

In examining overall commander fatalities to Soviet air attacks it is apparent that they mirror the rise of Soviet air power and the wane of the Luftwaffe. One German general was killed from the air in 1941, two in 1942, four in 1943, five in 1944 and three during the first four months of 1945.

GM Hellmuth Pfeifer (KIA April 22, 1945).

GL Baade – note Tank Destruction Badge on sleeve denoting that during the war he destroyed an enemy tank in close combat with a grenade or other small anti-tank weapon.

In Italy, Allied fighters also struck with devastating efficiency. A lone Allied fighter bomber strafed GL Hellmuth Pfeifer, commander of the 65th Infantry Division, as he was crossing a bridge over the Panaro River on April 22, 1945. Pfeifer, who was not accompanied by anti aircraft weapons, was killed by the plane's cannon and machine-gun fire.[23]

Another late war incident occurred in Germany itself. On April 24, 1945 near Gut Neverstaven in Holstein GL Ernst Baade, the outgoing commander of the LXXXI Army Corps, was strafed in his command vehicle by a British aircraft, as he was enroute to his estate. Shot through the neck and leg, he was rushed to a hospital at Bad Segeberg. Several of the rounds which struck him were apparently tracer. The phosphorous material from the base of the tracer round caused his wounds to become infected and he died two weeks later.[24]

MINEFIELDS

Generals Heitz, von Brauchitch and Strauss examine a mine detector, France 1940. Enemy mines were not always detected.

Surprisingly enough, at least nine commanders died in incidents involving minefields. The first was GM Kalmukoff, the commander of the 31st Infantry Division, who was killed in a Russian minefield along with his adjutant on August 13, 1941 near the Dnepr River.[25] On September 12, 1941, GO Ritter von Schobert, commander of the 11th Army, was killed when his Fieseler Stork aircraft attempted a forced landing and inadvertently landed in a Soviet minefield killing all aboard.[26] GL Ludwig Löweneck, commander of the 39th Infantry Division, drove into a minefield north of Petschenegi,[27] and

GL Friedrich Schmidt, commander of the 50th Infantry Division, blundered into another minefield in the Russian Kuban while visiting an artillery firing position.[28] GM Bruno Hippler, commander of the 329th Infantry Division, was also killed in a minefield. On March 23, 1942 he was riding to forward positions near Lake Ilmen to get a look at the front-line situation, as the Soviet 2nd Shock Army had made a penetration in the sector. However, his vehicle struck a mine, and the crew was finished off in close combat with Soviet infantry who swarmed over the immobilized panzer.[29] GL Werner Richter, the commander of the 263rd Infantry Division, was killed in a minefield of sorts. On May 21, 1944 he, along with elements of his division, occupied former Soviet positions which were mined with explosives. Somehow the explosive charges were detonated and Richter was seriously wounded. He was medically evacuated to a field hospital in Riga where he died of his wounds on June 3, 1944.[30]

GL Fischer (KIA February 1, 1943)

Two other commanders died in Africa from minefield effects. GM Heinz von Randow, commander of the 21st Panzer Division was killed near Tripoli, December 21, 1942 by a mine laid by the British Long Range Desert Group.[31]

"Friendly" minefields also took their toll. GL Wolfgang Fischer, commander of the 10th Panzer Division, was killed on February 1, 1943 near Mareth when his staff car driver inadvertently drove into a poorly marked Italian minefield.[32] Fischer, who had grievous wounds to both legs and one arm, tried to write a last note to his wife as he lay dying, but expired within a few minutes.

In a mine-related incident earlier in the war, GM Georg Braun, the commander of the 68th Infantry Division, was blown up in his headquarters in Kharkov on November 14, 1941 by a time-fused mine. The mine, along with hundreds of other explosive devices, had been emplaced by Soviet units just before they were forced to abandon the city in the face of the continuing German onslaught. Braun's headquarters had interestingly enough been previously used by Nikita Khrushchev, Communist Party boss of the area[33].

PARTISANS

We have to be thankful to the Germans that their policy enabled us to fan the flames of the partisan movement.

(Alexander Scherbakov, Member of the Soviet Politburo)[34]

The German military effort in World War II took many forms and went beyond traditional, conventional, combat. Many German units were engaged in rear area missions, or had extensive partisan problems in their own front-line areas. Post-war German historian Heinz Kühnrich in his seminal work *"Der Partisanenkrieg in Europa 1939-45"* estimates that overall, 1,933,000 partisans operated in the Soviet Union during the war, 370,000 fought in Yugoslavia and 350,000 were active in Poland.[35] The Germans referred to these guerrilla bands as "bandits" but whatever the name, they played a crucial role in operations. Partisans struck hard at rail lines and roadways as described in the following account of this brutal warfare in Russia:

> *Bridges were prime targets for sabotage, as they were the sole means by which a road could be cut for more than a few hours. Apart from mining, the main guerrilla tactic employed against roads consisted of direct attacks on enemy vehicles and convoys. These generally followed the same pattern. A German convoy traveling through a forest would meet a log barrier placed at a blind spot on the road; on coming to a halt, or attempting to turn, they would be exposed to devastating fire from all sides. If any vehicle managed to escape, it would be caught and destroyed by another roadblock set up in the rear. Single snipers were also used, espe-*

cially during the early days of the war, and, as the partisans became stronger, infantry-type assaults were made on convoys which had been brought to a halt; they usually ended with the destruction of the vehicles.[36]

At least seven German general officer commanders are known to have been killed in action against partisan units. On August 26, 1943 GL Kurt Renner, commander 174th Reserve Infantry Division, was ambushed near Ozarow while enroute to the Deba maneuver area and killed. Although the route was known to be in a partisan area, Renner was accompanied on his visit by only his adjutant, a staff veterinarian, and five other staff personnel.[37]

GM Walter Herold, commander of the 10th Motorized Division, was also killed in this manner when he was ambushed returning from a visit to an assembly area of the 110th Armored Reconnaissance Battalion near Bochnia, Poland, southeast of Cracow, November 28, 1944. He was traveling with just his aide, a lieutenant, when the ambush occurred.[38] His body was discovered the following day in a nearby woods, covered with leaves.

By the autumn of 1944 northern Italy was in a state of near civil war as partisan bands consisting of escaped prisoners of war, royalist army officers and Communist cells attacked German lines of communications through the Po River valley.

The fighting became intense – GFM Kesselring later estimated casualties from June to August at over 5,000 German soldiers killed.[39] By September German generals in the area were unable to move freely without danger. GL von Senger und Etterlin, the commander of the XIV Panzer Corps wrote:

Every time I drove to the front now, I had to pass through a guerrilla-infested district. Normally I drove in the little Volkswagen and displayed no general's insignia of rank – no peaked cap, no gold or red flags.[40]

Near Bologna GM Wilhelm Crisolli, commander 20th Luftwaffe Field Division, was caught and killed by partisans in the vicinity of the XIV Panzer Corps headquarters, September 12, 1944, as he returned from a conference with von Senger.[41] Apparently, he had not heeded his boss' warning.

Things were not much better in Poland any later in the war than they had been earlier. GdI Siegfried Hänicke, the chief of army security in the Government-General (occupied) Poland commented on many occasions about the deteriorating security there.[42]

The railways and roads can no longer be considered safe, when it is a question of directing reserves to the East ... a large number of the Members of the Forces do not seem to have realized that when they find themselves in the Government-General area, they are not in the Fatherland, but in a region where the majority of the population is hostile to us and opposes us with violence.

GM Crisolli (KIA September 12, 1944)

GdI Hermann Recknagel.
(KIA January 23, 1945)

During the Red Army offensive across Poland in 1945 the Soviet 5th Guards Army and 3rd Guards Tank Army unleashed a massive artillery bombardment from the Baranow bridgehead against the 4th Panzer Army, broke through German defenses and pushed toward the foothills of Cracow. This deep penetration of over sixty miles overran the headquarters of the XXXXII Army Corps on January 23, 1945 near Petrikau, Poland – killing or capturing the bulk of the corps staff. GdI Hermann Recknagel, its commander, avoided capture by regular Soviet Army forces, but fell into the hands of Polish partisans in the area and was killed.[43]

On April 9, 1945 GL Johann Mickl was severely wounded in the head during intense fighting at Vratnik Pass Yugoslavia at the front-lines of his 392nd Infantry Division. He was first transported to a field hospital at Senj but needed further treatment to the rear. Enroute to a hospital at Fiume, in a filled ambulance, his party was ambushed by Yugoslav partisans. The general was shot twice more in the lungs (everyone else was killed) which caused his death the following day in Fiume.[44]

German retribution against captured partisans fed the flames of partisan warfare rather than extinguished them.

ARTILLERY

To make the breakthrough a success, Rokossovsky will need one more artillery corps.

(Marshal Georgi Zhukov) [45]

Artillery continued to play a dominant role in warfare during World War II, and took a deadly toll of German generals. The amount of firepower available from artillery increased dramatically from World War I in several ways. Rocket artillery was revived and used extensively for area targets. Gun mobility increased through the use of self-propelled carriages and increased use of motorized prime movers for towed pieces. The use of recoilless guns enabled the WWII infantryman to carry his own artillery with him. Finally, radio communications and aerial observation enabled artillery to fire much more quickly and accurately than in 1918.

At least twelve German generals were killed by this system, and probably many more unknown deaths were in fact due to artillery. Especially hard hit were panzer generals. On December 6, 1941, GM Walter Neumann-Silkow, 15th Panzer Division, was fatally wounded by British artillery fire which landed next to his command tank, a Panzer Mark III.[46] When the rounds hit, Neumann-Silkow was exposed in the commanders hatch and had no time to seek safety inside the turret. He was promptly evacuated to Derna but died three days later.[47]

GM Neumann-Silkow exposed in the cupola giving directions (DOW December 6, 1941)

The following year, GM Georg von Bismarck, 21st Panzer Division, was probably killed by British mortar fire while advancing with a lead battalion near El Alamein.[48] GFM Erwin Rommel, however, believed that von Bismarck had been killed by a mine, illustrating the "fog of war" that surrounds many accounts of the fighting.[49]

On the Eastern Front four more panzer generals were killed by artillery. During the German 1942 offensive to seize the oil fields in the Caucasus region of southern Russia, GM Erwin Mack, 23rd Panzer Division, was killed by a Soviet mortar barrage on August 26, 1942 near Nowo Poltawskoje. At the time, approximately 10:00 AM, he was forward with the 128th Motorized Infantry Regiment.[50]

Killed with Mack were three other officers next to the general's halftrack command vehicle. The rounds struck so quickly that the general and his subordinates were unable to reach protective cover inside the vehicle.

On January 28, 1944, GM Adalbert Schulz, 7th Panzer Division, was hit in the head by mortar fragments while leading a panzer attack from his command tank near Schepetowka. Although medically evacuated, he died enroute to a field hospital.[51]

65

GM Mack (KIA August 26, 1942) with his panzer men

GLdSS Werner Ostendorff, 2nd SS Division *"Das Reich"*, was seriously wounded on March 8, 1945 near Lake Balaton, Hungary when his VW-Kübelwagen received a direct hit from Soviet artillery. He died of his wounds two months later. On March 26, 1945, GM Gustav von Nostitz-Wallwitz, 24th Panzer Division, was seriously wounded in the abdomen by artillery shrapnel as he was directing a withdrawal from his headquarters. Evacuated by motor boat to a field hospital, he underwent emergency surgery. Recuperating in the basement of a bombed-out Luftwaffe kaserne, his wounds became infected and he died May 31, 1945 at Eckernförde, Germany.[52]

Artillery was just as dangerous to non-panzer commanders as shown in the case of GL Stephan Rittau, 129th Infantry Division, who was killed by artillery riding in his command vehicle near Martinowo on August 22, 1942. At the time he was with the 427th Infantry Regiment "for a picture of the situation and the handling of the battle."[53] On August 8, 1941, while leading his

GL Rittau (KIA August 22, 1942) on right with GL Materna (left).

troops forward in the attack from his Kübelwagen, *SS-Gruppenführer* Arthur Mülverstedt, the commander of the SS *"Polizei"* Division, was struck in the chest by shrapnel from Soviet mortar fire. He was rushed to an aid station but died shortly thereafter.[54] He was wearing a camouflage jacket which was excellent concealment from snipers but no protection from artillery.

SS-Brigadeführer Friedrich von Scholz was struck in the head by shrapnel from a heavy Soviet artillery barrage during the Battle of Narva on July 27, 1944, as he was inspecting fighting positions of the 13th Company, 24th SS Regiment *"Danmark"* of the 11th Waffen SS Division *"Nordland"*. He was first transported to the division field hospital at Kothla-Jarva, and then to a surgery unit at Wesenberg. He died of his wounds however, enroute. Hitler posthumously promoted von Scholz, and awarded him the Swords to his previous decorations of the Knight's Cross and Oak Leaves.[55]

On July 13, 1944 spearheads of the *1st Ukrainian Front*, under General Koniev, pierced German lines, drove deep into the Army Group rear and met at the Bug River – some 30 miles west of the city of L'vov. Encircled were five divisions of the German XIII Army Corps. GdI Arthur Hauffe, commander of the corps, was killed by artillery fire while supposedly riding on a train inside the pocket near L'vov on July 22, 1944; according to an eyewitness who reached German lines in August.[56]

Later in the war, on April 9, 1945 during the Soviet siege of Königsberg, GM Erich Sudau, the commander of the 548th Volks-Grenadier Division, attempted to lead a desperate breakout of a few men and one assault gun from the doomed city. Soon after the assault began he was cut down by artillery fire in the vicinity of the Luisen Church near the city center.[57]

NAVAL GUNFIRE

German military operations in coastal areas frequently came under attack by Allied naval bombardment. Two German division commanders are known to have been killed by naval gunfire; one on the Eastern and one on the Western Front. The Soviet Black Sea Squadron played an important role in supporting the Red Army's 44th Army in the Crimean area from January to March 1942. During this defensive operation, the battleship *Sevastopol*, accompanied by three to four destroyers, conducted six coastal bombardments of German forces.[58]

GM Himer in more peaceful surroundings (KIA March 22, 1942).

Steaming from the port of Poti, on the southern shore of the Crimea, the ships conducted night attacks on enemy positions at Feodosiya, Vladislavovka, Nowo Michailowka, Staryy Krym, Saly and Taraktam. From March 11 through 22 several cruisers and additional destroyers joined in these bombardments with a further eleven strikes. These missions had one aim; that of disrupting enemy forces by attacking command and observation posts and communications centers.[59] GL Kurt Himer, commander of the 46th Infantry Division, was a victim of shelling by these units of the Soviet Black Sea Squadron near Nowo Michailowka on the Kerch Peninsula of the Crimea on March 22, 1942.[60]

On the Western Front, Allied naval power was a key ingredient in the success of the Normandy invasion. On D-Day itself, no less than 9 battleships, 23 cruisers, 104 destroyers and 71 corvettes provided support for Allied troops going ashore. As long as Allied units were in range of the ships' guns they were in receipt of naval gunfire support. Heavy capital ships literally expended their ammunition, returned to England for resupply, and then reappeared on station to fire again – thanks to Allied dominance of the air over the English channel.

SS-Brigadeführer Fritz Witt, commander of the 12th SS Panzer Division *"Hitlerjugend"*, was killed about noon, June 14, 1944 in Normandy by the effects of this overwhelming fire support. Controlled by an artillery spotter aircraft, British naval gunfire in this incident initially missed the division headquarters, which was located seventeen miles southwest of Caen.

Witt came out of the chateau, which was serving as the command post, apparently believing that the intended target of the attack was a battery of the division's 100mm artillery located several hundred yards to the southeast. However, the shelling continued and soon found the correct range. The general and several of his troops sought cover in nearby trenches; but at that moment, a 16" shell from a battleship exploded in the trees above showering the area with shrapnel. Witt was struck in the head by a fragment killing him instantly.[61]

It is possible that Allied intelligence gained from ULTRA helped locate these key assets of the 12th SS. On June 10, ULTRA was used to pinpoint the headquarters of *Panzergruppe West* and an airstrike was launched to bomb the location. It was a direct hit and so many officers were killed, that the headquarters was not functional for two weeks.[62]

AIRCRAFT SHOOTDOWNS

Three commanders were shot down and killed while flying near the battle area. The first involved *SS-Obergruppenführer* Theodor Eicke. During February 1943, the SS Division *"Totenkopf"* participated in GFM von Manstein's counteroffensive that retook Kharkov. On the afternoon of February 26, 1943 the division was involved in a lengthy pursuit of Soviet forces. A long radio silence from the division armored regiment caused

Eicke to take to the air in his Fieseler Storch observation plane to attempt to gain contact with the unit. Approximately 4:30 PM, Eicke and his pilot spotted a company from the silent regiment in the village of Michailovka and the aircraft approached to land. Dropping to 300 feet Eicke passed over some unseen Russian positions in an adjoining village of Artelnoye.

The enemy immediately opened fire with intense small arms and antiaircraft fire. The Storch was ripped apart in midair, crashed between the two villages and burned fiercely leaving no survivors. That night SS troops repeatedly attempted to reach the wreckage with no success. The following morning, a reinforced company succeeded, and recovered the charred bodies of Eicke, his division adjutant and his pilot.[63]

The 16th Army lost its commander in an aircraft shootdown as well. On August 29, 1944, GdI Paul Laux took off in a Fieseler Storch on a reconnaissance flight from Riga. His plane was shot down over the front-lines, most probably by a Soviet fighter aircraft, and the general received critical burns and died soon after in a field hospital in the city.[64]

GdI Laux (left) and GFM Busch, June 1943 south of Lake Ilmen (Laux DOW September 2, 1944).

GdPz Ludwig Crüwell, then commander of the Africa Corps, was shot down and captured in Africa. On May 29, 1942 Crüwell took his *Storch* to visit the headquarters of the X Italian Corps during the battles near Gazala. During the flight they inadvertently strayed over British lines, received a crippling burst of anti-aircraft fire. Flying at a height of only 150 meters, the first burst of machine-gun fire hit the plane's engine; the second struck and killed the pilot. Crüwell crashed in enemy positions and was promptly captured by British soldiers.[65]

Over the Mediterranean, British fighters also achieved success. GL Kurt Thomas, commander of the 999th Light Africa Division was shot down enroute to Tunis April 1, 1943.[66]

GL Crüwell (left, POW) and GM Bayerlein with command vehicle "Moritz"

Although not a ground commander, the Luftwaffe's GO Ulrich Grauert became the senior German general of the war to be killed in an aircraft shootdown, and the senior Luftwaffe officer to fall in combat. Grauert, the commander of the 1st *Flieger* Corps, which controlled German fighter squadrons in northwest France, was shot down and killed on May 15, 1941 over St. Omer by British fighter planes. He had led the corps with distinction since 1939 and would be sorely missed.

Admiral Günther Lütjens, Commander of the Fleet, was the senior Navy commander to be killed in action during the war. Sailing with the battleship *Bismarck*, the pride of the Kriegsmarine, he went down with the ship in the Atlantic after the British Home Fleet finally caught up with the German warship after a legendary chase from Norway through the Denmark Straits and at last toward France. The year before, Commodore Friedrich Bonte, Commander of Battle Group 1, was killed at Narvik on April 19, 1940 during the German invasion of Norway. Bonte's ship, the destroyer *Wilhelm Heidkamp,* was sunk along with several other German ships in the fjord but Narvik fell to the Germans and the Allies withdrew from Scandinavia. Finally, Rear Admiral Erich Bey was killed in action December 26, 1943 in the Norwegian Sea when the battleship *Scharnhorst* was ambushed and sunk by British naval forces led by the battleship Duke of York. Although other German admirals would die during the war, no others would be killed in naval surface combat as the High Seas Fleet became confined to the Baltic Sea.

GLIDER CRASH

GL Süssmann (KIA May 20, 1941)

One Luftwaffe commander, GL Wilhelm Süssmann of the 7th Airborne Division, the German's initial airborne organization was killed in a glider crash during the invasion of Crete in 1941. Riding in a DFS-230 glider, towed behind a JU-52 transport, he took off from the Eleusis airfield in Greece on May 20, 1941 leading one of the first waves of airborne troops enroute to Crete. An hour into the flight a HE-111 bomber, which had become separated from its own formation, suddenly approached the tow aircraft on a collision course. The pilot of the JU-52 went into an emergency dive to avoid a collision, but the maneuver snapped the tow rope and the glider broke free. Too far for either a landing on Crete or a return to Greece the pilot attempted to land the soaring craft on the small island of Aegina. However, during the approach run the left wing of the glider broke off and the craft crashed on the island killing all aboard.[67]

SNIPERS

Soviet snipers killed at least three general officers on the Eastern Front. As a lesson from the Finnish War, sniper training in the Soviet Army increased through inter unit competitions; and throughout the war snipers were greatly respected. Additionally, one of the most proficient characteristics of Soviet infantry and reconnaissance units during the war was their ability to infiltrate German positions, particularly in winter and in rough terrain.[68]

GM von Hünersdorff (DOW July 17, 1943)

Snipers first struck on April 7, 1942 when GM Franz Scheidies, 61st Infantry Division, was shot in the head and killed in operations near Gluschitza.[69] During the Battle of Kursk, another general fell to the proficient marksmen. GM Walther von Hünersdorff, 6th Panzer Division, was shot in the head on July 14, 1943. Although wearing a steel helmet, a fragment lodged in his brain. He was flown to a hospital at Kharkov, and was operated on by a German brain specialist who was flown to the city for the emergency. Despite these efforts, GM von Hünersdorff died three days later. At the time of the incident, he was enroute from a forward detachment to the division forward command post.[70]

The following year, a Soviet sniper shot GL Hermann Kress, commander of the 4th Mountain Division. This action occurred on a stable portion of the front. Near Novorossijsk on the Black Sea, the Germans had attempted to eliminate a Russian beachhead for several months. The dominant key terrain along the seven kilometer front was the Myschako Hill. Time and again the 4th Mountain Division had attempted to seize the heights, and time and again they were repulsed by the determined defenders. Finally, GL Kress ordered the division to shorten the lines and cease the attack. To facilitate removal of stockpiled ammunition and supplies from the rugged terrain, he ordered the construction of a small cable railroad from the hill west to the safety of more protected terrain. All types of supplies were lifted to safety as well as the steady transport of wounded personnel to the rear. However, so great was the threat from enemy snipers, that the commander ordered that the railway would not be used for routine movement of unwounded troops.

On the morning of August 11, 1943 at 6:00 AM, GL Kress visited the base station of the railroad and ordered the engineer to transport him up the hill to the forward defensive positions near the top. The engineer complied after reminding the general of his ban on the movement of personnel. Fifteen minutes later Kress arrived at the exposed position, again ignoring warnings about Soviet snipers, and began to survey the battlefield. As he raised his binoculars to his eyes to observe the enemy positions to the east, it is likely they reflected the morning sun to a waiting sniper, as he was almost instantly shot in the head and killed.[71]

One factor assisting the Soviets in this effort was the German generals' uniforms, which displayed prominent red and gold insignia designating this rank. Although camouflage clothing appeared in greater numbers as the war progressed, wartime photographs show that most German generals did not wear this tactical garment but stayed with the traditional uniform.

The old ways died hard. For example, GL Rudolf Bamler assumed command of the 12th Infantry Division in June 1944, after having served in occupied Norway for several years. On his first visit to a front-line regiment, he insisted on wearing his distinctive general's uniform to include the double red striped breeches and general's hat. His subordinate, *Oberstleutnant* (Lieutenant Colonel) Heinz-Georg Lemm described the visit.[72]

> *GL Bamler arrived at my regiment and was dressed in his distinctive general's uniform. I offered him my own cap and long overcoat for his visit which would conceal his rank from Russian observers. I stated that the Russians would like nothing better than to shoot a German general on his first day at the front. General Bamler declined my offer and became angry; saying that the problem was not his uniform, but that our trenches were obviously not deep enough to provide protection from Russian sharpshooters. He then left our positions, ordering us to report to him when our trenches were improved to permit his next visit.*

That visit back to Lemm's regiment never happened. Bamler, still dressed in his distinctive uniform, was captured by the Soviets a month later near Mogilev during the great Soviet offensive against Army Group Center. In retrospect, he was one of the fortunate ones.

GM Richard Schimpf (right) visiting Normandy wearing a camouflage uniform, and carrying an FG 42 (he survived the war).

General Schörner (right) in Bulgaria along the Greek border, March 7, 1941 wearing a Bulgarian army uniform as a disguise. Schörners's division was preparing for the invasion of Greece. Schörner wore camouflage uniforms throughout the war and survived.

TANK AND ANTI-TANK

Povernite tankove armii na Berlin.
Turn your tank armies on Berlin.
(Josef Stalin to Marshal Koniev)

Despite the fact that tank and anti tank weapons often accounted for decisive tactical successes, both played a lesser role in accounting for German general officer casualties, inflicting five and six fatlities respectively. Four generals were found to have been killed by Soviet tanks. GM Erich Gruner, 111th Infantry Division, was killed by main gun fire from a T-34 tank on May 12, 1944 during the attempted German evacuation of the Crimea as the German positions were overrun.[73]

GM Wüstenhagen (KIA June 26, 1944)

GM Albrecht Wüstenhagen, commander of the 256th Infantry Division, was killed in action June 26, 1944 as he attempted to break out of the encirclement of Army Group Center. As his command vehicle was moving across country to avoid Soviet forces, it received a direct hit from a Soviet tank round. The general was killed instantly.[74]

On January 27, 1945, a deep Soviet tank raid killed GM Arthur Finger, 291st Infantry Division, near Czestochowa, Poland. The general, leading a small battlegroup, was attempting to break out of a huge Soviet encirclement

76

that developed as his division was overwhelmed by the Soviet Vistula Offensive.[75]

It is believed one German division commander, GL Dietrich Kraiss of the 352nd Infantry, was killed by tank fire on the Western Front when an American tank column from the 2nd Armored Division overran his headquarters on August 2, 1944 near St. Lo, Normandy during the Allied breakout.

GdSS Heinrich Schuldt was struck and killed by Soviet anti-tank fire on March 15, 1944 while visiting the front-lines of the 1st Battalion, 42nd Waffen-SS Grenadier Regiment of the 19th Waffen-SS Division during defensive operations on the Velikaya River near the village of Sapronovo.[76] GM Werner Dürking, commander of the 96th Infantry Division, fell victim to a Soviet anti-tank round on September 11, 1944.

The general had gone forward to a regimental forward command post to coordinate a multi-regiment attack. At the conclusion of his orders briefing, Dürking asked one of his subordinate commanders to remain to discuss additional details. Standing in front of the command post, he was struck by a hail of sudden anti-tank fire coming from the village of Mokre. Mortally wounded, he was rushed to the division aid station where he died shortly thereafter.[77]

The year before during the winter battles in the Ukraine, GM Friedrich Sieberg, the commander of the 14th Panzer Division also died from the effects of an anti-tank round. On October 29, 1943 the division commenced an attack toward the village of Tolstaja, 30 miles east of Kirowograd. Shortly after the attack began, Sieberg was seriously wounded by shrapnel from Soviet anti-tank fire. He was flown to Kirowograd in a Fieseler Stork the next day, but died on November 2.[78]

GdA Wilhelm Stemmermann, commander of the XI Army Corps, was also killed in this manner. During the German breakout at Tscherkassy on February 18, 1944, his command car broke down near the small village of Pochapintsky. Searching for a replacement vehicle, he found a vehicle belonging to the division operations officer of the 5th Waffen-SS *"Wiking"* Division. The vehicle had a flat tire and was stuck in a ravine, but the general mounted up and the driver attempted to negotiate the slope with the damaged vehicle. Suddenly the vehicle was struck in the rear by a direct hit from a Soviet anti-tank round and the general was struck in the back full force and killed instantly by the shrapnel. At the time of the incident Stemmermann was observed brandishing a machine-pistol, urging his men forward through Soviet positions.[79]

Another general killed by anti-tank fire was GL Hans-Günther von Rost of the 44th Infantry Division. On March 22, 1945 near Stuhlweissenburg, Hungary, his division prepared to breakout from encircling Soviet units and move west. At 8:00 PM the division command group moved out in an armored half-track, well situated between combat units. The enemy defenses consisted of five successive defended roadblocks. In the darkness, von Rost and his comrades successfully negotiated the first two, but received a direct hit from an enemy anti-tank round killing the general and the division operations officer.[80]

Anti-tank fire earlier killed one general in Africa. On April 9, 1941 GL Erwin Rommel briefed GL Heinrich von Prittwitz und Gaffron, the 15th Panzer Division commander, on his role in the Africa Corps assault on the fortress of Tobruk the following day. On April 10, orders in hand, von Prittwitz was traveling at the front of the divisional units in his command car, complete with division commander pennant – having been given a report that the coastal road toward Tobruk was secure until the final 7 miles from the city. It was not, and he was struck in the chest and killed 25 miles west of Tobruk by Australian anti tank fire that morning. Ironically, the anti-tank weapon that fired the fatal shot was a 47mm gun which had earlier been captured from the Italians.[81]

SMALL ARMS AND GRENADES

Small arms include machine-guns, automatic rifles, rifles, machine pistols, grenades and pistols – but despite their lack of glamour often associated with larger weapons, these infantry weapons dispatched at least thirteen German generals. Many of the general officer casualties from small arms and grenade attacks came in the form of ambushes. Shortly after noon, September 6, 1942, GM Albert Buck, 198th Infantry Division, was ambushed and killed while driving in his command car over a bridge near Klutschewaja. A reconnaissance element from the 723rd Soviet Rifle Regiment was hiding under a bridge along this route, recognized the division commander's auto pennant on the vehicle, and destroyed the car with anti tank hand grenades.[82]

On the Western Front, soldiers of the American 82nd Airborne Division ambushed GL Wilhelm Falley, 91st Air Landing Division, on D Day in Normandy. Falley originally left his unit at 1:00 AM that day to attend war games at Rennes; unaware that the Allied invasion was about to begin. Enroute some two hours later, he heard the drone of aircraft and the explosion of bombs, and realizing something was amiss, turned back. The Horch staff car he was riding in, complete with general officer pennant, was hit by Browning Automatic Rifle fire shortly before he reached his headquarters at Picauville, which caused the vehicle to skid and strike a low wall. Crawling across the road to retrieve his weapon, he was shot and died instantly. The American officer in charge of the patrol noted that the general was wearing a dress uniform with gold insignia and twin red stripes on the trouser legs.[83]

GL Karl Eibl, the commander of the XXIV Panzer Corps, became the only high ranking commander to be killed by his own troops, albeit allies, when he was seriously wounded by a hand grenade thrown by a soldier from a passing Italian truck column. Eibl, who was sitting on the fender of his staff car at the time, was evacuated and underwent emergency amputation of his leg, without anesthesia – but died shortly thereafter of shock.[84]

Other small arms attacks came in a more traditional form of combat. During the 1940 French Campaign GdI Hermann von Speck led the XVIII

GM Falley (KIA June 6, 1944) earlier in the war with arm wound
– in conference with GL Gallwitzer.

Army Corps in its drive east of Paris to the Loire River. Upon reaching Pont sur Yonne, the Germans found the bridge over the Yonne River to be blown. On June 15, 1940 von Speck visited the lead combat elements as they attempted a river crossing. Approaching the waterline, he was hit and killed by fire from French machine-guns firing from the opposite bank.[85]

On the Russian Front, during the intense fighting before Moscow in December 1941 GL Friedrich Bergmann, commander of the 137th Infantry Division, ignored the warnings of the regimental commander, and accompanied the 449th Infantry Regiment in an attack. Approaching the edge of a woods north of Sjawki near Kaluga, he was mortally wounded by Soviet machine gun fire.[86]

SS-Gruppenführer Artur Phleps, commander of the V SS Volunteer Mountain Corps, was probably killed by enemy small arms fire in an unusual situation. While making a forward reconnaissance near Arad, Rumania, Phleps and his driver were captured by Soviet troops. Shortly thereafter, the Soviets were in turn attacked by German ground attack aircraft. In the confusion of the attack it appears that the Russian troops shot and killed both men.[87]

The same fate awaited GM Bogislav von Schwerin, commander of the

Site where von Speck was killed by machine-gun fire — Soldiers erect memorial marker shortly thereafter.

207th Security Division. On September 17, 1944 the front-lines east of Dorpat, Estonia collapsed and Soviet infantry threatened to overrun his division headquarters. As the staff command vehicle, signal troops, and division commander's vehicle started a withdrawal they were met by heavy small arms fire. Von Schwerin and the division ordnance officer jumped out of the vehicle and took up positions to the right of the road in a drainage ditch almost into the arms of a Soviet infantry platoon. As German soldiers on the opposite side of the road attempted to provide covering fire, von Schwerin was observed to stand up – whereupon he was shot by the enemy. It is not known if he was trying to surrender when killed.[88]

These close combat situations occurred in towns and cities as well as rural areas. At Stalingrad, on January 26, 1943, GL Alexander von Hartmann, commander of the 71st Infantry Division, led a small group of troops outside his headquarters in the southern portion of Stalingrad and began engaging Soviet troops advancing across the snow. Von Hartmann gave the order to commence firing and personally fired a machine pistol at the enemy, killing at least one enemy infantryman – but was shot in the head by machine gun fire and killed near a railroad embankment.[89]

During the night of February 2, 1943 GM Günther Angern of the 16th Panzer Division called his officers together and told them "Gentlemen, the battle is over. The Sixth Army no longer exists. We have done our duty to the end. I thank you. Each man must now decide for himself what he will do."[90] Angern, dressed in his camouflage uniform, along with his aide de camp, attempted to breakthrough Soviet troops at the vicinity of the Tractor Factory and was killed in the attempt. His body was later found by the Russians. This

Phleps examining captured partisan weapon (KIA September 21, 1944).

style of savage street fighting was not confined to Stalingrad alone. On the Western Front the 9th Panzer Division lost its commander, GL Harald von Elverfeldt, in street fighting in Cologne March 6, 1945. That morning, while climbing out of his command vehicle, he was felled by a burst from an American submachine-gun.[92]

Nor was close combat in cities limited to large urban areas. GL Heinrich Recke, commander of the 161st Infantry Division personally led an assault group attempting to regain the Russian village of Panskaja August 15, 1943. Shortly after the attack began at 3:00 PM, he was seen surrounded by five Soviet troops locked in close combat, and was presumably killed.[93]

UNKNOWN / SUICIDES / OTHER CAUSES

Regimental Commander: *I have 150 "Fritzes" here. What shall I do with them?*

Division Commander: *Keep a few for interrogation and have the others liquidated.*

(Telephone conversation between Soviet officers)

In the best of circumstances, war is confusion. During desperate fighting, when every man is trying to survive, it can be total chaos, so it is quite natural that the causes of death for many German generals remain unknown even to this day. Frequently, comrades present with the general, did not actually see him get killed. Often their bodies were not recovered. Many undoubtedly ended up in mass graves, with the circumstances surrounding their deaths entombed with them. Often, there were no survivors of the engagement to begin with or they were put to death immediately after capture.

This unpleasantry happens more often than civilized societies would like to admit. By May 8, 1945 more than three million German troops had fallen prisoner into Soviet hands. Over one million died in captivity – a great number of whom were killed shortly after capture. Of roughly 91,000 Germans who surrendered at Stalingrad, 73,000 perished before reaching their final prisoner of war camp in Tashkent; a further 12,000 died there.

After the destruction of Army Group Center in July of 1944, a full 37,000 did not survive their initial period of captivity. One month later after the demise of Army Group South in Rumania, 100,000 prisoners did not reach POW camps. At the fall of Budapest in February 1945 some 25,000 German prisoners could not be accounted for after the first few days. The list of staggering losses extends to many more battles and engagements. Although not nearly in the same scope, German soldiers attempting to surrender to Western Allied soldiers were sometimes summarily killed as well.[95]

Some of the generals were killed while actually leading troops into battle. GL Gerhard Berthold, commander of the 31st Infantry Division, was killed leading the 3rd Battalion 17th Infantry Regiment in an assault on April 14, 1942 near Saizewa-Gora. The unit was attempting to gain control of the Roslawl-Juchnow highway, a key line of communications in the sector of Army Group Center.

After stopping the German ill-fated Kursk offensive, Soviet forces took the offense themselves and began retaking the Ukraine. One of their breakthroughs cut off the withdrawal routes of the 19th Panzer Division near Achtyrka. As the Soviet 27th Army closed in from the southwest, German units were left with only one avenue of retreat. As the German columns fled down the road, Luftwaffe aircraft conducted mock attacks on friendly forces in a desperate attempt to deceive enemy forward observers into thinking the columns were the Red Army. The ruse failed and the Soviet air force, combined with massive artillery fire, struck hard, knocking out many German vehicles. GL Gustav Schmidt, the commander, his adjutant and two enlisted men found themselves on foot, attempting to make their way through the enemy forces in a woods when they were surprised by a band of Russians. Pinned down, Schmidt told his comrades they had only two choices, death or captivity. He added that as a general he could not allow himself to become a prisoner of war; but that the others should surrender to save their lives. The two enlisted men did, and were later brought back to identify and then bury their fallen commander.[97] Schmidt may have committed suicide or was shot by the enemy while trying to surrender.

Suicide is an interesting phenomenon that heavily afflicted the German general officer corps during the war. Josef Foltmann's study on general officer deaths lists at a minimum sixty-four generals who committed suicide. This is a conservative estimate. Writing in 1953, Foltmann did not have complete knowledge of the fates of many officers on the Eastern Front – as this information did not return until the final prisoner releases in 1956. In research concerning division, corps and army commanders it appears that at least sixteen may have committed suicide during the heat of battle (as opposed to committing suicide back in Germany and out of both immediate combat and danger). Although these acts seem to have occurred on the spur of the moment as defeat was closing in on their own units, the question remains – why so many?

Throughout the *Reichswehr* and World War II periods stress levels of the German Army officer corps were high. In the intensely competitive 100,000 man *Reichswehr*, much was expected of officers in all ranks. The German Army coined the phrase "General Staff Officer's stomach" as a description for stomach ulcers that many hard-driving, hard-working, ambitious officers of the period frequently were afflicted with. Most senior officers were self-confident, intelligent, with a high expectation level and with a strong desire to be in control – of themselves, their units and their situations. The idea of defeat was abhorrent to many.[98]

Added to this high occupational stress level was that imposed by wartime conditions – months on end of brutal fighting which fostered additional emotional, mental and physical stress on general officers making key decisions affecting the lives of thousands of soldiers. Later war defensive battles, where the Allies controlled the tempo and initiative of operations also facilitated a chronic shortage of rest for many German officers. Sleep deprivation became severe, especially in units that were encircled. Stories of brutal treatment prisoners could receive at the hands of their captors did little to ease the minds of many generals who themselves had ordered, permitted or at the least known about their own units mishandling of Allied prisoners earlier in the war. From 1943 onward the Reich was crumbling and many generals sensed an end to their way of life and their importance in society.[99]

The most famous incident of a German commander committing suicide in the face of the enemy was GFM Walter Model. As the commander of Army Group B in the Ruhr pocket April 1945, he ordered the army group dissolved rather than surrender the unit to the Allies. For four days Model evaded capture by American forces and brooded his fate. After dismissing his staff, he finally chose suicide as the only way out. As he told GL F.W. von Mellenthin during the crisis "I would never have thought that I would ever be so disappointed. My only aim was to serve Germany." [100] On April 21, 1945 he walked into a forest near Duisburg, Germany and killed himself with a single shot from his Walther pistol. His body was buried in a secret, unmarked grave. Several years later his gravesite was identified by a comrade on the wish of Model's son, and his body reinterred in a cemetery in the Hürtgen Forest. After the war von Mellenthin wrote the following of Model's decision to commit suicide: "Following the collapse of the *Wehrmacht*, which to Model was synonymous with the crumbling of all his life's desires, aims and ideals, one can scarcely imagine any other end for him than the suicide he chose. It was his way of remaining true to himself." [101]

Other suicides were less prominent, but were significant losses none-the-less. In the last stages of the battle for Stalingrad, many German generals discussed suicide and surrender among themselves. GL Richard Stempel, in conversation with generals Moritz von Drebber and von Hartmann, chose suicide stating "I have lost my son, who was my hope and pride. I will not let myself be taken prisoner, but will shoot myself." [102] The next day, January 26, 1943, he retired to his room and shot himself.[103] During the fall of 1943, Soviet forces successfully thwarted the German attack at Kursk and then drove west liberating much of the Ukraine. A bitter fight ensued for Kiev during which the German 88th Infantry Division was overrun and fell back towards the city. GL Heinrich Roth, the division commander, attempted to halt the broken formations but was killed in action against the spearheads of enemy infantry.[104]

When Army Group Center collapsed under the weight of the Soviet 1944 Summer Offensive many divisions simply splintered – with individuals and small groups of soldiers moving westward through miles of Soviet occupied territory in desperate attempts to seek the safety of German lines far to the west. Called *Rückkämpfer*, or behind-the-lines warriors, their trek often lasted weeks, with those who could not go further, were wounded or could simply not endure were left behind to die alone or face capture and an uncertain fate. The Soviets did everything to attempt to catch these men, using reconnaissance aircraft, Cossacks, partisans, roadblocks and even propaganda leaflets. Only a few *Rückkämpfer* survived to tell the tales of thousands who perished in the attempt. One of these survivors sheds light on the fate of GL Drescher, whose division was overrun in June but still had small groups evading west as late as August.[105]

> One of the many tragic fates was that of a larger group under the command of the commander of the 267th Division, General Drescher. Its flight was halted by the Niemen River, as too many of the men were non-swimmers. After attempts to build rafts from the willows growing along the river failed, they fashioned a chain from their belts. It must have been a fairly strong one, as the river at this location was 110-120 meters wide. Once the chain was completed, several swimmers crossed to the west side of the river with one

end. Too many non-swimmers tried to cross at one time, however, and the end of the belt slipped from the hands of the men on the west bank. There was no time for another attempt, as dawn was breaking and the German troops were soon coming under fire from Russian sentries. The Soviets deployed motorized troops to attack the group, and in the ensuing combat General Drescher and his staff met their end [on August 13, 1944].

During the fighting in Rumania in August 1944, elements of the German Sixth and Eighth Armies became encircled by elements of the *2nd* and *3rd Ukrainian Fronts* and attempted to breakout near Vutcani, between the Pruth and Barladuhl Rivers, on August 29. On this day it was rumored that GdI Friedrich Mieth, the commander of the IV Corps, had died of a heart attack.

GdI Mieth (third from left) June 1944 with Rumanian and German officers.

Also during this encirclement, the 294th Infantry Division commander faced a similar dilemma. Sensing that all form of organized resistance was crumbling, he ordered the survivors of the division to form small battle groups to force a breakout. As the battle groups moved into their positions, *Generalmajor* Werner von Eichstedt was observed to pick up a rifle and lead the attack. Running forward, the Germans were engaged by Soviet machine guns, anti-tank guns and finally tank fire. Most were killed in the wild melee, but they were not successful and had to fall back toward Guragalbina, south-west of Kishinew. The general was not among the survivors.[106]

In late December 1944 elements of the Soviet 2nd and 3rd Ukrainian Fronts surrounded the Hungarian capital of Budapest. Some 188,000

GM Schmidhuber – badge at top right is the Infantry Close Assault Badge, awarded for 15 days of close combat with the enemy. Silver oval badge on bottom right denotes that Schmidhuber received three wounds.

German and Hungarian troops were thus surrounded in and near the city, including the 13th Panzer Division. In January the Germans commenced four successive, but unsuccessful, counteroffensives toward the beleaguered garrison and penetrated to within a few kilometers of Buda before they failed. However, the city could not be held indefinitely; by early February the German garrison had been squeezed into the Citadel area on the western bank of the Danube.

On February 11, the city commander *SS-Obergruppenführer* von Pfeffer-Wildenbruch ordered his units to begin to conduct breakout operations. GM Gerhard Schmidhuber, commander of the 13th Panzer Division began moving the remnants of his division out of the city but was killed almost immediately in the attempt.[107] Two Waffen-SS commanders died as well. SS-Brigadeführer Joachim Rumohr was also a casualty of Budapest. On February 11 his unit, the 8th SS Cavalry Division *"Florian Geyer"*, attempted to breakout of the besieged city, as did *SS-Brigadeführer* August Zehender commander of the 22nd SS Cavalry Division *"Maria Theresa"*. Although reports vary, it is possible both were wounded, were unable to keep up with breakout forces, faced certain capture with all ramifications as Waffen-SS officers, and therefore committed suicide shortly before Soviet troops overran their headquarters elements.[108]

SS-Brigadeführer Franz Augsberger also died in uncertain circumstances as commander of the 20th Waffen-SS Grenadier Division (Estonian) when his unit was surrounded near Falkenberg in Silesia. On March 17, 1945 the unit divided into three assault groups and attempted to breakout to the west. Augsberger led the northernmost battle group and fell near Grottkau. Several reports indicate he may have committed suicide rather than fall captive to the Soviets.[109] Waffen-SS soldiers faced this dilemma more than other German soldiers as the Soviets often did execute German prisoners of war wearing the dreaded SS runes on their collars. In fact, eight of the sixteen Waffen-SS senior commanders who died at the head of their troops appear to have committed suicide.

On April 18, 1945, GL Hans Källner, the commander of the XXIV Panzer Corps, was killed in action during a large tank battle at Sokolniza, not far from the Napoleonic battlefield at Austerlitz. The corps was attempting to check the advance of Russian tank forces as they advanced north from Vienna.[110] It is not known exactly how the general was killed.

Just a few days later, GdPz Karl Decker, commander of the XXXIX Panzer Corps, also died in uncertain circumstances; although it is most likely he committed suicide. By April 21, 1945 Allied forces had driven German units deep into Germany. On that date Decker, with two command cars, an armored reconnaissance vehicle and several soldiers were in the midst of advancing American troops near the village of Wendhausen near Fallersleben.

Hiding in a woodline, they heard shots; and realizing they could not proceed mounted, disabled the reconnaissance vehicle and began to make their way on foot. In the midst of their attempt to escape toward friendly lines, Decker became separated from his troops and was seen heading into a large group of trees. The next day a resident of the village found Decker's body lying with a pistol in his hand. Nearby lay a framed photograph of a mother and two small children. Perhaps the general had committed suicide to avoid capture.[111]

SS-Obergruppenführer Walter Krüger, commander of the VI SS Corps, sought to avoid capture as well. At the surrender of German forces in Courland, Krüger vowed not to be taken to Moscow in captivity and began a trek, with a few companions southwest in an almost hopeless attempt to reach East Prussia, and a possible opportunity to go into hiding. On May 20, they ran into a group of Soviet soldiers in a small woods. GdSS Krüger, who had been hindered over the journey by a wound received in World War I, realized the hopelessness of the situation and ordered the others to attempt to go on without him. He remained in the woods alone and almost certainly shot and killed himself.[112]

In reviewing these accounts of general officer fatalities several conclusions can be drawn. First, most of the deaths occurred from quick unexpected

GL Källner (KIA April 18, 1945)

attacks. Air bombardments, artillery barrages, hidden minefields, snipers, and partisan attacks were quite different than the deadly but more methodical operations these men had experienced in World War I. Second, a great many deaths occurred in vehicles moving through the battle area. Such movement attracted air attacks and set up potential ambush situations.

Although the commanders had to move by vehicle to better control the battlefield, it appears most did so without an adequate escort capable of discouraging some of the attacks. Much of this movement was done in hours of very good visibility which facilitated enemy air attacks. Some of their disdain for enemy capabilities may have resulted from Luftwaffe reports of friendly air superiority over the battlefield or perhaps the belief that a single staff car was too small a target to be effectively engaged.

Third, many of these fatal incidents transpired during overrun attacks – a breakdown in defensive lines by the Germans which culminated in command posts being threatened by enemy mechanized and even infantry forces. Additionally, many seemed to have occurred during last ditch defensive efforts, many ordered by Hitler, where senior commanders attempted to lead breakouts after organized resistance was no longer possible. They following chart, showing just corps commanders killed in action lists the type of military operation the corps was undertaking at the time of the commander's death:

Corps Operations

Name		Unit	Date Killed	Corps Operation
GL	von Speck	XVIII AK	15.6.40	River Crossing
GdI	von Briesen	LII AK	20.11.41	Offense
GdPz	von Langermann und Erlenkamp	XXIV PzK	3.10.42	Offense
GdA	Wandel	XXIV PzK	14.1.43	Withdrawal
GL	Eibl	XXIV PzK	21.1.43	Withdrawal
GsI	Zorn	XXXXVI PzK	2.8.43	Defense
GdA	Stemmermann	XI AK	18.1.44	Breakout
GdA	Marcks	LXXXIV AK	12.6.44	Defense
GdA	Martinek	XXXIX PzK	28.6.44	Overrun
GL	Schünemann	XXXIX PzK	29.6.44	Overrun
GdI	Hauffe	XIII AK	22.7.44	Defense
GdI	Mieth	IV AK	2.9.44	Defense
GdSS	Phleps	V SS K	21.9.44	Defense
GdI	Wegener	L AK	24.9.44	Overrun
GdI	Schneckenburger	AK Belgrade	14.10.44	Defend City
GdI	Priess	XXVII AK	21.10.44	Defense
GdI	Recknagel	XXXXII AK	23.1.45	Overrun
GdI	Block	LVI PzK	26.1.45	Overrun
GL	Källner	XXIV PzK	18.4.45	Counterattack
GL	Baade	LXXXI K	8.5.45	Retreating
GdI	Erdmannsdorff	LXXXXI AK	8.5.45	Retreating
GdI	Dostler	LXXV AK	8.5.45	Surrendered
GdPz	Fehn	XV GebK	5.6.45	Surrendered

Many of the conditions in overrun and breakout operations were truly appalling, almost on a medieval "fight to the death" scale between warring barbaric empires. Two battles on the Eastern Front, the Cherkassy encirclement and the collapse of the Crimea characterize these last ditch efforts. Some front-line descriptions of them truly capture the desperation of these events:

Cherkassy

· *The road from Gorodische in the southeast to Korsun is jammed with giant columns. Thousands of vehicles of every type, often three abreast, are crawling along a 20 kilometer stretch of road through muck and holes, offering the enemy air force targets which could scarcely be better. The Russian machines buzz like angry wasps and dive on columns mired in the mud every ten minutes. Trucks are burning everywhere. By night the way to Korsun is marked by flames from a hundred burning vehicles... The surrounded units are nearing the end of their strength. There is little ammunition and no regular rations. The men are dead tired and have been completely soaked for days... Every few minutes the enemy breaks through the positions somewhere... The men in their dirty, mud-covered winter uniforms are exhausted. There is almost nothing to eat and only dirty water from the sides of the road to drink... The men, without sleep, and shivering from the cold, have received nothing, [to eat] hot or cold, for three days... A collective farm which has been transformed into a field hospital is hit by fire from a Stalin Organ. Dozens of wounded create a bloody shambles. More than 1,200 wounded have already spent several days and nights in the open in straw filled, light panje wagons requisitioned from villages inside the pocket. After the rain of the previous weeks they have become soaked to the skin; now they must face the biting cold and lie half-frozen beneath their snow-covered blankets. One scarcely hears any moaning or groaning; many have given up, and no longer ask for anything.*

General der Artillerie Stemmermann, the leader of all German forces inside the pocket was killed during a command post move in the midst of these conditions.[113]

Crimea

The unending columns, mostly train units and surviving German and Rumanian units, streamed south in the direction of the fortress of Sevastopol. There was no one who could restore order... The bright morning sun illuminated the depressing scene of long columns in flight. At the sides of the coastal road along which the army columns were moving lay burning vehicles and dead and dying horses... There were battles of insane bitterness, deep penetrations and crises, and finally the entire B-Stellenberg position was lost. Losses among our troops climbed alarmingly... In the thunder of exploding bombs the desperate men jostled down the bluffs, hanging from ladders, climbing over one another and falling on the dead, the wounded and the boulders tossed up by the sea. More low-flying enemy aircraft approached the bluffs from the sea, however, and fired their guns into the clusters of men... Russian tanks rolled forward on a broad front and began to fire. The wounded wailed. Many men were as if lost in thought, many ran into the enemy fire.[114]

Generalmajor Gruner attempted to surrender his forces in this inferno, but was killed by Soviet tank fire in the attempt.

Nor were these catastrophes confined to the Eastern Front. GM Fritz Bayerlein, the commander of the Panzer Lehr Division in Normandy 1944, describes the massive Allied firepower, the application of which signaled the St. Lo breakout.[115]

Normandy

...back and forth the carpets [from American B-17 heavy bombers] were laid, artillery positions were wiped out, tanks overturned and buried, infantry positions flattened and all roads and tracks destroyed. By midday the entire area resembled a moon landscape, with the bomb craters touching rim to rim...All signal communications had been cut and no command was possible. The shock effect on the troops was indescribable. Several of my men went mad and rushed around in the open until they were cut down by splinters. Simultaneously with the storm from the air, innumerable guns of the American artillery [in fact 552] poured drumfire into our field positions.[116]

Finally, throughout the war German generals retained distinctive but dangerous markings of their grade – continued to wear distinctive uniforms and flew vehicular pennants advertising their position. Both provided target information to snipers, ambushes, and partisans. If the Allied forces were learning how to conduct lethal operations against German command and control, what were the Germans learning to combat these dangers?

CHAPTER NOTES

[1] B.H. Liddell-Hart, *The Rommel Papers*, New York: Da Capo Press, 1989, p. 491.

[2] R. James Bender and Richard D. Law, *Uniforms, Organization, and History of the Afrikakorps*, San Jose, CA: R. James Bender, 1973, p. 74.

[3] Max Hastings, *Overlord, D-Day and the Battle for Normandy*, New York: Simon and Schuster, 1984, pp. 173-174.

[4] William B. Breuer, *Hitler's Fortress Cherbourg*, New York: Stein & Day, 1984, p. 164.

[5] Richard D. Law and Craig W.H. Luther, *Rommel*, p. 322.

[6] *Ibid.*

[7] Max Hastings, *Overlord*, pp. 274-275.

[8] The Soviet designers referred to the *Sturmovik* as the "flying tank". At various stages of the war, the 40,000 of these aircraft produced (!) were armed with 7mm machineguns, 23mm cannons, 37mm cannon, rockets, PTAB 2.5 kg hollow-charge anti-tank bombs and conventional bombs up to 1,000 pounds.

[9] Ray Wagner, *The Soviet Air Force in World War II*. Translated by Leland Fetzer, New York: Dobleday & Company, 1973, pp. 120-121 and 208.

[10] Wrner Haupt, *Das war Kurland*, Bad Nauheim, FRG: Podzun Verlag, 1987, p. 170.

[11] Microfilm, LII Armeekorps, Ia, "Kriegstagebuch", 20.11.41, National Archives Microfilm Publication T-314, Roll 1276, Washington, D.C.: The National Archives Records Service, General Services Administration, 1970, Frame 510.

[12] Microfilm, XXXXVI Panzerkorps, Ia, "Kriegstagebuch", 2.8.43, National Archives Microfilm Publication T-314, Roll 1086, Washington, D.C.: The National Archives and Records Service, General Services Administration, 1970, Frame 533.

[13] "Die Gebirgstruppe", München, FRG: Geschäftßtelle des Kameradenkreises der Gebirgstruppe e.V., Heft 2-4, 1969, p. 39.

[14] Alex Buchner, *Ostfront 1944*, Friedberg, FRG: Podzun-Pallas-Verlag, 1988, p. 171.

[15] Gerd Niepold, *Battle for White Russia*, p. 142.

[16] Microfilm, L Armeekorps, Ia, "Kriegstagebuch", 24.9.44, National Archives Microfilm Publication T-314, Roll 1249, Washington, D.C.: The National Archives and Records Service, General Services Administration, 1970, Frame 707.

[17] *Kriegstagebuch* Ia, 22.3.42, 294, Infanterie Division.

[18] *Tagebuch Russland 1.7.1941 - 13.5.1945* (46 I.D.) Kellberg b. Passau, 1989, p. 59.

[19] Ernst Ott, *Jäger am Feind*, München, FRG: Kameradschaft der Spielhahnjäger, 1966, p. 294.

[20] Wilhelm Meyer-Detring, *Die 137. Infanteriedivision im Mittelabschnitt der Ostfront*. Nördlingen, FRG: C.H. Beck'schen, 1966, pp. 186-188.

[21] Roland Kaltenegger, *Die deutsche Gebirgstruppe, 1933-1945*, München, FRG: Universtitas Verlag, 1989, p. 431.

[22] Reinhard Tiemann, *Geschichte der 83. Infanterie-Division, 1939-1945*, Friedberg, FRG: Podzun-Pallas-Verlag, 1986, pp. 330-331.

[23] Wilhelm Velten, *Vom Kugelbaum zur Handgrenate, der Weg der 65. Infanterie Division*, Neckergemuend, FRG: Kurt Vorwinkel Verlag, 1974, p. 194.

[24] Franz Thomas und Günter Wegmann, *Die Ritterkreuzträger der Deutschen Wehrmacht 1939-1945*, Teil III: Infanterie, Band 1: A-Be, Osnabrück, FRG: Biblio-Verlag, p. 139, and "Der Landser" Magazine, Nummer 422, pp. 63-64.

[25] Friedrich Hossbach, *Infanterie in Ostfeldzug 1941/42*, Osterode, Germany: Giebel & Öhlschlägel, 1951, p. 67.

[26] Richard Brett-Smith, *Hitler's Generals*, San Rafael, CA: Presidio Press, 1977, p. 30.

[27] Microfilm, 39 Infanterie Division, Ia, "Kriegstagebuch", 14.5.43, National Archives Microfilm Publication T-315, Roll 907, Washington, D.C.: The National Archives and Records Service, General Services Administration, 1970, Frame 623.

[28] Microfilm, 50. Infanterie Division, Ia, "Kriegstagebuch", 26.6.43, National Archives Microfilm Publication T-315, Roll 948, Washington, D.C.: The National

Archives and Records Service, General Services Administration, 1970, Frame 782.

[29] *329. (Hammer) Infanterie Division Erinneringen aus dem Kampfgeschen 1942-1945*, Traditionsband der Ehemaligen 329. Infanterie Division. Düsseldorf, FRG: Selbstverlag, 1968, p. 23.

[30] *Alte Kameraden*, October 1960, p. 23.

[31] Paul Carell, *The Foxes of the Desert*, New York: E.P. Dutton, 1961, p. 289.

[32] R. James Bender and Warren W. Odegard, Uniforms, Organization and History of the Panzertruppe, San Jose, CA: R. James Bender, 1980, p. 92.

[33] Paul Carell, *Scorched Earth*, London: George G. Harrap & Co., 1970, pp. 207-208.

[34] Matthew Cooper, *The Nazi War Against Soviet Partisans, 1941-1944*, New York: Stein & Day, 1979, p. 59.

[35] Jörgen Hästrup, *European Resistance Movements, 1939-1945: A Complete History*, Westport, CN: Meckler Publishing, 1981, pp. 471-472.

[36] *Ibid.*, p. 140.

[37] Microfilm, 174. Reserve Infanterie Division, Ia, "Kriegstagebuch", 26.8.43, National Archives Microfilm Publication T-315, Roll 1536, Washington, D.C.: The National Archives and Records Service, General Services Administration, 1970, Frame 27.

[38] August Schmidt, *Geschichte der 10. Division*, Bad Nauheim, FRG: Podzun-Pallas-Verlag, 1963, p. 256.

[39] Douglas Orgill, *The Gothic Line*, New York: W.W. Norton & Company, 1967, p. 35.

[40] *Ibid.*

[41] Werner Haupt, *Kriegßchauplatz Italien 1943-1945*, Stuttgart, FRG: Motorbuch Verlag, 1977, p. 200.

[42] Hästrup, *European Resistance*, p. 423.

[43] John Erickson, *The Road to Berlin*, Boulder, CO: Westview Press, 1983, p. 457.

[44] Roland Kaltenegger, *Operationszone "Adriatisches Küstenland"*, Graz, Austria: Leopold Stocker Verlag, 1993, pp. 223-224.

[45] G.K. Zhukov, *The Memoirs of Marshal Zhukov*, New York: Delacorte Press, 1971, p. 499.

[46] Bender, *Afrikakorps*, p. 26.

[47] Carell, *Foxes*, p. 91.

[48] Bender, *Afrikakorps*, p. 67.

[49] Liddel-Hart, *Rommel Papers*, p. 277.

[50] Ernst Rebentisch, *Zum Kaukasus und zu den Täern: Die Geschichte der 23. Panzer-Division, 1941-1945*, Forcheim, FRG: Sperl, 1982, p. 87. The Soviets used a wide variety of artillery but three pieces – the 122mm light howitzer, the 152mm medium howitzer and the 132mm multiple rocket launcher, were found in large numbers. The 122mm could fire five 48 lb. projectiles per minute to a range of

11,800 meters. The 152mm howitzer could fire four 96 lb. projectiles per minute to 15,800 meters. The rockets in the multiple rocket launcher weighed 58 lbs. each and had a range of 6,000 meters.

[51] Hasso von Manteuffel, *Die 7. Panzer-Division im Zweiten Weltkrieg*, Friedberg, FRG: Podzun-Pallas-Verlag, 1986, pp. 390-391.

[52] Dr. F.M. von Senger und Etterlin, *Die 24. Panzer Division*, Neckargemünd, FRG: Kurt Vorwinkel Verlag, 1962, pp. 287-298.

[53] Microfilm, 129. Infanterie Division, Ia, "Kriegstagebuch", 22.8.42, National Archives Microfilm Publication T-315, Roll 1086, Washington, D.C.: The National Archives and Records Service, General Services Administration, 1970, Frame 169.

[54] Friedrich Husemann, *Die Guten Glaubens Waren, Band I, 1939-1942*, Osnabrück, FRG: Munin Verlag, 1984, pp. 53-54.

[55] Landwehr, *Narva 1944*, pp. 88-89.

[56] Dermot Bradley & Richard Schulze-Kossens, *Tätigkeitsbericht des Chefs des Heerespersonalamtes General der Infanterie Rudolf Schmundt*. Osnabrück, FRG: Biblio Verlag, 1984, pp. 210-211. The eyewitness, a *Major* Pick, reported on August 18, 1944 that Häffe had been killed by a direct hit from enemy artillery while riding on a train.

[57] Otto Lasch, *So Fiel Königsberg*, Stuttgart, FRG: Motorbuch-Velag, 1976, pp. 100-101.

[58] The *Sevastopol* was begun in 1909 at St. Petersburg. She was renamed in 1921 as the *Parizhskaya Kommuna* (Paris Commune) and transferred to the Black Sea Fleet in 1930. Her main armament consisted of two turrets, each with three 12 inch guns. The *Sevastopol* was heavily bombed in 1942 and spent the rest of the war in the port of Poti.

[59] V.I. Achkasov and N.B. Pavlovich, *Soviet Naval Operations in the Great Patriotic War*, Annapolis, MD: Naval Institute Press, 1981, pp. 186-187.

[60] *Tagebuch Rußland* 1.7.1941 - 13.5.1945 (46 I.D.), p. 37.

[61] Craig W.H. Luther, *Blood and Honor: The History of the 12th SS Panzer Division "Hiter Youth", 1943-1945*, San Jose, CA: R. James Bender Publishing, p. 205.

[62] Ralph Bennett, *ULTRA in the West*, New York: Scriber's, 1979, p. 68.

[63] Charles W. Sydnor, Jr., *Soldiers of Destruction*, Princeton, N.J.: Princeton University Press, 1977, p. 271.

[64] Werner Haupt, *Heeresgruppe Nord, 1941-1945*, Bad Nauheim, FRG: Podzun Verlag, 1966, p. 277.

[65] Law, *Rommel*, p. 139.

[66] Bender, *Afrikakorps*, p. 84.

[67] G.C. Kiriakopoulos, *Ten Days to Destiny*, New York: Franklin Watts, 1985, pp. 128-131.

[68] John A. English, *A Perspective on Infantry*, New York: Praeger, 1981, pp. 121, 127, and 128.

[69] Microfilm, 61. Infanterie Division, Ia, "Kriegstagebuch", 7.4.42, National

Archives Microfilm Publication T-315, Roll 1016, Washington, D.C.: The National Archives and Records Service, General Services Administration, 1970, Frame 123.

[70] Paul Carell, *Scorched Earth*, London: George G. Harrap & Co., 1970, p. 87.

[71] Roland Kaltenegger, *Gegirgssoldaten unter dem Zeichen des "Enzian", Schicksalsweg und Kampf der 4. Gebirgs-Division, 1940-1945*, Graz, Austria: Leopold Stocker Verlag, 1983, p. 258.

[72] *Generalleutnant a.D.* Heinz-Georg Lemm in a personal interview with the author after the annual Association of the Knight's Cross reunion, September 24, 1989 at Regensburg, Germany. Lemm survived the Soviet onslaught and went on to receive both the Oakleaves and Swords to his Knight's Cross. After the war he entered the *Bundeswehr* and rose to general officer rank before retiring.

[73] Carell, *Scorched Earth*, p. 476.

[74] Barbara Selz, *Das Grüne Regiment*, Freiburg, FRG: Otto Kehrer Verlag, 1970, p. 206.

[75] Werner Conze, *Die Geschichte der 291. Infanterie-Division, 1940-1945*, Bad Nauheim, FRG: Hans Henning Verlag, 1953, p. 79.

[76] Arthur Sigailis, *Latvian Legion*, San Jose, CA: R. James Bender Publishing, 1986, p. 75.

[77] Hartwig Pohlmann, *Geschichte der 96. Infanterie-Division*, Bad Nauheim, FRG: Hans-Henning Verlag, 1959, p. 335.

[78] Rolf Grams, *Die 14. Panzer-Division*, Friedberg, FRG: Podzun-Pallas-Verlag, 1986, pp. 130-131.

[79] Buchner, *Ostfront 1944*, p. 41, 50 and Carell, Scorched Earth, p. 428.

[80] Friedrich Dettmer, Karl Lamprecht and Anton Schimak, *Die 44. Infanterie Division*, Wien: Verlag Austria Press, 1968, pp. 343-344.

[81] Wolf Heckmann, *Rommel's War in Africa*, Garden City, N.Y.: Doubleday and Company, 1981, pp. 72-73.

[82] Gerhard Graser, *Zwischen Kattegat und Kaukasus, Weg und Kämpfe der 198. Infanterie-Division 1939-1945*. Tuebingen, FRG: Traditionsverband der ehemaligen 198. Infanterie-Division, 1961, pp. 184-185.

[83] Cornelius Ryan, *The Longest Day*, New York: Simon and Schuster, 1959, pp. 269-270.

[84] Bradley, *Tätigkeitsbericht*, p. 42.

[85] Erwin Böhm, *Geschichte der 25. Division*, Stuttgart, FRG: Kameradenhilfswerk 25 e.V., 1983, pp. 72-73.

[86] Wilhelm Meyer-Detring, *Die 137. Infanteriedivision*, pp. 105-106.

[87] Jost W. Schneider, *Their Honor was Loyalty! An Illustrated and Documentary History of the Knight's Cross Holders of the Waffen SS and Police, 1940-1945*, San Jose, CA: R. James Bender Publishing, 1977, p. 281.

[88] G. Müller und F.W. Guttmann, *Geschichte der 207. und 281. Infanterie Division*, Kiel, FRG: 1958, pp. 213-214.

[89] Carell, *Hitler Moves East*, p. 619.

[90] Heinz Schröter, *Stalingrad*, New York: E.P. Hutton, 1958, p. 258.

[91] Wolfgang Werthen, *Geschichte der 16. Panzer Division, 1939-1945*, Friedberg, FRG: Podzun-Pallas-Verlag, 1958, p. 137.

[92] Johann Raabe, Secretary of the 9th Panzer Division Kameradschaft, letter to the author, January 24, 1990.

[93] Kriegstagebuch Ia, 161. Infanterie Division, 15.8.43.

[94] Martin K. Sorge, *The Other Price of Hitler's War*, New York: Greenwood Press, 1986, p. 8.

[95] *Ibid.*, pp. 76-78. GdI Joachim vom Kortzfliesch was very likely shot by American troops April 20, 1945 **while** surrendering near Wükwesort, Germany. In another incident, a British officer, Lieutenant Colonel, A.D. Lewis, commander No. 6 Commando, 1st Commando Brigade, 2nd British Army, admitted killing GM Friedrich-Wilhelm Deutsch, Commandant of the city of Wesel, **after** his capture March 27, 1945. Lewis found Deutsch and his staff in an underground bunker, and stated: "Deutsch became very aggressive, quite dangerous – he had to be shot" Source: W. Denis Whitaker, Rhineland, New York: St. Marten's Press, 1989, pp. 297-298.

[96] Franz Thomas und Günter Wegmann, *Die Ritterkreuzträger der Deutschen Wehrmacht 1939-1945, Teil III: Infanterie, Band 1: A-Be*, p. 440.

[97] Otto von Knobelsdorff, *Geschichte der niedersächischen 19. Panzer-Division, 1939-1945*, Friedberg, FRG: Podzun-Pallas-Verlag, 1958, pp. 219-220.

[98] Conversations between Burkhart Müller-Hillebrand, author of *Das Heer 1933-1945* and Dr. Samuel Lewis, historian at the Combat Studies Institute, U.S. Army Command and General Staff College, Fort Leavenworth, Kansas, recounted for the author by Dr. Lewis. Müler-Hillebrand had a distinguished career to include Chief of Staff 3rd Panzer Army, Chief of Staff XXXXVI Panzer Corps, Commander of the 24th Panzer Regiment and Operations Officer 93rd Infantry Division.

[99] Opposite this view and resulting suicides were those generals who chose capture and a degree of collaboration with Allied forces. The most notable group in this category was the National Committee for a Free Germany formed in July, 1943 from German emigres and prisoners of war held in the Soviet Union. This organization published a manifesto which called on the German people to overthrow Hitler, establish a non-Nazi government, stop the war and relinquish all occupied territories. Membership in the committee was open to all; however the Soviets encouraged higher ranking officers to join in order to legitimize the movement. The High Command and Hitler naturally condemned the members as traitors. Reaction of junior military personnel seems to have been mixed, perhaps leaning against the activities of the committee (After the war many highly decorated junior officers refused to and included: GdI Erich Buschenhagen, GdI Friedrich Gollwitzer, GdA Ernst Hell, GdI Ludwig Müller, GdA Walter von Seydlitz-Kurzbach, GdI Karl Strecker, GdI Paul Völckers, GL Rudolf Bamler, GL Gottfried von Erdmannsdorff, GL Walter Heyne, GL Edmund Hoffmeister, GL Kurt von Lützow, GL Vincenz Müller, GL Georg Postel, GL Helmuth Schlömer, GL Hans Traut, GL Alexander Conrady, GM Joachim Engel, GM Gustav Gihr, GM Adolf Hamann, GM Günther Klammt, GM Herbert Michälis, GM Claus Müller-Bülow, GM Freidrich von Steinkeller and GM Adolf Trowitz. Source: Bodo Scheurig, *Free Germany; The*

National Committee and the League of German Officers, Middleton, CN: Wesleyan University Press, 1969.

[100] Correli Barnett, *Hitler's Generals*, New York: Grove Weidenfeld, 1989, pp. 330-331.

[101] *Ibid.*

[102] Schröter, *Stalingrad*, p. 231.

[103] An account in the historical novel *Stalingrad*, written by Theodor Pliever in 1948, is extremely accurate in its description of the battle. In this work Pliever describes the death of General Stempel as being caused by poison. Perhaps the actual cause of death may never be known considering the few survivors of the encirclement.

[104] Carell, *Scorched Earth*, p. 365.

[105] Alex Buchner, *Ostfront 1944: The German Defensive Battles on the Russian Front 1944*, West Chester, PA: Schiffer Publishing, 1988, pp. 203-204.

[106] *Ibid.*, pp. 263 and 283.

[107] *Der Schicksalsweg de 13. Panzer-Division 1939-45*, Friedberg, FRG: Podzun-Pallas-Verlag, 1986, p. 211.

[108] Schneider, *Their Honor*, p. 320.

[109] Ernst-Günther Krätschmer, *Die Ritterkreuzträger der Waffen-SS*, Oldendorf, FRG: K.W. Schütz Verlag, 1982, p. 886.

[110] Von Knobelsdorff, *19. Panzer-Division*, p. 284.

[111] Ulrich Saft, *Krieg in der Heimat*, Langenhagen, Germany: Verlag-Saft, 1990, p. 370.

[112] Hans Stöber, *Die lettischen Divisionen*, Osnabrück, FRG: Munin Verlag, 1981, pp. 250-256.

[113] Buchner, *Ostfront*, pp. 25-69.

[114] *Ibid.*, pp. 99-139.

[115] The Panzer Lehr Division was a unique organization. It was formed in November 1943 at the Potsdam and Bergen training areas from demonstration units of German Army training schools, and was looked on as an elite unit. The division was a mainstay in the German defenses at Normandy before suffering severe losses at Caen and St-Lo. The Panzer Lehr participated in the Ardennes Offensive before being trapped in the Ruhr Pocket in April 1945, where it surrendered to American forces.

[116] John Keegan, *Six Armies in Normandy*, New York: The Viking Press, 1982, p. 231.

✠ CHAPTER 9 ✠
WARTIME LESSONS LEARNED AND SENIOR OFFICER TRAINING

GFM von Schobert (left) leaving a command meeting held to discuss tactical problems. He was killed shortly thereafter.

The German Army had a fairly comprehensive system of capturing pertinent lessons from combat. The following are some excerpts from GM Alfred Topp regarding lessons learned during the campaign in Africa – applicable to reducing general officer casualties as well.

(1) For the first time, all German units were exposed to lively enemy activity in the air, a feature they were to experience daily from now on. At first, several instances occurred where severe losses were suffered owing to the bunching up of vehicles and troops. It was weeks before the troops learned to counter this new combat factor by a wide dispersal of units in breadth and depth – a particularly important requirement in the desert, where no cover whatever is to be found. (The minimum distance between vehicles should be 50 and if possible 100 meters.) It also proved necessary to dig in immediately all vehicles that were halted for any considerable time. They were to be dug into the ground to at least a depth that protected the axles in order to lesson the effects of bomb fragments. In the same measure, it was also necessary to camouflage the vehi-

cles. This was only possible with the use of camouflage nets so that it was extremely difficult. Furthermore, it was now necessary for each and every man to dig a foxhole as protection during air raids.

(2) The danger of radio stations being intercepted and located made it imperative to have all radio instruments, and particularly central radio stations, removed at least one kilometer from headquarters sites in order for them not to interfere with the functioning of staff headquarters. The resultant delay in the transmission of orders and reports had to be accepted as an unavoidable disadvantage. This delay had to be reduced as far as possible by the use of messengers with motor vehicles.[1]

Given this high level of battlefield lethality and the German system for capturing these and many other significant battlefield lessons, it would seem that general officer training would be tailored to reflect these dangers. Unfortunately it did not. In January 1943 a four to six week pre-command course for division and corps commanders was established. It was commanded from July 1943 to the end of the war by GdI Kurt Brennecke, a Knight's Cross winner and former commander of the XXXXIII Army Corps. Students visited the panzer, assault gun, infantry, artillery, engineer, and signal schools, where they discussed the latest technical achievements and witnessed live-fire demonstrations.

Additionally, they conducted map exercises and professional discussions on principles of command in operations against an enemy superior in strength and material, flexibility of command in combat operations and camouflage as a means of conducting combat operations.[2] Students also received evaluations with similar comments as those found in officer efficiency reports. However, no battlefield lethality classes or protective countermeasures were included in the lessons – and no amount of school visits or map training would serve any constructive purpose if the senior commander were killed shortly after arriving at the front.[3] This was a fatal flaw in the curriculum that was never addressed throughout the war. The overall result of these losses was a degraded command and control system that occurred during German campaigns throughout the war. The fortunes of the German Army mirror this degradation and can be seen in reviewing the campaigns chronologically, and by examining general officer losses during them.

CHAPTER NOTES

[1] Major General Alfred Toppe, *Desert Warfare: German Experiences in World War II*, Fort Leavenworth, Kansas: U.S. Army Command and General Staff College Combat Studies Institute, 1991, p. 33.

[2] Helmuth Reinhardt, "Training of Senior Officers", U.S. Army Historical Division Study MS# P-080, Washington, D.C.: Office of the Chief Military History, 1951, pp. 8, 13.

[3] Letter received by the author from Dr. Dermot Bradley, October 7, 1988. Dr. Bradley, a noted German Historian, stated that in most cases German generals took over divisions and corps without having attended such courses. He additionally interviewed GL Hellmuth Reymann, a former commander of the 212th Infantry and 11th Infantry Divisions, who did attend this course from January 3 to 28, 1945, but who did not recall any instruction concerning general officer safety or battlefield lethality.

✠ CHAPTER 10 ✠
GENERAL OFFICER CASUALTIES – THE CAMPAIGNS –

1939

No German high ranking commanders were killed in action during this first year of the war. Operations during the period were characterized as generally offensive in nature, with German forces holding the initiative and avoiding unfavorable force ratios in their battles.

POLAND - 1939

On September 1, 1939, under a pre-dawn air bombardment, 60 divisions of the German Army attacked Poland from the north, west and south. GO Fedor von Bock's Army Group, comprised of the 3rd and 4th Armies encircled the Polish Corridor, while GO Gerd von Rundstedt's Army Group, with the 8th, 10th and 14th armies overran Upper Silesia and Galicia.

After the battles near the frontiers, the 3rd Army advanced on Brest-Litovsk in the east, while the 14th Army swept past Cracow. German panzer divisions surrounded the overmatched Polish forces under Marshal Edward Smigly-Rydz at Czestochowa, Kutno, Lwow, Modlin and finally Warsaw. The Poles made numerous gallant attempts to break out, often attacking German armored formations with cavalry, but incessant Luftwaffe air attacks and continued ground pressure finally caused the Poles to surrender.

On September 17, in conformity with the German-Soviet Pact from the previous month, Soviet troops invaded eastern Poland, dashing Polish hopes for anything other than total surrender.

German casualties for the campaign were 10,570 killed, 30,322 wounded and 323 missing in action (MIA).[1] No division or corps commanders were killed. However, retired GO Werner von Fritsch, who had resigned his position of Commander in Chief of the German Army in disgrace in 1938 amid false accusations of homosexual conduct, returned to front-line service as the honorary commander of his old regiment, the 12th Artillery, as they were preparing for war in East Prussia. He accompanied that unit during the campaign, and on September 22 moved ahead of German lines with several forward observers as they conducted a reconnaissance near the outskirts of Warsaw. Wearing his general's overcoat with distinctive red lapels, he was shot by a Polish sniper and seriously wounded in the thigh. A German officer braved death and rushed to his side and attempted to stem the flow of blood but the general ordered him away. Minutes later Fritsch died of massive bloodloss.[2] He had sought and found an honorable death in battle – and a Polish sniper became the first official killer of a German general in World War II.

1940

The Germans conducted two major campaigns during the year. The first was directed against Norway and Denmark commencing in April 1940, and the second against France beginning in May. No German generals were among the 4,975 killed in the Norwegian Campaign.[3] One German corps commander was killed during the French Campaign. German operations, although rising in scope of forces committed and in corresponding casualties, were still extremely favorable, with the German Army maintaining the initiative throughout the year.

FRANCE - 1940

By the beginning of May approximately two and one-half million German soldiers in 104 infantry, 10 panzer and 9 motorized divisions assembled to attack France and the Low Countries. The German Plan called for a quick thrust by Army Group B into the Netherlands – a move designed to pull Allied forces north. Then a slower developing, but more powerful, assault through Belgium would be made by Army Group A which would then drive to the Channel coast, thus isolating the British Expeditionary Corps from other Allied elements in northern France.

German *Fallschirmjäger* and panzer elements quickly seized key areas in the Netherlands on May 10, 1940 causing that nation to seek negotiations within four days. GdF Kurt Student, commander of the German 7th Parachute Division missed becoming the first division commander fatality by literally millimeters when he was struck in the head by small arms fire at Rotterdam on May 14. At the time the general was in conference with German officers in the northwest portion of the city, and had just donned his officer's overcoat replete with distinctive general officer collar facing and insignia as the late afternoon turned cooler. It is not known whether the shots were aimed enemy fire or errant rounds.[4] Student was rushed to a Rotterdam hospital where emergency surgery saved his life.

The German drive through Belgium and northern France proved equally successful with panzer formations crossing the Meuse River on the 13th, the Channel on the 21st and isolating Dunkirk and Calais on the 25th. Belgium surrendered, but in a historical decision that has been argued ever since, Hitler stopped the advancing panzers from assaulting Dunkirk which permitted 338,000 Allied soldiers to escape to Britain.

Then the German Army turned its undivided attention to the French Army to the south. Army Group B, led by von Kleist's panzers struck from the Somme, smashing the French Tenth Army and reaching Paris by June 9. Von Rundstedt and Army Group A meanwhile, broke through the center of the French lines at Chalons and headed south as well. It was during this operation that the Germans suffered their sole senior commander fatality of the campaign. A subordinate element of the army group, under GdI Hermann von Speck, the XVIII Army Corps drove east of Paris to the Loire River.

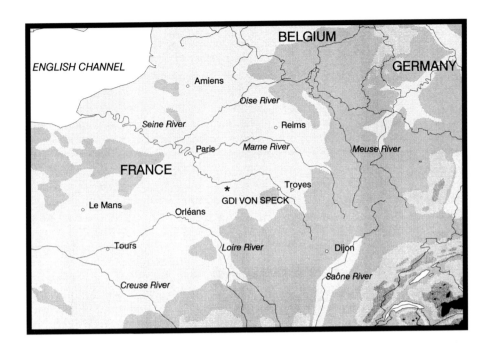

Upon reaching Pont sur Yonne, the corps found the bridge over the Yonne to be blown, and the lead engineers and infantry attempted a river crossing on June 15. Personally leading his troops, while approaching the waterline, von Speck was hit and killed by a hail of bullets from French machine-guns firing from the opposite bank.[5] His death shocked the corps troops but did not adversely affect the campaign for the Germans, and the French sued for peace six days later. German losses in the campaign rose significantly from that suffered the previous year in Poland; 27,074 men were killed, 111,034 wounded, and 18,384 missing – but many of the missing were later liberated by advancing German units.[6] General officer deaths and overall casualties would increase even more dramatically before too long.

1941

The German Army expanded operations to two continents – Europe and Africa, during 1941 and the resulting increase in the size of operations led to ten general officer fatalities during the year. Overall casualties rose as well; for the year, estimates of fatalities totaled 291,000. Ominously, missing in action rose as well to some 27,996.[7] Most were on the Russian Front; and as later years would reveal in that theater, missing in action most likely equated to never seeing Germany again.

CRETE - 1941

After the successful invasion of Greece the German High Command turned its attention to the island of Crete in an attempt to expand its control of the eastern Mediterranean. The invasion was primarily to be conducted by air assault and was led by parachute and glider troops. GL Wilhelm Süssmann of the 7th *Flieger* Division, was killed in a glider crash during the invasion of Crete in 1941 on the small island of Aegina when the left wing of the glider broke off and the craft crashed on the island.[8]

The loss of Sümmermann and many other key leaders almost scuttled the attack. On April 25, 1941 Hitler ordered the seizure of Crete as a base for air warfare against Great Britain in the eastern Mediterranean. The attack, code-named Operation Mercury, initially had a limitation that it be undertaken only with elements from the Luftwaffe – to allow Army units to continue to prepare for the upcoming attack on Russia; but later, elements of the 5th Mountain Division were earmarked to take part as well. GL Kurt Student, now recovered from his wounds the previous May, planned for the operation to be conducted in two phases – a morning attack with two battle groups. Task Force Comet, the western group, would seize the Maleme airfield and the dominant terrain around it. It would be commanded by GM Eugen Meindl. The central group, Task Force Mars, would attack the capital of Canea, and would be commanded by GL Süssmann. Phase two would be an afternoon attack to seize the cities of Iraklion and Rethimnon. Süssmann was killed early on, but Student – having incomplete information – did not designate *Oberst* Richard Heidrich as his successor until noon.

Major Walter von Braun, the lead commander of the Parachute Assault Regiment was killed as soon as his glider hit the ground. *Major* Otto Scherber, the commanding officer of the Third Assault Battalion of Meindl's regiment was shot and killed while still in his parachute. *Major* Wulf Derpa,

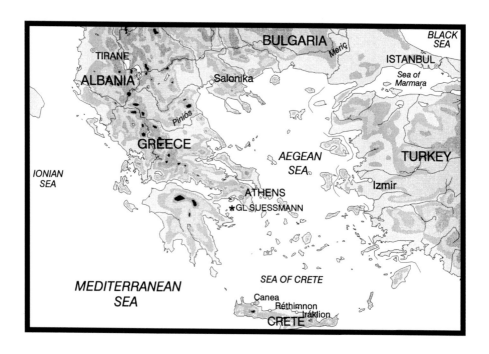

104

the commander of the Second Paratroop Battalion, 3rd Parachute Regiment, was bayoneted in the stomach and died of his wounds. GM Meindl himself was severely wounded in the chest by machine-gun fire. *Oberst* Sturm, the commander of the 2nd Paratroop Regiment was taken prisoner.

Student requested to leave Athens and go directly to Crete to take charge of the operation on the ground but was denied permission by GO Alexander Löhr, the commander of the German Fourth Air Fleet. Finally, GL Julius Ringel, the commander of the 5th Mountain Division, was dispatched to Crete to take command.

The battle seesawed but the Germans finally wrested control of the island. Over 6,000 German troops were listed as casualties – of these 1,990 were killed in action. Crete served as a microcosm of the effect the loss of senior leadership could have on an operation – the loss in paratroop leadership was so great that Hitler never again employed the *Fallschirmjäger* in mass, stating that Crete had become the graveyard of the German paratrooper.

AFRICA - 1941

By 1941 it became obvious that Italy was unable to defeat British forces in North Africa; in fact General Sir Archibald Wavell had administered one defeat after another on the hapless Italian Army. By February German reinforcements were arriving in Tripolitania, and by March 24 Rommel began his first offensive aimed at capturing Tobruk. British General Wavell, determined to hold Tobruk to the last man, landed the 7th Australian Division and some armor to stiffen the defenses. The *Afrika Korps* advanced on the garrison, and on April 9, 1941 GL Erwin Rommel briefed GL Heinrich von

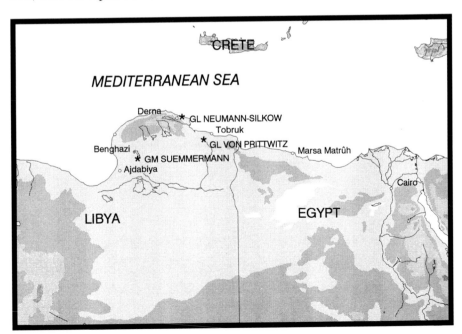

Prittwitz und Gaffron, the 15th Panzer Division commander, on his role in the assault which was to begin the following day. On April 10, von Prittwitz began the assault, traveling at the front of the divisional units and was killed 25 miles west of Tobruk by British anti-tank fire that morning.[9] The situation was confused to say the least. Rommel himself admitted "We had at that time no real idea of the nature or position of the Tobruk defenses."[10] Von Prittwitz's death contributed to the ill-prepared assault which was finally repulsed after three days. The window of opportunity lost, Tobruk would not fall to Rommel until the following year.

In November 1941 General Sir Claude Auchinleck regained the initiative and launched the British Eighth Army from Mersa Matruh northwest to isolate the German-Italian Sollum-Bardia defensive zone. The Axis withdrawal had commenced when on December 6, 1941, GM Walter Neumann-Silkow became the second commander of the 15th Panzer Division to be killed, when he was fatally wounded by British artillery fire which landed next to his command tank.[11] Four days later, GM Max Sümmermann, commander of the 90th Light Division, was killed by a strafing British aircraft. He was riding in his command vehicle when hit.[12] These two German divisions were the mainstay of the Axis force; disorganized, they were unable to stem the British advance, and Rommel was forced to withdraw all the way to El Agheila, his original jump-off position from the previous March.

RUSSIA - 1941

The largest German land operation of the war commenced June 22, 1941 as Hitler launched Operation Barbarossa against the Soviet Union. One hundred sixty two divisions, some 3 million men, simultaneously attacked along a 2,000 mile front in a campaign Hitler envisioned as lasting not more than 4 months, with anticipated equally light casualties. He was wrong on both counts and German senior commanders felt the harshness of the fight almost immediately.

In the northern sector of the Eastern Front, the first division commander killed during the campaign was GM Otto Lancelle who was felled by small arms fire on July 3 while leading his 121st Infantry Division near Kraslawa, near Daugavils on the Dvina River. His replacement, GM Martin Wandel, reported to the division five days later; in the interim a colonel was in command. On August 8, SS-Gruppenführer Arthur Mülverstedt, the commander of the SS "Polizei" Division, while leading his troops forward in the attack from his Kübelwagen, was struck in the chest by shrapnel from Soviet mortar fire. He was rushed to an aid station near Luga but died shortly thereafter.[13]

In the center sector, GM Karl von Weber of the 17th Panzer Division died near Krassnyj, south of Smolensk, on July 20. The division, a part of Army Group Center, had just completed the encirclement of Soviet forces at Minsk – where on July 9 it had destroyed one hundred enemy tanks near Orscha in a single day. The division reported no gains of territory the day after the general was killed.[14] Perhaps some momentum of his unit had been lost with his

sudden death. On August 13, 1941, GM Kurt Kalmukoff died in a minefield east of Smolensk while leading his 31st Infantry Division. Later, *SS-Gruppenführer* Paul Hausser, commander of the SS *"Das Reich"* Division narrowly escaped death on October 14 when he was hit in the eye by enemy fire, but cheated death and went on to lead some of the largest formations in the armed forces.

Finally, during the fighting before Moscow on December 21, GL Friedrich Bergmann, commander of the 137th Infantry Division, was mortally wounded by Soviet machine gun fire southeast of Kaluga at Sjawki, as he became the tenth German commander killed in 1941.[15] His division's attack on Soviet units approaching the major city of Kaluga from the south failed with his death, and the division went over to the defense. Kaluga fell to the Red Army on December 30. The division was then commanded by an *Oberst* Heine for one week, followed by an *Oberst* Muhl for eight days. Neither distinguished himself in the interim and neither commanded a division again.

They in turn were followed by GM Hans Kamecke who added some stability by commanding the unit for a year and a half. Every senior commander casualty adversely affected Army Group Center's drive on Moscow during the fall and early winter of 1941. This ill-equipped, desperate lunge by the German Army, with many divisions struggling along at fifty percent strength or less, exceeded the Wehrmacht's culminating point in the East – and the German Army would find in front of Moscow that it could not even hold on to what it had conquered – much less capture the Soviet capital.

GFM Gerd von Rundstedt and Army Group South's role in the attack east in 1941 has often been overshadowed by the exploits and struggles of the

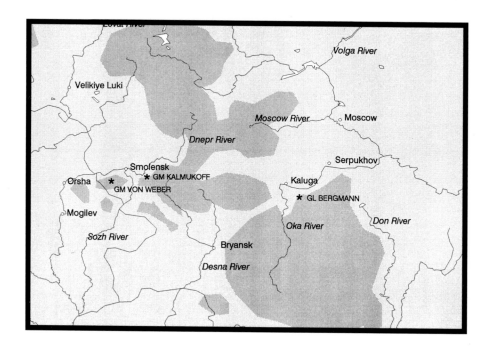

The map shows various locations and rivers including:
Volga River, Velikiye Luki, Moscow River, Moscow, Dnepr River, Serpukhov, Smolensk, GM KALMUKOFF, Orsha, GM VON WEBER, Kaluga, GL BERGMANN, Mogilev, Oka River, Don River, Sozh River, Bryansk, Desna River

two more northern army groups but the fighting in the south during the year was just as vicious and claimed three senior commanders' lives. On September 12, 1941, GO Ritter von Schobert, commander of the 11th Army, was killed by mines when his Fieseler *Storch* aircraft attempted a forced landing and inadvertently landed in a Soviet minefield killing all aboard.[16] The army at the time was poised to break into the Crimea. GdI Erich von Manstein assumed command of the army a day later, but the Crimea would not fall until mid-1942.

This incident had an interesting side effect. In taking command of the 11th Army, Manstein relinquished command of the LVI Panzer Corps. At the time the corps was advancing to Demyansk, northwest of Kalinin. Later that autumn the corps would continue its advance – under a somewhat less talented GdPz Ferdinand Schaal to Taritsa, Klin and the Moscow-Volga Canal – but the corps and the German Army could never capture Moscow. Could the corps, still under von Manstein, have succeeded in capturing the Soviet capital? A fascinating historical question that was made moot when a small German aircraft landed in an enemy minefield.

GdI Kurt von Briesen, LII Corps, was not so lucky, and was killed November 20, 1941 southeast of Andrejewka by attacking Soviet aircraft.[17] He was replaced by the unheralded GM Albert Zehler, who was never given command of a front-line division or corps for the remainder of the war. Von Briesen's death was only the first of nineteen German corps commanders who would be killed on the Eastern Front during the war. Also in November, GM Georg Braun of the 68th Infantry Division, was killed by a mine explosion at his headquarters in at Kharkov on November 14. He was replaced by

a colonel before the arrival of a permanent commander.

The year ended with the German forces reeling west from Moscow. The front was forced back some 100 to 200 miles in a series of piecemeal withdrawals and Soviet attacks. Tens of thousands of German soldiers were killed and even more were crippled by frostbite and illness. But this setback was only the beginning. Later years would prove even bloodier.

1942

For three years the German Army had run up one victory after another but this would change in 1942. The year started with grand plans for Final Victory. In Africa GFM Rommel believed that Egypt could be taken and envisioned a final strategic objective as an attack through Persia and Iraq into southern Russia to seize the oil fields at Baku. His aims were not shared by the German Army High Command who continually thought of the theater as a side show.

In the East, Hitler wanted to resume Army Group South's offensive towards the Caucasus, seize the oil fields there, and continue the attack south to seize more oil in Iran and Iraq. Additionally, Hitler insisted that Leningrad be taken in the north – but he allocated no increase in resources to do so; the main effort or *Schwerpunkt* would be in the south. For Hitler the seizure of Stalingrad would ensure the protection of the northeast flank for the drive to the oil fields. Once again, the Army High Command – OKH (*Oberkommando des Heeres*) held a different understanding of the Führer's intentions and believed that Stalingrad, not the Caucasus, was the principle objective. In their view the advance into the Caucasus was to serve only as a flank guard for the main effort racing east to the Volga River. The generals reasoned that once Stalingrad was secure the German Army could pursue a number of options; drive east to the Urals, north to Moscow or south to the Caucasus – and thus bring the war in the East to a successful conclusion.

These strategic differences of opinion proved disastrous. German territorial gains peaked during the year and then began to ebb. The Wehrmacht suffered massive setbacks at El Alamein in Africa and Stalingrad on the Eastern Front during the year. German ground units, often severely understrength, now frequently found themselves on the defensive in ground operations – while enemy air activity markedly increased as the Luftwaffe found itself stretched too thin fighting a multi-front war against Britain, the United States and the Soviet Union. Materiel losses mounted and casualties began to rise at an alarming rate. Fourteen senior general officer commanders were killed during the year; two in Africa and twelve in Russia. This compared with overall German Army deaths of 443,322 and of 94,600 missing in action.

AFRICA - 1942

GM Georg von Bismarck, 21st Panzer Division, was probably killed by British mortar fire while advancing with a lead battalion near El Alamein August 31, 1942, during the high-water mark of Rommel's offensive in Egypt, as the Germans failed in their effort to drive to Alexandria and the operational initiative passed to Field Marshal Montgomery.[19]

Von Bismarck was replaced by a colonel. The British commander meanwhile, struck back on October 23, 1942 at the pivotal battle of El Alamein and smashed through the German defenses after a furious 13-day fight. Montgomery maintained the initiative by conducting a methodical pursuit for the next two months, hoping to keep unremitting pressure on the Germans. During their withdrawal, GM Heinz von Randow, commander of the 21st Panzer Division was killed near Tripoli, December 21, 1942 by a mine laid by the British Long Range Desert Group.[20] His replacement for twelve days was a colonel. Two commanders of the same division were thus struck down in less than four months. Between the two, the division was forced to place a colonel in temporary command for a three-week period during the crucial fighting near El Alamein.

GdPz Georg Stumme, the commander of Panzer Army Africa, died of a heart attack during this time. On October 23, 1942 at approximately 10:00 PM, he drove forward in his Kübelwagen to get first hand information on the rapidly developing British offensive. Suddenly his command car came under British machine-gun and anti-tank fire. A colonel in the car was killed immediately; Stumme jumped out of the vehicle to avoid the fire and suffered a massive heart attack in the process.[21] While not technically killed in action, the result was still the same – impaired command and control during a crucial battlefield situation.

These losses were exacerbated by Rommel's own ill health and more frequent absences from the battlefield. In 1941 he experienced jaundice and

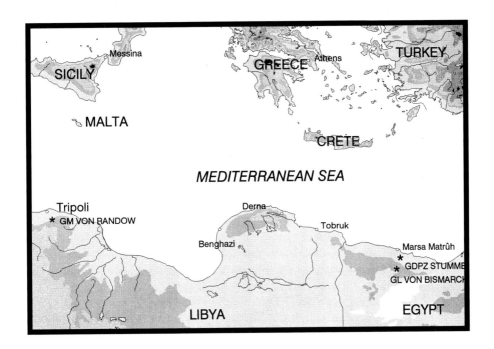

suffered continually from heat diarrhea. On September 23 he flew to Germany after receiving the following diagnosis from his personal doctor:

> *GFM Rommel suffers the results and symptoms of low blood pressure with a tendency towards fainting spells. The present condition dates back to a stomach and intestine disorder existing for some time, which is being intensified by the excessive physical and psychological demands of the last weeks, especially considering the unfavorable climactic conditions. A full employment, especially under heavy stress, is at present not advisable at all, and only to be expected again after a prolonged home leave under medical care.* [22]

Rommel returned on October 25 in the emergency caused the British offensive, but the initiative – so critical to success in the fluid desert war characteristic of the fighting in North Africa, had passed to Field Marshal Montgomery and the British Eighth Army.

Rommel's health continued to deteriorate, despite his month long stay in Germany and he left the African Theater for good on March 9, 1943. Leadership had proven to be a key ingredient in German operations in Africa during the year – and the loss of key leaders, whether permanent caused by death, or temporary due to illness, often had a direct effect on tactical and operational initiative.

RUSSIA - 1942

Nineteen forty-two began with German forces still reeling in front of Moscow, and the German High Command seeking other areas of the front to renew offensive operations. General officer casualties reflected these situations. In the south, GL Kurt Himer the commander of the 46th Infantry Division, was a victim of naval gunfire by units of the Soviet Black Sea Fleet near Nowo Michailowka on the Kerch Peninsula of the Crimea on March 22, 1942.[23] For ten days thereafter a colonel was in command.

In late summer, Army Group A reorganized its two subordinate armies and continued the advance against elements of the *South and Independent Coastal Fronts*. The mission of the 1st Panzer Army was to cross the Terek River, take Ordzhonikidze and open the Grusinian Military Road for future advances toward Grozny. GM Erwin Mack, the commander of the 23rd Panzer Division of the 1st Panzer Army, was killed by a Soviet mortar barrage on August 26, 1942 near Nowo Poltawskoje.

At the time he was forward with the 128th Motorized Infantry Regiment, as the Germans attempted to drive deep into the Caucasus, and secure oil sources. The drive started well. Maykop fell to the Germans on August 9 and at the same time Pyatigorsk, some 150 miles to the southeast, was captured as well. After twelve days the Germans reached the foothills of the Caucasus. Then the pace slowed and the 1st Panzer Army did not reach the area of Ordzhonikidze until November 2. The drive ultimately failed, the Baku oil fields remained 300 miles inside Soviet control, and Germany was plagued the entire war by fuel shortages.[24]

The 17th Army, meanwhile, was to continue to attack to seize the Black

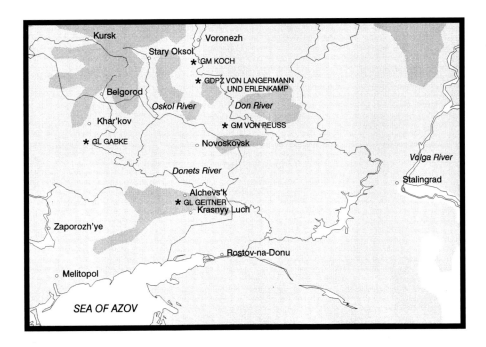

Sea port of Novorossiysk, thrust along the road running southwest from Maykop to Tuapse, and to push the XXXXIX Mountain Corps through the mountain passes to Sukhumi in order to clear the Soviets from the eastern shore of the Black Sea which would then eliminate the Soviet Navy in this theater. On September 6, 1942, GM Albert Buck, of the 198th Infantry Division in the 17th Army, was ambushed and killed while driving in his command car over a bridge near Klutschewaja in the Kuban.[25] He was succeeded by a colonel.

Also with Army Group South, GL Otto Gabcke, commander of the 294th Infantry Division was killed when two Soviet aircraft bombed Michailowka and the headquarters for the division, on March 22, 1942.[26] GdPz Willibald von Langermann und Erlencamp was killed near Storoshewoje, northwest of Stalingrad, on October 3, while leading the XXIV Panzer Corps – his obituary gives little details of his demise, but presents much on his impact to the Army.

Obituary for the fallen General of Panzer Troops Freiherr Willibald von Langermann and Erlencamp

On 3 October, 1942, the Commanding General of an Army Corps, General of Panzer Troops, Freiherr Willibald von Langermann and Erlencamp, Bearer of the Oak Leaves to the Knight's Cross of the 1939 Iron Cross fell in Russia.

Leading a veritable soldier's life, shining with impassioned devotion and extreme joy in responsibility for his people and fatherland, [GdPz von Langermann and Erlencamp] has finished his last accomplishment through his heroic death. He was a proven young officer in the World War; during the campaign in the West, this well-deserved General led his division onto the battlefields of France with courage and astuteness to decisive successes. Carried by the unconditional trust of his soldiers, he was inspiring in the march against Bolshevist Russia to more glorious acts. The victorious battles near Roslavl and Bachmatch have gone into the history of the Army. As Commanding General of an Army Corps he stood alone with a fierce aggressive spirit; as an inspired officer constantly in the front lines and was a shining example to his soldiers of courageousness and devotion until his last breath. Our Army will eternally remember his devotion in their thoughts.

The 13th of November, 1942.

[signed] Der Führer,
Adolf Hitler

Clearly, this senior commander would be sorely missed.

The Soviet Stalingrad counteroffensive began November 19, 1942 and within four days elements of the *Don* and *Stalingrad Fronts* had encircled the German 6th Army and the bulk of the 4th Panzer Army, and severely mauled the Rumanian 3rd and 4th Armies. Shortly thereafter the *Stavka* planned to launch a follow-on offensive with the *Voronezh* and *Southwestern Fronts* to seize Rostov and thus trap Army Group A. However, this plan had to be modified. Now the *Southwestern Front* would envelope the Italian 8th Army and Army Detachment Hollidt. The offensive began on December 16, 1942 and within two days had ruptured the German and Italian defenses. On

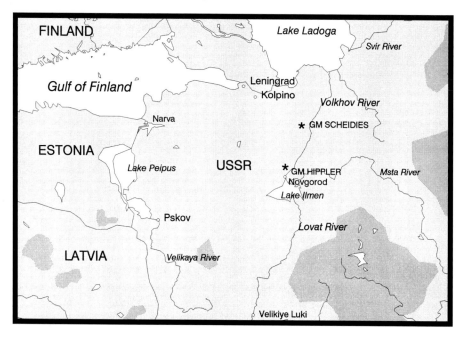

114

the 19th the 62nd Infantry Division was encircled by units from the 1st and 3rd Guards Armies. The division tried to fight its way out to the west of Bokovskaya, on the Chir River, pursued by the 266th Rifle Division and 94th Rifle Brigade. GM Richard von Reuss was killed in action in this desperate fighting on December 22, 1942. GM Viktor Koch of the 323rd Infantry Division died near Voronezh on the same day. He was replaced by *Oberst* Andreas Nebauer, who in turn was killed five weeks later, who was succeeded by an *Oberst* Koschella, who commanded the division until it was disbanded.

To the north, GM Bruno Hippler, commander of the 329th Infantry Division, was killed in a minefield on March 23, 1942 as he was riding to forward positions near Lake Ilmen to get a look at the front-line situation.[27] On April 7, 1942 GM Franz Scheidies, 61st Infantry Division, was shot in the head by a sniper and killed in operations near Gluschitza in the vicinity of Leningrad.[28] Both units were conducting counterattacks against the Soviet 2nd Shock Army of the *Northwest Front* which had attacked across the Volhov River north of Lake Ilmen. The counterattacks succeeded but neither general lived long enough to share in the victory.

In front of Moscow on January 24, 1942 GL Gerhard Berthold, commander of the 31st Infantry Division, was killed in an assault near Saizewa-Gora, northwest of Kaluga.[29] Again, a unit had lost two commanders in a relatively short period of time. GM Karl Fischer of the 267th Infantry Division also died northwest of Kaluga on March 31 at Uljewo near Vyasma. He was replaced by *Oberst* Friedrich Stephan.

On July 16, 1942 the Stavka instructed Marshal Zhukov, then commander

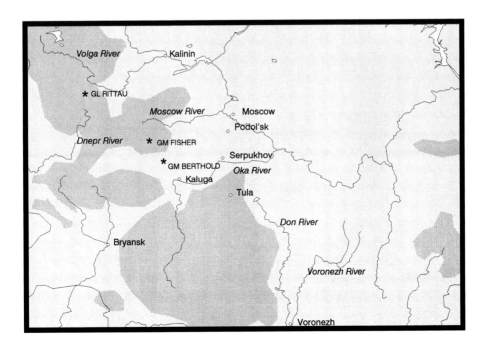

of the West Front and General Koniev, the commander of the Kalinin Front, to conduct an offensive to take the cities of Rzhev and Zubstov, 125 miles west of Moscow. Koniev commenced the assault on July 30 while Zhukov followed suit five days later. The fighting raged for four weeks – by August 17, the German 9th Army had lost 20,000 casualties in close-in fighting reminiscent of World War I. GL Stephan Rittau, 129th Infantry Division, was killed by artillery riding in his command vehicle near Martinowo, a few miles northeast of Rzhev, on August 22, 1942.[30] His immediate replacement was a colonel.

The fighting continued at Rzhev into 1943 when Hitler authorized the 9th and 4th Armies to withdraw from the salient to form defensive positions over 100 miles to the west in front of Smolensk. The 129th Infantry Division, as part of Army Group Center, thus began a long, tortuous two year retreat which would only end with the defeat of Germany.

1943

The turning point on the German road from victory to defeat occurred in 1943. The year opened with German forces still deep in Russia, still a powerful force in North Africa and with no Allied troops north of the Mediterranean Sea. But the plans for continued operations were no way as clear as in previous years. This dilemma is perhaps best described by GFM Erich von Manstein:

> *The question now was how the German side should continue the struggle the following summer [1943]. Obviously, after so many major formations had been lost, there would no longer be the forces available to mount another crucial offensive on the scale of 1941 and 1942. What did seem possible – given proper leadership on the German side – was that the Soviet Union could be worn down to such an extent that it would tire of its already excessive sacrifices and be ready to accept a stalemate.[31]*

Neither the Soviet Union, nor the Western Allies, however, were worn down during 1943. It was the German Army at Kursk and Tunisia that were ground down through excessive losses which marked the end of Germany's true offensive capability. With the fall of Africa, the German southern theater of operations was no longer restricted to the North African coastline, but was expanded to include possible Allied landings anywhere on the northern Mediterranean littoral. The war in Yugoslavia dragged on – by mid-year no fewer than fifteen German divisions were stationed in the Balkans. The year ended with the loss of most of the Ukraine; Africa completely captured by the British and Americans, and the Allies halfway up the boot of Italy.

Even more telling than territorial losses, were overall army casualties. During the year, 449,096 soldiers lost their lives while a further 343,608 were listed as missing.[3] Once again, many of these missing in action later turned up in Allied prisoner of war camps while others had in fact been killed in action. General officer fatalities almost doubled from the previous year. Twenty-six perished, two in Africa, twenty-three in Russia and one in France.

AFRICA - 1943

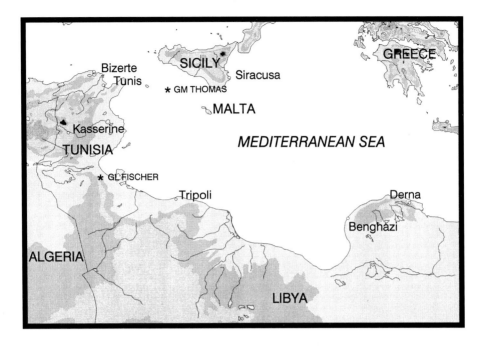

GL Wolfgang Fischer, commander of the 10th Panzer Division, was killed on February 1, 1943 near Mareth when his staff car driver inadvertently drove into a poorly marked Italian minefield.[33] The last German senior commander to be killed in the African Campaign didn't actually die in Africa at all. Over the Mediterranean, GL Kurt Thomas, commander of the newly formed 999th Light Africa Division was shot down enroute to Tunis April 1, 1943 by British fighters.[34] One month later, the Axis forces on the continent surrendered and 275,000 soldiers, a quarter of them German, including many senior commanders marched into captivity.

Seven senior commanders had been killed during the African campaign from 1941 through 1943 and 12,808 soldiers lost their lives.[35] Many of these losses can be directly attributable to Rommel's insistence on front-line leadership. Rommel recalled in 1944 that in Africa "from my officers I demanded the utmost self-denial and a continual personal example, and as a result the army had a magnificent esprit de corps."[36] Numerous other senior commanders narrowly avoided death in battle; GL von Värst, 15th Panzer Division commander was seriously wounded in May 1942, GdPz Nehring was wounded in August 1942 near Alam Halfa, and GL Kleemann, 90th Light Africa Division, was wounded the following month. Rommel had been correct in his assessment – much had been expected of the senior commanders in the theater and much had been paid in their quest to seize the desert sands for Germany. The following table shows all the casualties to the commanders of the major units in the Africa Corps, prior to the surrender:

Africa Corps Commander Casualties

Name		Unit	Date	Casualty Type
GdK	Stumme	Panzer Army Africa	24.10.42	Killed
GL	Crüwell	Africa Corps	29.5.42	Prisoner
GL	Nehring	Africa Corps	31.8.42	Wounded
GdPz	von Thoma	Africa Corps	4.11.42	Prisoner
GdPz	Fehn	Africa Corps	16.1.43	Wounded
GM	von Liebenstein	Africa Corps	17.2.43	Wounded
GL	Fischer	10 Panzer Division	1.2.43	Killed
GM	von Prittwitz	15 Panzer Division	5.7.41	Wounded
GM	Meumann-Silkow	15 Panzer Division	8.12.41	Killed
GL	von Värst	15 Panzer Division	26.5.42	Wounded
GM	von Ravenstein	21 Panzer Division	29.11.41	Prisoner
GM	von Bismarck	21 Panzer Division	17.7.42	Wounded
GM	von Bismarck	21 Panzer Division	31.8.42	Killed
GM	von Randow	21 Panzer Division	21.12.42	Killed
GM	Sümmermann	90 Light Division	10.12.41	Killed
GM	Kleemann	90 Light Division	2.9.42	Wounded
GL	Thomas	999 Light Division	1.4.43	Killed

In May 1943 final German resistance in Africa ceased and those Axis soldiers and generals remaining in Tunisia became prisoners of war. The generals included GO Hans-Jürgen von Arnim, commander of Army Group Tunis, GL Willibald Borowietz, 15th Panzer Division, GM Fritz von Broich, 10th Panzer Division, GM Heinrich-Hermann von Hülsen, 21st Panzer Division, GdPz Gustav von Värst, 5th Panzer Army and GM Kurt von Liebenstein, 164th Light Africa Division.

RUSSIA - 1943

By early January 1943 the Red Army again massed troops to conduct an offensive – this time the *Voronezh Front* under General Golikov against the 2nd Hungarian Army near Voronezh. On January 12 this new offensive ripped a gaping hole in the German front from south of Voronezh to Voroshilovgrad which opened the potential for seizing the Donbas, the Donets and perhaps even the Dnepr crossings or the Sea of Azov. The northern group of forces consisting primarily of the 40th Army headed for Alekseyevka, where it would link up with the southern force, the 3rd Tank Army launching from Kantemirovka and attacking northwest. The 3rd Tank Army commenced operations on the 14th; and by evening had advanced 12 miles. A subordinate unit, the 15th Tank Corps overran the headquarters of the XXIV Panzer Corps this day killing its commander GdA Martin Wandel near Chilino. The situation deteriorated further and by the 19th 56,000

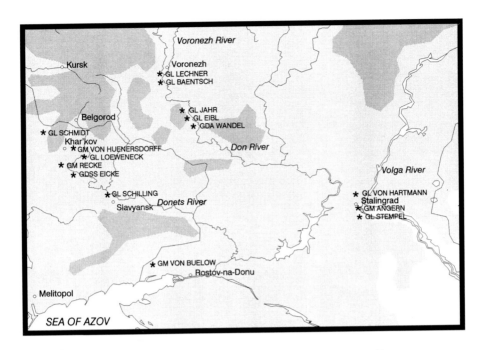

German soldiers and their allies had been captured as well as numerous stocks of supplies and weapons. GL Arno Jahr took command after Wandel on January 15; but by January 20 he considered the situation so hopeless that he committed suicide near Podgornoje. Once more the command of the corps passed to new hands – unfortunately with similar results. GL Karl Eibl, the commander of the XXIV Panzer Corps within seven days, became the only high ranking commander to be killed by his own troops when he was seriously wounded by a hand grenade – thrown by a soldier from a passing Italian truck column.[37] GL Alfred Bäntsch of the 82nd Infantry Division became the fourth commander to die in this Soviet offensive when he was seriously wounded on January 27, 1943 near Voronezh and died of his wounds four days later. He was replaced by *Oberst* Walter Heyne who was promoted to *generalmajor* in June. On January 29, GL Adolf Lechner of the 377th Infantry Division was killed in the same area. Both divisions were part of the German 2nd Army which was being driven back by the winter offensives as well.

At Stalingrad, on January 26, 1943, GL Alexander von Hartmann, commander of the 71st Infantry Division was shot in the head by machine gun fire and killed near a railroad embankment in the southern portion of Stalingrad.[38] GL Richard Stempel of the 371st Infantry Division committed suicide the same day in his headquarters. A few days later on February 2, 1943 just after the final radio call announced the surrender of the division and other elements of the 6th Army, GM Günther Angern, commander of the 16th Panzer Division, attempted to breakthrough Soviet troops in the vicinity of the Tractor Factory and was killed in the effort.[39]

119

Eibl (head only, behind artillery piece) (DOW January 21, 1943)

The *Voronezh Front* continued its advance west and seized Kharkov on February 15, 1943. GFM von Manstein counterattacked, trapping and destroying several Red Army formations which were strung out and at the end of a tenuous supply line. *SS-Obergruppenführer* Theodor Eicke, SS Division *"Totenkopf"* was shot down and killed February 26, 1943 on a reconnaissance flight near the villages of Michailovka and Artelnoye, as the 4th Panzer Army approached Kharkov from the south.[40] The *"Totenkopf"* would take part in the greatest tank battle in history some five months later, but the charismatic Eicke would not be in command. In the spring, GL Ludwig Löweneck, commander of the 39th Infantry Division, drove into a minefield north of Petschenegi and died on May 14.[41] His replacement was a colonel who commanded the unit which was now reduced to a *kampfgruppe* (a battle group).

At Kursk several commanders were killed as Hitler tried to seize the operational initiative on the Eastern Front for a last time. In the southern pincer of the German attack, GL Walther von Hünersdorff, commander of the 6th Panzer Division – a subordinate unit of the III Panzer Corps, was shot in the head by a sniper on July 14, 1943 and died three days later. At the time of the incident, he was enroute from a forward detachment to the division forward command post, during the height of the battle.[42] His replacement was *Oberst* Wilhelm Crissoli who commanded the division for a month. The *Voronezh* and *Steppe Fronts* opposite the southern German pincer, went over to the offensive on August 3, and headed for Kharkov. They captured the city and continued the push west through the Ukraine. Shortly thereafter, a Soviet breakthrough during the battle cut off the withdrawal routes of the 19th

Panzer Division, another III Panzer Corps unit, near Achtyrka – northwest of Kharkov, on August 7. As the German columns passed the Soviet 13th Guards Rifle Division the Soviet division commander ordered the 39th Guards Rifle Regiment to capture the German divisional headquarters. GL Gustav Schmidt, the commander of the 19th Panzer Division, probably committed suicide to avoid capture by the enemy, but may have been shot.[43] GL Heinrich Recke, commander of the 161st Infantry Division, a part of the XLII Army Corps and Army Detachment Kempf, southwest of Kharkov, personally led an assault group attempting to regain the Russian village of Panskaja August 15, 1943 and was killed as the Soviet torrent kept expanding through German held territory.[44] His replacement was *Oberst* Otto Schell who would be killed himself thirteen months later while still a colonel, now in command of the 320th Infantry Division.

Not all general fatalities during this time on the southern sector involved units that were part of the Kursk battle. GL Walter Schilling of the 17th Panzer Division was killed along the Donets River on July 21 – after serving in command for only one month. *Oberst* Karl von der Meden replaced Schilling but was not promoted until October. Further south, GM Werner von Bülow was killed near Obronoje west of Rostov on the 28th of August while leading his 111th Infantry Division as part of the newly reconstituted 6th Army. He was replaced by *Oberst* Werner von Bülow who in turn was posted missing in action shortly thereafter.

In the northern pincer at Kursk, GL Richard Müller of the 211th Infantry Division, was killed northeast of Orel on July 16. By July 12 the German attack had fizzled; the *Bryansk Front*, under General Popov, and the *West Front*, under General Sokolovskiy, opened a three pronged offensive to

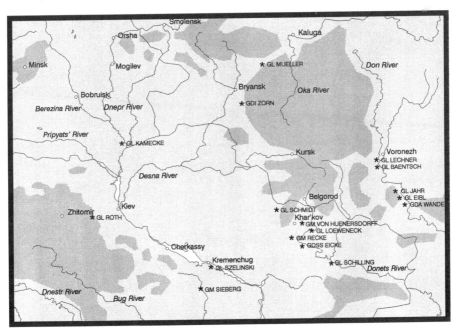

retake Orel and trap elements of the German 2nd Army. Three Soviet mobile corps smashed through the German defenses, caved in the 211th Division near Sikejewo, and made several deep penetrations which threatened the city. Orel was saved when GFM Kluge diverted four divisions from the offensive, but Müller was not among the survivors.

Soviet pressure against the Orel salient did not slacken, and the Germans began to prepare fall-back field fortification positions – called the Hagen Position, at the base of the Orel salient about 50 miles west of the city. Withdrawing on August 1, the operation almost immediately came under pressure from the enemy. GdI Hans Zorn, commander XXXXVI Panzer Corps – of the withdrawing 9th Army, was killed from the air near Krassnaja, enroute to a front-line unit on August 2, 1943.[45] GL Hans Kamecke, the 137th Infantry Division commander, was a victim of another Soviet air attack. On October 15, 1943, on his return trip to division headquarters from visiting front-line units, he was mortally wounded by Soviet fighters near Kolpen.[46] He was replaced by *Oberst* Egon von Neindorf, and the division was disbanded one month later. To von Neindorf this was merely a temporary reprieve, he was killed the following April while serving as the Commandant of Tarnopol. On November 3, after several attempts to break out of several bridgeheads north and south of Kiev, the Soviet 3rd Guards Tank, 38th and 60th Armies blasted out of the Lutezh and Yasnogorodka enclaves north of the city and immediately made progress. The German 4th Panzer Army front collapsed and by November 5 both sides were involved in heavy street fighting in the city – on the 6th the Germans retreated south. That day, GL Heinrich Roth, the 88th Infantry Division commander, was killed in action against the spearheads of enemy infantry.[47] His replacement was a colonel.

Street Fighting

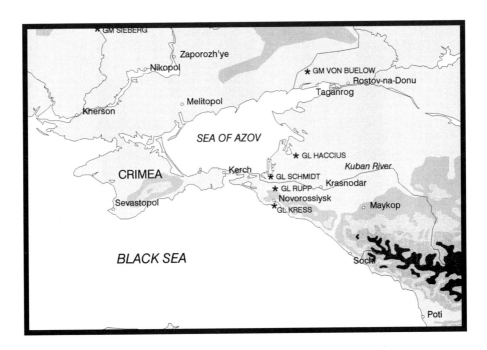

The situation was no better for the Germans on other sectors. Army Group A became dangerously exposed in the Kuban area of the Caucasus. With the *Trans-Caucasus Front* to its front, the Black Sea and the Sea of Azov to its rear, and the Soviets bearing down on escape routes through Rostov in the north, the army group made plans to withdraw west to the *Gotenkopf* Position on the Taman bridgehead. GL Ernst Haccius of the 46th Infantry Division was killed February 14, 1943 by an air attack near Taman as German forces completed their withdrawal.[48] He was replaced by *Oberst* Karl Le Suire who was not promoted to *generalmajor* until May. Le Suire proved his mettle and commanded several other divisions later in the war. Soviet aircraft, dropping bombs and strafing with machine guns, attacked the headquarters of the 97th Jäger Division May 30, 1943.

GL Ernst Rupp, the division commander, was killed by a bomb fragment during the incident.[49] He was replaced by Oberst Friedrich Otte, who commanded the division for four days before returning to his regiment – he was killed one year later during the last days of the fight for the Crimea. GL Friedrich Schmidt, commander of the 50th Infantry Division, blundered into a minefield in the Russian Kuban while visiting an artillery firing position on June 26.[50] He was followed by *Oberst* Hermann Böhme, who went on to later command the 73rd Infantry Division but was never awarded the Knight's Cross. Finally, a Soviet sniper shot and killed GL Hermann Kress, commander of the 4th Mountain Division, in the Kuban, near Novorossijsk on the Black Sea on August 11. GM Julius Braun replaced Kress; he too was never awarded a Knight's Cross for his military exploits.

On August 26, 1943 GL Kurt Renner, commander 174th Reserve Division, was ambushed by partisans near Ozarow while enroute to the Deba maneuver area and killed.[52] Renner's replacement was a colonel who filled in for nineteen days before a general officer took command. GM Karl von Groddeck was mortally wounded by Soviet aircraft on August 28 as commander of the 161st Infantry Division. He would die several months later in Breslau of his wounds. He too, was replaced by a colonel. During the winter battles in the Ukraine, GM Friedrich Sieberg, the commander of the 14th Panzer Division died from the effects of an anti-tank round. On October 29, 1943 his division commenced an attack toward the village of Tolstaja, 30 miles east of Kirowograd. Sieberg was seriously wounded by shrapnel from Soviet anti-tank fire and died on November 2.[53]

Finally, at the end of the year, GL Arnold Szelinski of the 376th Infantry Division was killed in action December 12 near Kremenschug, along the Dnepr River. He was replaced by *Oberst* Otto Schwarz, an extremely experienced General Staff officer but with limited front-line combat experience.[54] The year had ended as poorly as it had begun – but 1944 would prove even worse.

1944

The German Army and general officer corps received mortal blows in 1944 that sealed the fate of the Third Reich. During the year the Soviet Army drove Germany back to her pre-war boundaries and beyond, as well as liberating parts of Hungary and Poland, and knocking Rumania and Finland from the Axis camp. In Normandy, the Western Allies conducted Operation Overlord and retook France, Belgium and most of the Netherlands before being temporarily halted by Hitler's Ardennes Offensive.

Finally, in Italy the stalemate at Cassino was finally broken, Rome taken, and Axis troops inexorably pushed up the peninsula toward the Alps. Twenty-one general officer commanders were killed in action during the year, while 457,965 troops were killed and 1,069,718 became missing in action for the year through November, when finally the efficient German records system became overloaded and lost an accurate count.[55] Demobilization offices were set up for each division, corps and army that had been completely destroyed.

These organizations attempted to establish the names of all those who had been killed or who were now missing – especially hard as all papers and documents had been destroyed with the unit. Frequently, this amounted to over twelve thousand names per division. Notices were then sent to each next-of-kin and orders were written formally disbanding the particular division if it were decided not to reform it at a later date. The task would be daunting enough in the age of the computer – in 1944 it had to be done by pencil and paper only.

EASTERN FRONT - 1944

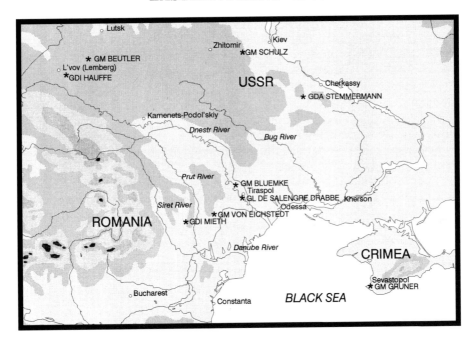

The year started out poorly when GM Adalbert Schulz, commander of the 7th Panzer Division and winner of the Diamonds to the Knight's Cross, was hit in the head by mortar fragments and mortally wounded while leading a panzer attack from his command tank near Schepetowka.[56] He had been in command of the division for only two days when he was killed. His immediate replacement was an *Oberst* Gläsemer.

On January 26, the *1st* and *2nd Ukrainian Fronts* executed a double envelopment west of the Dnepr River, some 60 miles southeast of Kiev, and trapped the German XI and XXXXII Army Corps in the vicinity of Korsun.[57] On February 1, the 1st Panzer Army began relief operations and advanced to within 5 miles of the pocket – which began to move southwest on February 16, to facilitate the link-up. GdA Wilhelm Stemmermann, commander of the XI Army Corps, was killed by a direct hit from a Soviet anti-tank round during movement of his command post near Khil'ki as the general was riding in his command car leading the breakout on February 18.[58]

In the winter of 1943-44 the 17th Army sat cut-off from other German forces in the Crimea. On April 8, 1944 the *4th Ukrainian* Front attacked south out of the Sivash bridgehead and overran several Rumanian units. By April 10, German forces were in retreat toward the fortress of Sevastopol, which was the only other defensible position in the Crimea – and closed into position there by the 17th. The Red Army began a siege, and by the beginning of May was in position to attack. On May 5 the Russians attacked north of Sevastopol but this was a feint. The main assault came two days later at

Balaklava and quickly gained the Sapun Heights which gave them clear observation of all evacuation beaches to the tip of Cape Khersonyes, where the Germans were attempting a Dunkirk-style withdrawal. For the next several days they squeezed the Germans closer to the sea. GM Erich Gruner, 111th Infantry Division, was killed by cannon fire from a T 34 tank on May 12, 1944 on the beach as the final German positions were overrun.[59] Over 26,700 other soldiers fell into enemy hands.

While Army Group South was getting pounded into submission, to the north Army Group North Ukraine was experiencing its own significant problems. The *1st Ukrainian Front*, under General Koniev, had ten armies of its own to hurl against the 1st and 4th Panzer Armies. Koniev opened his attack on July 13 – by the 18th Soviet armored spearheads from the north and south had pierced German lines, driven deep into the army group rear and had met on the Bug River –30 miles west of the city of L'vov. Encircled were five divisions of the German XIII Army Corps. GM Otto Beutler, 340th Infantry Division, was killed near Brody, 50 miles east of L'vov, Poland on July 21, 1944; the next day the division was destroyed and the corps disintegrated. Groups of soldiers frantically struggled west to breakout from the encirclement. Perhaps 12,000 succeeded; but a further 30,000 men were killed and 17,000 captured – GdI Arthur Hauffe, the commander of the beleaguered XIII Corps, fell near L'vov on July 22.

South of the *1st Ukrainian Front,* the *2nd* and *3rd Ukrainian Fronts* began their offensives against Rumania on August 20, 1944. Immediately two war-weary Rumanian divisions threw down their weapons and ran while others simply refused to fight the Red Army. By the 24th Soviet spearheads had achieved another breakthrough and encirclement. The German 6th Army, which had been reformed in 1943 after the disaster at Stalingrad, and the 8th Army were hardest hit by this latest Soviet steamroller. GL Hans de Salengre-Drabbe of the 384th Infantry Division was killed on the 25th; when the IV Army Corps became encircled and attempted to breakout near Vutcani. On August 29 GdI Friedrich Mieth, the commander died, probably of a heart attack, during the fighting. Also killed during this encirclement, was GM Werner von Eichstedt of the 294th Infantry Division.[60] GM Friedrich Blümke, 257th Infantry Division, severely wounded in a Soviet air attack near Tighina by Tirasopol on August 24, 1944, died of his wounds on September 4 at a Soviet prison camp at Odessa.

To the far north of the Eastern Front conditions were almost as bad for German generals. At the beginning of 1944 the German 16th and 18th Armies were opposed by the *Leningrad Front*, under General Govorov, with 33 rifle divisions, the *Volkhov Front*, under General Meretskov, with 22 rifle divisions and the *2nd Baltic Front*, commanded by General Popov, which had 45 rifle divisions assigned. GM Hermann von Wedel of the 10th Luftwaffe Field Division was mortally wounded on January 29 near Dorpat, Estonia and died six days later. The division was so hard hit that it was disbanded February 3. On February 22nd, GM Paul Gurran died while leading the 23rd Infantry Division. *SS-Brigadeführer* Hinrich Schuldt fell on March

15, 1944 near Velikaya as the 19th Waffen-SS Division was locked in fierce fighting with the Soviets. GL Werner Richter, the commander of the 263rd Infantry Division, was mortally wounded in a minefield on May 21, 1944.[61] He was replaced by *Oberst* Ernst Meiners. *SS-Brigadeführer* Friedrich von Scholz, commander of the 11th Waffen SS Division *"Nordland"*, was struck in the head by shrapnel from a heavy Soviet artillery barrage during the Battle of Narva and died of his wounds on July 27, 1944.

Later in the summer, the 16th Army lost its commander on August 29, 1944, when GdI Paul Laux took off on a reconnaissance flight from Riga, and his plane was shot down over the front-lines. Suffering from massive burns, he died shortly thereafter.[62] Soviet air attacks killed GdI Wilhelm Wegener, commander L Corps, on September 9, 1944 as he was enroute to visit a subordinate infantry division.[63] GM Bogislav von Schwerin, commander of the 207th Security Division, was killed by small arms fire on September 17, 1944 near the front-lines in the vicinity of Dorpat, Estonia, as pressure in the north continued to force the German Army west.

But it was in the center that disaster struck the German Army on a scale that overshadowed every other debacle of the war. On June 22, 1944, Josef Stalin launched Operation Bagration – the Soviet attack to destroy Army Group Center. The *1st Baltic, 3rd Belorussian, 2nd Belorussian and 1st Belorussian Fronts*, with some 2,500,000 Russian troops, backed by a revitalized air force, smashed into GFM Busch's 400,000 overextended German troops. The result was predictable, not only on a strategic level, but also concerning general officer losses. GM Hans Hahne of the 197th Infantry Division died as Soviet troops overran German positions at Vitebsk on June

24. GM Albrecht Wüstenhagen, commander of the 256th Infantry Division, was killed in action June 26, 1944 as his command vehicle was moving across country to avoid Soviet forces and received a direct hit from a Soviet tank round.[65] The following day, GL Pistorious, commander of the 4th Luftwaffe Field Division, fell in action at Gankowitsch. The division was so completely destroyed, that it was never reformed. GL Ernst Philipp, in command of the 134th Infantry Division, saw his division cut off and smashed by the Soviet 9th Tank Corps and the 41st Motorized Corps; and dealt with this catastrophe by retiring to his bunker and committing suicide.[66] On June 28, 1944 GdA Robert Martinek was killed by a bomb splinter east of the Beresina River while commander of the XXXIX Panzer Corps.[67]

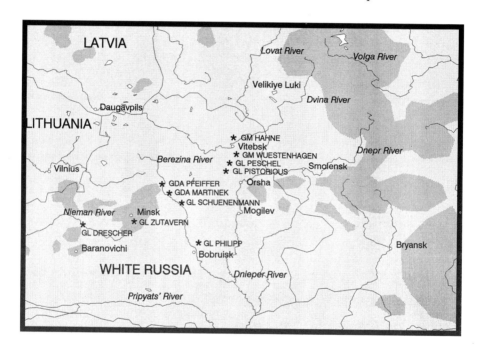

That same day, GdA Georg Pfeiffer, commander VI Corps, was killed from the air in the vicinity of Mogilev.[68] GL Otto Schünemann became the second commander of the XXXIX Panzer Corps to be killed in forty-eight hours, at Pagost on the Beresina River on June 29. GL Rudolf Peschel of the 6th Luftwaffe Field Division died at Vitebsk on June 30, as German defenses collapsed along the entire sector. The 18th Panzer Grenadier Division retreated toward Minsk but the situation appeared hopeless and the commander GL Karl Zutavern committed suicide just east of the city. GL Otto Drescher, 267th Infantry Division, fell near the Niemen River on August 13 after more than fifty days of trying to regain German lines when his division was overrun. The destruction of Army Group Center was the single most costly defeat for German military arms in history. For the first time entire formations simply vaporized to a degree that not only were they unable to be reconstituted, but also most knowledge concerning their last days and hours – and the fates of hundreds of thousands of men, has disappeared from history as well. The scope of this catastrophe to just general officers is shown on the following table:

Army Group Center Commander Casualties

Name		Unit	Casualty Type
GdI	Gollwitzer	LII Army Corps	Prisoner
GM	Müller-Bülow	246 Infantry Division	Prisoner
GL	Pistorius	4 Luftwaffe Field Division	Killed
GL	Peschel	6 Luftwaffe Field Division	Killed
GL	Hitter	206 Infantry Division	Prisoner
GdA	Pfeiffer	VI Army Corps	Killed
GM	Hahne	197 Infantry Division	Killed
GM	Wüstenhagen	256 Infantry Division	Killed
GdA	Martinek	XXXIX Panzer Corps	Killed
GL	von Kurowski	110 Infantry Division	Prisoner
GL	Schünemann	XXXIX Panzer Corps	Killed
GL	Bamler	12 Infantry Division	Prisoner
GL	Ochsner	31 Infantry Division	Prisoner
GL	Müller	XII Army Corps	Prisoner
GL	Zutavern	18 Panzer Grenadier Division	Suicide
GL	Drescher	267 Infantry Division	Killed
GM	Trowitz	57 Infantry Division	Prisoner
GdI	Völkers	XXVII Army Corps	Prisoner
GL	Traut	78 Assault Division	Prisoner
GM	Klammt	260 Infantry Division	Prisoner
GL	von Lützow	XXXV Army Corps	Prisoner
GL	Philipp	134 Infantry Division	Suicide
GM	Heyne	6 Infantry Division	Prisoner
GM	Engel	45 Infantry Division	Prisoner
GL	Hofmeister	XXXXI Panzer Corps	Prisoner
GM	Conrady	36 Infantry Division	Prisoner
GM	Michaelis	95 Infantry Division	Prisoner
GM	Gihr	707 Infantry Division	Prisoner
GM	von Steinkeller	*"Feldherrnhalle"* Division	Prisoner

Losses slackened somewhat after the lethal days of summer. GM Werner Dürking, commander of the 96th Infantry Division, fell victim to a Soviet anti-tank round on September 11, 1944 near Sanok, Poland.[69] GdI Hellmuth Priess of the XXVII Corps fell near Hasenrode, East Prussia on October 21, 1944.[70] GM Walter Herold, commander of the 10th Motorized Division, was ambushed by partisans and killed near Bochnia, Poland on November 28, 1944. He was replaced by a colonel. But the apparent slow pace of the Soviet advance was deceiving; Soviet units opposite Warsaw were building strength for an early offensive in January 1945, while Soviet pressure shifted to clearing the Balkans.

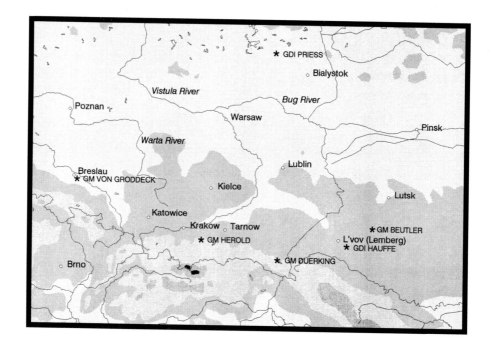

WESTERN FRONT - 1944

German general officers felt the effects of the Allied invasion at Normandy almost immediately. On D-Day, soldiers of the American 82nd Airborne Division ambushed and killed GL Wilhelm Falley, commander of the 91st Air Landing Division, as he raced to his headquarters.[71] Thus, during the first few critical hours of the invasion, the 91st, which held a key sector of the defenses, was deprived of its commander. He was followed by *Oberst* Bernhard Klosterkemper. GdA Erich Marcks, commander LXXIV Corps, was killed enroute to Carentan on June 12 when a strafing fighter struck his automobile.[72] *SS-Brigadeführer* Fritz Witt, commander of the 12th SS Panzer Division *"Hitlerjugend"*, was killed June 14, 1944 in Normandy by Allied naval gunfire.[73] On June 17, GL Heinz Hellmich, commander 243rd Infantry Division, was killed by a strafing fighter near Cherbourg.[74]

The remnants of his division also fell under the command of *Oberst* Bernhard Klosterkemper. One day later, GM Rudolf Stegmann, commander of the 77th Infantry Division, was struck in the head by 20 mm cannon fire from a strafing Allied fighter plane near Briebeque France and died. *Oberst* Rudolf Bacherer took command, but the division was destroyed near St. Malo in August. GL Viktor von Drabich-Wächter, 326th Infantry Division, and GL Dietrich Kraiss, 352nd Infantry Division both fell on August 2, 1944 near St. Lo as the Allies started their breakout from Normandy in Operation Cobra. Von Drabich-Wächter was replaced by an *Oberst* Kertsch, the 352nd, however, was destroyed along with Kraiss.

GL Edgar Arndt of the 708th Infantry Division died near Troyes later in the

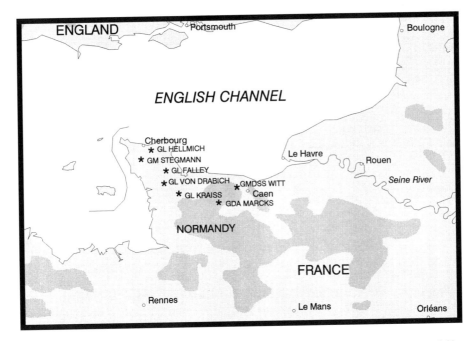

month as Patton's 3rd Army raced east overrunning many less mobile German units. In southern France, GL Johannes Bässler of the 242nd Infantry Division, a part of the German 19th Army at Toulon, France was seriously wounded August 26 (He died at Vienna, Austria on November 8.) The 242nd was destroyed in late August and was never reformed.

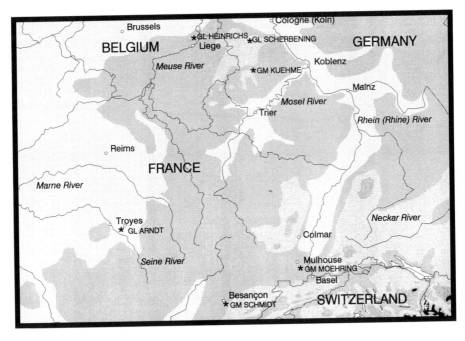

Two more German generals were killed on the Western Front in September. GM Axel Schmidt of the 159th Infantry Division was killed at Besancon, France on September 8. The same day GL Conrad-Oskar Heinrichs of the 89th Infantry Division fell in combat near Liege, Belgium. He was followed in command by an *Oberst* Rösler. GM Oschmann of the 338th Infantry Division died in action near Fraunbe, France November 14, 1944 (and was replaced by *Oberst* Rudolf von Oppen); and three more generals fell in December. GM Kurt Möhring, 276th Infantry Division, and GL Gerd Scherbening, 406th Infantry Division, died on December 18, at Belfort, France and Urft, Germany respectively. Finally, GM Kurt Kühme, the commander of a security division fell near Hallschlag in the Eifel on Christmas Day. Moehring was followed in command by Oberst Hugo Dempwolff.

BALKANS - 1944

The cancer of Yugoslavia turned worse for the German Army in 1944; by mid-year a full twenty-five German divisions were stationed in the Balkans. All attempts to eliminate Josef Tito had failed, and the communists had solidified resistance factions against the Nazis. To make matters worse for the Germans, the Soviet Army reached the frontiers of many Balkan nations during the year.

SS-Gruppenführer Artur Phleps, commander of the V SS Volunteer Mountain Corps, was probably killed by small arms fire near Arad, Rumania on September 21, as the 53rd Army of the *2nd Ukrainian Front* completed seizure of the country.[75] This drive by the Soviets foreshadowed a catastrophe in the making for many German units in the Balkans. By October 5, the 3rd

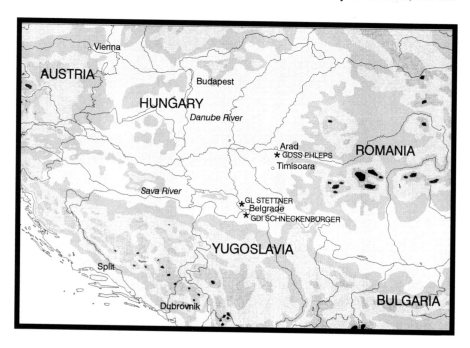

Ukrainian Front was standing on the north bank of the Danube River outside Belgrade, Yugoslavia. To the west and south of the city Tito's Yugoslav National Liberation Army, already a formidable fighting force, were gaining even more strength. And caught in the middle in Belgrade was the German 1st Mountain Division and other units from Army Group E. On October 14 the Red Army broke through the southern defenses of the city. GdI Willi Schneckenburger, the commander of Army Corps Belgrade was killed near the Avala Hill leading a counterattack of the 750th Jäger Regiment and the 1st Brandenberger Regiment. Twenty-nine enemy tanks were destroyed and many buildings were set afire, but the general's attack was unsuccessful.[76]

On October 18, GFM von Weichs finally ordered a general breakout from the besieged city. More than 5,000 soldiers from the 1st Mountain Division alone were killed or taken prisoner, as the defense became little more than individual pockets of resistance. During the day, the commander of the division, GL Walter von Stettner von Grabenhofen was seriously wounded. It is possible that further enemy fire killed the general – although a soldier in Soviet captivity after the war, who claimed he had been the general's driver, stated that von Stettner took his own life.[77] The "soft underbelly of Europe", as Winston Churchill referred to the region, was proving to be a cancerous drain on overall German manpower as well as German general officers. And the cancer caused by resistance movements was spreading west to Italy.

ITALY - 1944

One German general was killed in Italy in 1944. In northern Italy near Bologna, GM Wilhelm Crisolli, commander 20th Luftwaffe Field Division, was killed by partisans in the vicinity of the XIV Panzer Corps headquarters, September 12, 1944.[78] The following year more generals would meet their fate at the hands of the resistance movement.

1945

By the final year of the war Allied forces stood poised on the borders of the *Reich* ready to deliver the death blow to Hitler's empire. As previously mentioned, the German casualty reporting system lost all accuracy the previous November; and casualty figures for 1945 are at best an estimate. Given these limitations it is generally accepted that roughly 250,000 German troops perished during the year and 1,000,000 were missing in action. Fifty-nine senior commanders died in action as well during the cataclysmic year. Suicides increased among these senior commanders as even the most hard-core believers in "Final Victory" were forced to face the reality of impending defeat.

The German Ardennes Offensive was smashed by the Western Allies, who had amassed sufficient supplies to return to their own offensive, vault the Rhine and drive deep into Germany. The Soviets too caught their second wind and advanced along a broad front to finally take Berlin and bring about the German surrender.

Nor did the official end of hostilities in Europe on May 8, 1945 mean safety for the leaders of the German Army. Several were murdered by their captors shortly after the surrender while others were tried for war crimes and later executed.

EASTERN FRONT - 1945

Five senior commanders were killed on the Eastern Front during January as the Soviet Army resumed its offensive to liberate Eastern Europe and storm Germany itself. On January 12, 1945 nine armies of the *1st Ukrainian Front*, under Marshal Koniev, in the Sandomierz Bridgehead on the western side of the Vistula River roared west, pulverizing the defending German 4th Panzer Army. By January 16, Soviet armored and mechanized forces had reached objectives which had originally been set for much later in the advance. Operations transitioned from breakthrough to pursuit. The rates of advance were the highest achieved by the Red Army in the war so far – rifle units moved up to 30 kilometers per day, while tank and mechanized forces achieved between 45 and 70.

GM Harald von Hirschfeld of the 78th Volks-Grenadier Division was mortally wounded by a bomb fragment January 18, 1945 at the Dunajec Bridge near Tarnow, Poland.[79] GL Siegfried Rein died the same day near Schlossberg, East Prussia while in command of the 69th Infantry Division. An *Oberst* Grimme replaced Rein – by this stage in the war inexperienced under-ranking replacements didn't matter anymore as the German Army was on the run on every front. Two corps commanders were next to meet their fates. The Soviet 5th Guards Army and 3rd Guards Tank Army broke through German defenses and pushed west. This deep penetration overran the headquarters of the XXXXII Army Corps, killing or capturing the bulk of the corps staff. GdI Hermann Recknagel, the corps commander, avoided capture by regular Soviet Army forces, but fell into the hands of Polish partisans in the area and was killed on January 23 near Petrikau, Poland. GdI Johannes Block of the LVI Panzer Corps fell on January 26 near Lask, Poland.[80]

On January 27, 1945, a deep Soviet tank raid killed GM Arthur Finger, 291st Infantry Division, near Czestochowa, Poland. The general, leading a small battlegroup, was attempting to break out of a huge Soviet encirclement that developed as his division was overwhelmed by the Soviet Vistula Offensive; the entire division was destroyed.[81] In February, GM Kirschner, commanding the 320th Infantry Division fell in action near Saybusch, Poland on the 11th. GM Georg Kossmala of the 344th Infantry Division was killed on March 5 near Oberglogau, Silesia. *SS-Brigadeführer* Franz Augsberger, commander of the 20th Waffen SS Grenadier Division (Estonian), fell near Grottkau, Silesia on March 17, 1945, possibly a suicide.[82]

In late December 1944 elements of the Soviet *2nd* and *3rd Ukrainian Fronts* surrounded the Hungarian capital of Budapest, trapping 188,000 German and Hungarian troops. After two months of heavy fighting, the city could not be held and on February 11, the city commander *SS-Obergruppenführer* Karl von Pfeffer-Wildenbruch ordered units to conduct breakout operations. Sixteen thousand German and many Hungarian defenders attempted to force their way west from Buda – the portion of the city west of the Danube River – along the Italian Boulevard and a parallel subterranean drainage canal from the Castle Hill and Citadel which were their last strongholds. The wounded had to be left behind. Many troops were killed at the castle gates – few ever managed to reach the suburbs. GM Gerhard Schmidhuber, commander of the 13th Panzer was killed almost immediately in the attempt.

That same day, *SS-Brigadeführer* Joachim Rumohr, commander of the 8th SS Cavalry Division *"Florian Geyer"*, and *SS-Brigadeführer* August Zehender, the commander of the 22nd SS Cavalry Division *"Maria Theresa"*, also attempted to breakout of the besieged city, and probably committed suicide shortly before Soviet troops overran their headquarters.[84]

Both men had been invested with the Knight's Cross with Oak Leaves at the beginning of the month, perhaps in part due to the hopeless nature of the mission. The city finally fell on February 13; of the original garrison less than 700 reached German lines. Later in Hungary, GdSS Werner Ostendorff, commander of the 2nd SS Division *"Das Reich"*, was seriously wounded near Lake Balaton on March 8, 1945. He died of his wounds in Austria May 4, 1945. GL Hans-Günther von Rost of the 44th Infantry Division was killed by anti-tank fire was on March 22, 1945 near Stuhlweißenburg.[85] His replacement was an *Oberst* Hoffmann.

In the first week of March, Marshal Rokossovskii's *2nd Belorussian Front* drove through East Pommerania to the Baltic, thus isolating Danzig from the rest of the *Reich*. In the action, GL Karl Rübel, 163rd Infantry Division was mortally wounded at Schievelbein, Pommerania on March 8, while his division was being destroyed. The Soviets then turned the 49th, 65th and 70th Armies east to take the coastal ports. Danzig and its neighboring city Gotenhafen were jammed with 1.5 million German civilian refugees, 100,000 wounded soldiers and the remnants of the 2nd German Army.

On March 15 the Soviets began a major assault; by the 22nd, the 2nd Shock Army had penetrated the German defenses and seized the city of Zoppat, effectively cutting the German defenses into two isolated pockets. By March 27 resistance was further diminished by the news that GL Clemens Betzel, commander of the 4th Panzer Division and remnants of the 539th Infantry Division, had been killed by Soviet artillery fire that day. Danzig fell shortly thereafter but German forces continued to hold the Hela peninsula north of Gotenhafen, and the Danziger Werder – the flooded marshlands of the Vistula River delta east of Danzig until the end of the war.

The northern sector of the front proved a tougher nut for the Soviets to crack. On April 6 the 3rd Belorussian Front, under Marshal Vasilevski, with the 11th Guards Army from the south and the 50th and 43rd Armies from the north began the final assault on the German city of Königsberg, which had been encircled by the Red Army since February. At Königsberg, as at other late-war urban battles on the Eastern Front, Soviet regiments attacked with "assault squads" consisting of a rifle battalion, a company of engineers, a section of 76mm guns, a battery of 120mm mortars, a section of flame-

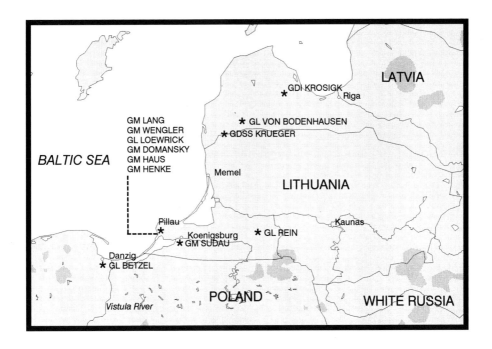

throwers, a tank company and several self-propelled assault guns. On the 9th, GM Erich Sudau, the commander of the 548th Volks-Grenadier Division, attempted to lead a breakout of soldiers, Nazi Party officials and civilians from the city. Leading the ragged column from an armored car, GM Sudau was mortally wounded by artillery fire near the Luisen Church close to the city center.[86]

The East Prussian port city of Pillau lay some 30 miles west of Königsberg on the tip of the Samland Peninsula. It lay on a spit of land with the Frisches Haff Bay to the south and east, and the Baltic Sea to the north and west. To the southwest across a narrow inlet was the small city of Neutief, on the Nehrung – a sandsplit paralleling the coast, and leading west to Danzig. Three days after the fall of Königsberg, where the Red Army reported 42,000 Germans killed and 92,000 taken prisoner, Marshal Vasilevskii turned the *3rd Belorussian Front* against the German forces on the Samland Peninsula. The Russians broke through two divisions, and flooded the area with tanks.

Two commanders died in the defense near Pillau on April 16; GM Georg Haus of the 50th Infantry Division, and GM Joachim-Friedrich Lang, of the 95th Infantry Division. Pockets of resistance fought on; German units made a stand at a defensive line near the village of Tenkitten, only 8 miles from the city center. One more general would also die at Pillau. GM Maximilian Wengler and his 83rd Infantry Division made a last ditch stand at the citadel and he was killed by a Soviet air attack along with members of his staff on April 25.[87] The last German positions in the city were wiped out on April 27.

German forces in the Courland region of Latvia suffered general officer casualties as well. Thirty divisions and over two hundred thousand German soldiers, were cut off by the advancing *1st* and *2nd Baltic Fronts* on October 13, 1944. GdI Ernst von Krosigk, commander of the 16th Army, was the next casualty – killed at his headquarters at Zabeln by a Soviet fighter bomber attack March 16, 1945.[88] Despite five successive major offensives against the enclave, Army Group Courland held out until the end of the war, and became one of the last major German groupings of forces to lay down their arms.

GL Erpo von Bodenhausen, commander of the L Corps committed suicide immediately following the surrender of German forces in Courland on May 9. GdSS Walter Krüger, commander of the VI SS Corps committed suicide on May 20, 1945 as his command group attempted to evade capture as they made their way from Courland to East Prussia where they hoped go into hiding. Twenty-six thousand troops were successfully evacuated by sea to safety, but 42 generals and 189,000 troops fell into long years of Soviet captivity.

In the center of the front the Soviets pressed toward Berlin. By April 15, the *1st Belorussian Front* was poised along the Oder River some 40 miles east of the German capital. The *Front*, under Marshal Georgi Zhukov, fielded 768,000 soldiers and over 3100 tanks and self-propelled assault guns. Opposing this juggernaut were elements of the German 9th Army with less than 500 fully operational armored vehicles.

The 20th Panzer Grenadier Division initially was defending near Seelow, but after heavy losses was withdrawn to Berlin and given the mission of defending the crossing sights over the Teltow Canal in the Grunwald-Wannsee area of southwest Berlin. These crossing sights would serve to facilitate the German 12th Army's desperate advance to relieve the city. It was a hopeless situation.

On the 28th of April the *1st Ukrainian Front's* 9th Guards Tank Corps assaulted elements of the division defending Potsdam. Later in the day the Soviet 10th Tank Corps launched an attack across the canal to Wannsee, quickly established a small bridgehead and began connecting pontoon bridges across the Teltow. The 20th Panzer Grenadier again resisted with fierce determination. GM Georg Scholze, commander of the 20th Panzer Grenadier Division, and whose wife and children had been recently killed in an air raid on Potsdam, committed suicide sometime during the day.

Southeast of Berlin the bulk of the 9th Army had been bypassed by the *1st Belorussian Front* to the north and the *1st Ukrainian Front* to the south and, surrounded in the heavily forested lake district of the Spreewald, had to break out of the encirclement to the west or risk total destruction. On the 28th of April GdI Theodor Busse, the commander of the 9th Army, met with his subordinate commanders at the small village of Hammer to discuss the breakout plan.

The XI SS Corps would face west and begin the breakout, attempting to split the junction of the 3rd Guards and 28th Armies. Once the pocket began moving, the corps would cover the northern flank of the breakthrough. The V Corps would cover the southern flank of the breakout and take over the spearhead of the breakout when needed. The V SS Mountain Corps would

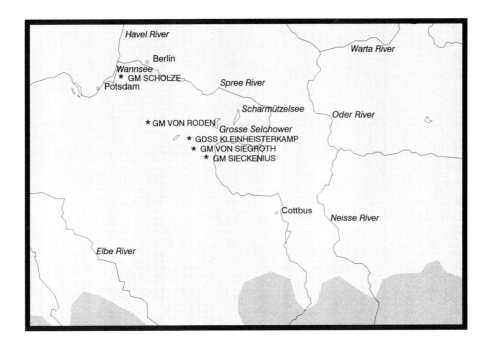

cover the breakout from the east and cover the rear of the pocket. The break-out started at dusk and almost immediately GM Sieckenius, commander of the 391st Security Division of the XI SS Corps, sensed the hopelessness of the situation and committed suicide near Märkish-Buchholz.

GdSS Matthias Kleinheisterkamp, XI SS Corps, is reported to have gone forward in his armored staff car with three officers that night when he was ambushed by Soviet forces near Halbe. Only one *Hauptsturmführer* (captain) survived the encounter; he was unsure if the general had been killed outright or had committed suicide. Some of the 9th Army managed to break west but the V SS Mountain Corps became trapped in the cauldron. The hard-pressed German effort continued into May with some 9th Army elements finally reaching the 12th Army to the west. But most of the 9th Army never made it. Of Busse's original 200,000 only 40,000 reached the 12th Army.

Although Hitler committed suicide and the *Reich* surrendered in early May general officer casualties did not stop for the 9th Army. GM Joachim von Siegroth of the 712th Infantry Division of the XI SS Corps fell on May 2 near Halbe by Berlin. The next day GM Emmo von Roden died near Berlin while in command of the 286th Security Division.

Some generals died of their wounds after the war was over. For example, on March 26, 1945, GM Gustav von Nostitz-Wallwitz, 24th Panzer Division, was seriously wounded in the abdomen by artillery shrapnel while directing a withdrawal; he later died May 31, 1945 at Eckernförde, Germany.[89] GL Henning von Thadden, 1st Infantry Division, was mortally wounded south-west of Königsberg on April 26, was evacuated by sea to Vordingborg Denmark, and died shortly thereafter of his wounds.

CZECHOSLOVAKIA - 1945

The conventional front-lines reached Czechoslovakia in April. On April 17, 1945, GL Gustav Hundt was killed while leading his 1st Ski Division near Troppau, Czechoslovakia. He had only recently been awarded the Knight's Cross for leading his division during these last defensive struggles. On April 18, 1945, GL Hans Källner, the commander of the XXIV Panzer Corps, was killed in action during a large tank battle at Sokolniza, near Olmütz, Bohemia.[90]

GM Robert Bader, commander of the 97th Jäger Division was posted missing in action and later killed in action near Prosnitz, Czechoslovakia on May 9, 1945. Also in Czechoslovakia, GL Richard Baltzer of the 182nd Infantry Division was probably killed by Czech partisans at Prague on May 10, 1945; while GM Oskar Krämer, the commander of the 11th Flak Division, died of unknown circumstances near Rattaj, Czechoslovakia the next day.

Our knowledge about German general officer casualties at the end of the war in Czechoslovakia is sketchy even to this day as Czech retribution against their former conquerors was swift, brutal and not well-documented. For six and one-half long years German occupation had grown harsher with each passing day. *SS-Obergruppenführer* Reinhard Heydrich assumed the role of Protector, literally its governor-general. Heydrich ruled with an iron fist until Czech resistance fighters, supplied by the British, ambushed him in a Prague suburb in 1942. Mortally wounded, Heydrich died several days later – and German revenge resulted in the massacre at Lidice. Heydrich was followed by the equally oppressive *SS-Obergruppenführer* Karl Frank, who ruled until the end of the war.

On April 18 Patton's Third Army advanced into western Bohemia, while the *2nd Ukrainian Front* captured Brun by the 26th. On May 1, German radio announced that Hitler had died in Berlin, but much of central Czechoslovakia remained in control of Army Group Center under GFM Ferdinand Schörner. By this time even a fanatic like Karl Frank could visualize ultimate defeat, and he began planning for a forced march from Prague west to American lines. Not all German officials or civilians joined in the exodus. On May 5 the Czech people in Prague started to rise against the Germans. That night the Waffen-SS Grenadier Regiment *"Der Führer"* was ordered to advance into the city, link up with the Army commandant of the city, open and hold the road west from Prague. It did and by the 9th had evacuated many Germans west to Pilsen. On May 10, 1945 the Soviet Army captured Prague, officially ending German rule. In keeping with many other Waffen-SS officers, SFdSS Heinrich Petersen, commander 18th SS Division *"Horst Wessel"* committed suicide on May 9, near Pilsen while GMdSS Fritz Freitag, 14th SS Division did the same near the village of Andra in Austria on May 10.

During the first two weeks of May, GL Paul Kern the 1st Panzer Army surgeon, GM Georg von Majewski a rear area commander, GL Peter Hermann the commander of the *Volkssturm* in Bohemia/Moravia, and *SS-Gruppenführer* Karl von Pückler-Burghauss, the commander of the Waffen-

SS in Bohemia/Moravia, also died under uncertain circumstances.

Undoubtedly some of these generals may well have been murdered at the hands of vengeful Czechs. But nowhere was retribution more widespread than in Yugoslavia.

YUGOSLAVIA - 1945

GL Johann Mickl, 392nd Infantry Division (Croatian), was severely wounded by small arms fire near Vratnik Pass, Yugoslavia on April 10, was shot again by partisans enroute to medical care and died at a reserve hospital at Fiume, while GdI Werner von Erdmannsdorff of the LXXXXI Corps was probably killed by Yugoslav partisans near Laibach (Ljubljana) Yugoslavia on May 5, 1945. Rear Admiral Georg Waü, Commandant of the Fortress of Pola, was shot May 8, 1945 upon his capture. GdPz Gustav Fehn fell to partisans on June 5, 1945 somewhere in Yugoslavia. For several moths after cessation of hostilities the victorious Yugoslav forces under Marshal Tito conducted a forced march of some 2,000 kilometers throughout the country of captured German soldiers as a display of the final total victory of partisan forces. Casualties were staggering – some sixty percent of the Germans involved are believed to have died during the ordeal.

Yugoslav justice continued after formal hostilities ended with predictable verdicts and sentences: GO Alexander Löhr, commander of German forces Southeast – hanged February 26, 1947, GdF Heinrich Danckelmann, Governor-general of Serbia in 1941 – hanged October 30, 1947, GdF Martin Fiebig, commander of Luftwaffe forces Southeast in 1943-44 – hanged October 24, 1947, *SS-Gruppenführer* Josef Grassy, commander of the 25th Waffen-SS Division *"Hunyadi"* – hanged November 5, 1946, *SS-Brigadeführer* Karl von Oberkamp, Inspector of Waffen-SS Mountain Troops – hanged 1947, GM Adolf Fischer, commander of a battle group – hanged October 1947, GL Johann Fortner, commander of the 718th Infantry Division – hanged 1947, GM Hans Gravenstein, commander of the 373rd Infantry Division – hanged 1947, GL Hans von Hösslin, commander of the 188th Reserve Mountain Division – hanged 1947, GdGeb Ludwig Kübler, Governor General of the Adriatic Coast – hanged August 18, 1947, GL Josef Kübler, commander of the 118th Jäger Division – shot February 1947, GM Adalbert Lontschar, Commandant of Belgrade – hanged 1947, GdI Hartwig von Ludwiger, commander of the XXI Mountain Corps – hanged May 5, 1947, GL Fritz von Neidholdt, commander of the 369th (Croatian) Infantry Division – shot 1947, *SS-Obergruppenführer* Erwin Rösener, commander of SS District Alpenvorland – hanged 1946, *SS-Brigadeführer* August Schmidhuber, commander of the 21st Waffen-SS Mountain Division *"Skanderbeg"* – hanged 1947, GM Hubert Strohmaier, commander of the 373rd Artillery Regiment – hanged 1947, *SS-Brigadeführer* Jürgen Wagner, commander of the 4th Waffen-SS Panzer Grenadier Brigade *"Nederland"* – hanged April 5, 1947, GLdSS Behrens, SS commander in Serbia – hanged 1947 and GL Eugen Wurster – hanged 1948. In total more than 1,000 German soldiers were sentenced to death in Yugoslavia after the war.

WESTERN FRONT – 1945

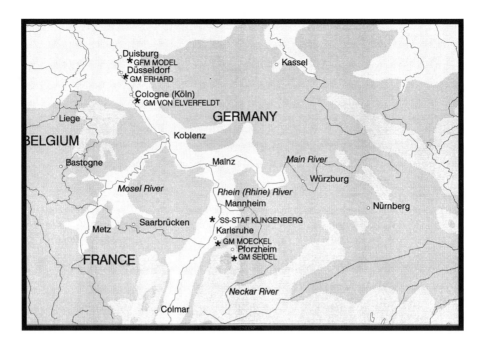

No commanders died on the Western Front during the first two months of the year, but this hiatus was broken soon thereafter. On March 3, 1945 near Aalsmeer, Netherlands, GL Kurt Schmidt of the 526th Infantry Division fell in combat.

Further south, by the beginning of March, the lead elements of the 1st US Army reached Cologne and penetrated to the center of the city. The 9th Panzer Division lost its commander, GL Harald von Elverfeldt, in street fighting in Cologne March 6, 1945, as the division was backed into a narrow corridor along the Rhine River.[92] Elements of the division were able to escape under the command of a colonel to the east bank of the river, but for all practical purposes the division was finished as a fighting force.

SS-Brigadeführer Klingenberg of the 17th SS *"Götz von Berlichingen"* Panzer Grenadier Division was killed in action near Herxheim on the Rhine River on March 22, during an American tank attack. He was replaced by an *Obersturmbannführer* (lieutenant colonel).[93] Just two days later, GM Alexander Möckel of the 16th Volks-Grenadier Division died near Karlsruhe not far from Herxheim.

GM Erich Seidel was the next to die, when he fell in action on April 11 while leading the 257th Infantry Division near Dobel-Wildbach, Germany. GM Alfred Erhard, the commander of the Luftwaffe's 7th Flak Division, committed suicide at Düsseldorf during the final stages of the Ruhr encirclement on April 17, 1945; GFM Walter Model followed suit four days later near Duisburg. GdPz Karl Decker apparently committed suicide on April 21, near Fallersleben while leading the remnants of the XXXIX Panzer Corps.

On April 24, 1945 near Gut Neverstaven in Holstein GL Ernst Baade, the outgoing commander of the LXXXI Army Corps, was mortally wounded by a strafing British aircraft; he died two weeks later.[94]

ITALY - 1945

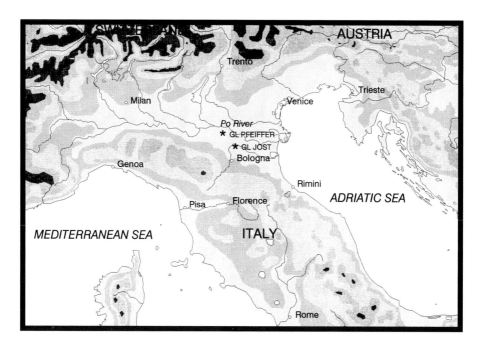

In Italy, three German generals fell in combat during the year. A lone Allied fighter bomber strafed GL Hellmuth Pfeifer, the commander of the 65th Infantry Division, as he was crossing a bridge over the Panaro River on April 22, 1945.[95] GL Walter Jost, commander of the 42nd Jäger Division, was killed this day also at Villadosa.

The final death in Italy occurred May 2, when GM Martin Strahammer of the 114th Jäger Division was killed in action in northern Italy as the division, along with the LI Mountain Corps was destroyed.[96] On May 5, GL Friedrich Stephan, 104th Jäger Division died in the Carinthia district of Austria.

OVERALL GENERAL OFFICER LOSSES

Theater Casualties

Theater	Dead	Missing	Generals KIA
Poland 1939	16,343	320	0
Norway 1940	4,975	691	0
France 1940	27,074	968	1
France 1941 - June 6, 1944	39,192	3,218	1
Western Front:			
June 6, 1944 - May 7, 1945	80,819	480,624	17
Africa 1941 - 1943	12,808	90,052	7
Balkans 1941 - 1944	24,267	12,060	6
Italy:			
May 1943 - Nov. 30, 1944	47,873	97,154	1
Eastern Front:			
June 21, 1941 - Jan. 1945	1,419,728	1,018,365	82
Eastern Front 1945:			
February - May	@ 150,000	@ 750,000	26
Balkans 1945	@ 40,000	@ 200,000	3
Italy 1945	@ 30,000	@ 50,000	4

The overall losses by theater for both general officers and overall casualties are shown above. It can be seen that some ten percent of German general officer casualties were inflicted in Africa and twelve percent in Italy and France at the hands of the Western Allies, for a total of twenty-two percent. Almost seventy-five percent of general officer losses fell as a result of actions by the Soviet Army. Lethality for German generals was present on every front and quality senior commanders fell on every theater. However, the leadership of the German Army can truly be shown to have received mortal wounds on the Eastern Front. The meat grinder in the vast steppes of Russia devoured not only the body of the German Army but it's head as well.

CHAPTER NOTES

[1] R. Ernest Dupuy and Trevor N. Dupuy, *The Encyclopedia of Military History*, New York: Harper & Row, 1986, p. 1051.

[2] Graf Kielmansegg, *Der Fritschprozess 1938*, Hamburg, FRG: Hoffmann and Campe Verlag, 1949, pp. 144-145.

[3] Burkhart Müller-Hillebrand, *Das Heer, 1933-1945, Band II - Die Blitzfeldzuge 1939-1941*, Frankfurt, FRG: E.S. Mittler & Sohn, 1956, p. 102.

[4] Frans S.A. Beekman and Franz Kurowski, *Der Kampf un die Festung Holland*, Herford, FRG: E.S. Mittler & Sohn, 1981, pp. 206-207.

[5] Boehm, *25. Division*, pp. 72-73.

[6] Telford Taylor, *The March of Conquest: The German Victories in Western Europe - 1940*, New York: Simon & Schuster, 1958, p. 313.

[7] Müller-Hillebrand, *Das Heer, Band III*, p. 266.

[8] Kiriakopoulos, *Ten Days*, pp. 128-131.

[9] Heckmann, *Rommel's War*, pp. 72-73.

[10] Ronald Lewin, *The Life and Death of the Afrika Korps*, New York: Quadrangle, 1977, p. 48.

[11] Bender, *Afrikakorps*, p. 62.

[12] *Ibid.*, p. 74.

[13] Husemann, *Die Guten, Band I*, pp. 53-54. The Soviet Army lost several generals as well during the summer of 1941. Major General Sushchii, 124th Rifle Division, Major General Shurba, 14th Rifle Division, Major General Pavlov, 23rd Motorized Division, Lieutenant General Kachalov, 28th Army, Major General Karpezo, 15th Rifle Corps, Major General Versin, 173rd Rifle Division and Major General Karmanov, 62nd Army Corps were all killed between June and August 1941.

[14] Kurst Mehner, *Die Geheimtagesberichte der Seutschenwehrmachtführung im Zweiten Weltkrieg 1939-1945, Band 3*, Osnabrück, Germany: Biblio Verlag, 1992, p. 199 (21. Juli 1941).

[15] Meyer-Detring, *Die 137.*, pp. 105-106.

[16] Brett-Smith, *Generals*, p. 30.

[17] Microfilm, LII Armeekorps, Frame 510.

[18] Müler-Hillebrand, *Das Heer, Band III*, p. 266.

[19] Bender, *Afrikakorps*, p. 67.

[20] Carell, Foxes, p. 289.

[21] "Der Landser" Magazine, Nummer 586, p. 66.

[22] Law, *Rommel*, p. 170.

[23] Tagebuch Russland (46 I.D.), p. 37.

[24] Rebentisch, *Zum Kaukasus*, p. 87.

[25] Graser, *Kattegat*, pp. 184-185.

[26] Kriegstagebuch Ia, 22.3.42, 294. Infanterie Division

[27] *329. Infanterie Division*, p. 23.

[28] Microfilm, 61. Infanterie Division, Frame 123.

[29] Thomas, *Ritterkreuzträger, Teil III: Infanterie, Band I: A-Be*, p. 440.

[30] Microfilm, 129. Infanterie Division, Frame 169.

[31] Matthew Cooper, *The German Army 1933-1945*, New York: Stein and Day, 1978, p. 456.

[32] Müller-Hillebrand, *Das Heer, Band III*, p. 266.

[33] Bender, *Panzertruppe*, p. 92.

[34] Bender, *Afrikakorps*, p. 84.

[35] Müller-Hillebrand, *Das Heer, Band III*, p. 265.

[36] Lewin, *Afrika Korps*, p. 48.

[37] Bradley, *Tätigkeitsbericht*, p. 42.

[38] Paul Carell, *Hitler Moves East*, Boston: Little, Brown and Company, 1964, p. 619.

[39] Wolfgang Werthen, *Geschichte der 16. Panzer Division, 1939-1945*, Friedberg, FRG: Podzun-Pallas-Verlag, 1958, p. 137.

[40] Sydnor, *Soldiers*, p. 271.

[41] Microfilm, 39 Infanterie Division, Frame 623.

[42] Carell, *Scorched Earth*, p. 87.

[43] Von Knobelsdorff, *19. Panzer-Division*, pp. 219-220. Captured German officers gave their interrogators some photographs and personal documents belonging to General Schmidt.

[44] *Kriegstagebuch Ia, 161. Infanterie Division*, 15.8.43.

[45] Microfilm, XXXXVI Panzerkorps, Frame 533.

[46] Meyer-Detring, *Die 137.* pp. 186-188.

[47] Carell, *Scorched Earth*, p. 365.

[48] *Tagebuch Rußland* (46 I.D.) p. 59.

[49] Ott, *Jäger*, p. 294.

[50] Microfilm, 50 Infanterie Division, Frame 782.

[51] Kaltenegger, *Gebirgssoldaten*, p. 258.

[52] Microfilm, 147. Reserve Division, Frame 27.

[53] Grams, *Die 14. Panzer-Division*, pp. 130-131.

[54] Schwarz served previously in the office of the Military Governor of the General Government (formerly the eastern half of Poland), an instructor in the Artillery School and in the *Führer Reserve*.

[55] Müller-Hillebrand, *Das Heer, Band III*, p. 266.

[56] Von Manteuffel, *Die 7. Panzer-Division*, pp. 390-391.

[57] The Germans referred to the ensuing fight as the "Cherkassy Pocket", or more specifically "the pocket near Cherkassy". The Soviet histories refer to the operation as the "Battle of Korsun'Shevchenkovskiy".

[58] Buchner, *Ostfront 1944*, pp. 41 and 50.

[59] Carell, *Scorched Earth*, p. 476.

[60] Buchner, *Ostfront 1944*, pp. 262 and 283.

[61] *Alte Kameraden*, Oktober 1960, p. 23.

[62] Werner Haupt, *Heeresgruppe Nord, 1941-1945*, Bad Nauheim, FRG: Podzun Verlag, 1966, p. 227.

[63] Microfilm, L Armeekorps, Frame 707.

[64] Müler, *207. und 281. Infanterie Division*, pp. 213-214.

[65] Selz, *Grüne Regiment*, p. 206.

[66] Werner Haupt, *Geschichte der 134. Infanterie Division*, Bad Kreuznach, FRG: Kameradenkreis der 134. Infanterie Division, 1971, pp. 225-227.

[67] "Die Gebirgstruppe", p. 39.

[68] Niepold, *White Russia*, p. 142.

[69] Pohlmann, *96. Infanterie-Division*, p. 335.

[70] August Schmidt, *Geschichte der 10. Division*, Bad Nauheim, FRG: Podzun-Pallas-Verlag, 1963, p. 256.

[71] Ryan, *The Longest Day*, pp. 269-270.

[72] Hastings, *Overlord*, pp. 173-174.

[73] Luther, *Blood and Honor*, p. 205.

[74] Breuer, *Hitler's Fortress*, p. 164.

[75] Schneider, *Their Honor*, p. 281.

[76] Karl Hnilicka, *Das Ende auf dem Balkan 1944/45*, Göttingen, FRG: Musterschmidt Verlag, 1970, p. 75.

[77] Kaltenegger, *Gebirgstruppe*, pp. 446-447 and 534.

[78] Werner Haupt, *Italien Kriegßchauplatz 1943-1945*, Stuttgart, FRG: Motorbuch Verlag, 1977, p. 200.

[79] Kaltenegger, *Gebirgstruppe*, p. 431.

[80] Erickson, *The Road*, p. 457.

[81] Conze, *291. Infanterie-Division*, p. 79.

[82] Krätschmer, *Ritterkreuzträger*, p. 886.

[83] *Schicksalsweg der 13. Panzer-Division*, p. 211. Von Pferrer-Wildenbruch himself took to the sewers to avoid capture. After a harrowing journey he emerged in the middle of a Soviet unit however.

[84] Schneider, *Their Honor*, p. 320.

[85] Dettmer, *Die 44. Infanterie Division*, pp. 343-344.

[86] Lasch, *So Fiel*, pp. 100-101.

[87] Reinhard Tiemann, *Geschichte der 83. Infanteri-Division, 1939-1945*, Friedberg, FRG: Podzun-Pallas-Verlag, 1986, pp. 330-331.

[88] Haupt, *Kurland*, p. 170.

[89] Von Senger, *Die 24. Panzer Division*, pp. 287-298.

[90] Von Knobelsdorff, *19. Panzer-Division*, p. 284.

[91] Schneider, *Their Honor*, p. 271.

[92] Raabe, Letter to author.

[93] The daily log for the division states Klingenberg died during an American tank attack, but provides no details. His body was never recovered to this day.

[94] Thomas, *Ritterkreuzträger, Teil III: Infanterie, Band I: A-Be*, p. 139.

[95] Velten, *Kugelbaum*, p. 194.

[96] Samuel W. Mitcham, Jr., *Hitler's Legions - The German Army Order of Battle, World War II*, New York: Stein & Day, 1985, p. 328.

✠ CHAPTER 11 ✠
EVACUATIONS

But since the value of men is not immaterial, and since we need men the entire war, I am definitely of the opinion that it was right to bring Hube out.

(Adolf Hitler, 1943) [1]

Not all of Hitler's orders were the stand-fast variety. At times, realizing that a particular defensive operation would ultimately end in the death or capture of all senior officers, Hitler permitted the limited evacuation of specialists and selected officers – to live and fight another day. During the encirclement of the 6th Army at Stalingrad at least six general officers were flown out of the pocket to avoid their loss. GdPz Hans Hube, then commander of the XIV Panzer Corps, left command of the surrounded corps on January 19, 1943 some two weeks before the final surrender of German forces there. Hube later commanded the 1st Panzer Army. Hube's escape was nerve-racking. On the 18th *Leutnant* Hans Gilbert landed his FW 200 Condor on the war-torn German airfield of Gumrak in the surrounded pocket. There was a heavy snow storm and visibility was reduced to fifty yards. The heavy aircraft snapped its rear skid landing device upon touchdown; a fellow pilot describes the scene:

The airfield is easy to pinpoint from 4,500 - 5,000 feet owing to its rolled runway, its wreckage and the numerous bomb craters and shell holes. The landing cross was covered with snow. Directly my machine came to a standstill the airfield was shot up by ten enemy fighters ... simultaneously it was under artillery zone fire. I had just switched off the engines when my aircraft became an object for target practice. The whole airfield was commanded by both [enemy] heavy and medium guns... When I returned to my aircraft I found that it had been severely damaged by artillery, and my flight mechanic had been killed.

GdPi Erwin Jänecke, commander of the IV Panzer Corps, also left after having been wounded several times.[2] On January 12, GM Wolfgang Pickert, commander of the 9th Flak Division, flew out of the pocket to Novocherkassk on a mission from GFM Paulus to attempt to get more help for the pocket. After attempting to persuade Luftwaffe units to deliver more supplies by air, Pickert flew back to Stalingrad on January 13 but his aircraft was unable to land at Pitomnik airfield. GL Richard von Schwerin flew out of the encirclement January 8 to reform a new 79th Infantry Division as did GM Otto Kohlermann of the 60th Infantry Division and GM Bernhard Steinmetz of the 305th Infantry Division. Ninety-one thousand lower ranking

German soldiers were not so fortunate and went into Soviet captivity – and less than six thousand ever returned to Germany.

Tunisia was the site for the second large evacuation of senior German officers. GFM Rommel, chronically ill for over a year, departed from Africa on March 9, 1943. GdPz Walter Nehring departed the 5th Panzer Army and avoided captivity; he later commanded numerous armored formations. GM Friedrich Weber, 334th Infantry Division, was evacuated before the final surrender as was GM Hasso von Manteuffel, then commander of "Division von Manteuffel". Von Manteuffel later played a pivotal role in the 1944 Ardennes Offensive. GM Siegfried Westphal left his position as Chief of Staff for the German-Italian Panzer Army – he later served as the chief of staff for several army groups. GM Fritz Bayerlein also was evacuated from the pocket – earlier in the campaign he had been Chief of Staff for the Africa Corps.

These, and other evacuations, saved some German leadership for future operations. They were too little, too late though as Hitler's obstinacy caused most officers to have to stand and die.

CHAPTER NOTES

[1] William Craig, *Enemy at the Gates: The Battle for Stalingrad,* New York: E.P. Dutton, 1973, p. 338.

[2] The historical novel Stalingrad, by Heinz Schroeter, asserts that several generals left the encirclement under less than honorable circumstances –abandoning their troops and leaving solely to save their own lives. Jänecke and GM Pickert are specifically singled out in this work as being in this group.

CHAPTER 12

OBITUARIES AND STATE FUNERALS

Today I buried some more of my former parishioners, Gebirgsjäger, who have died in this frightful land. Three more letters to write to add to the total of all those which I have already written in this war. The deleted names of the fallen are now more numerous in my pocket diary then the names of the living. My parish is bleeding to death on the plains of this country. We shall all die out here.

(Battalion chaplain, Eastern Front) [1]

OBITUARIES

The deaths of so many national military figures posed a serious problem for the Nazi leadership – how to use these deaths to spur the German war effort to greater output, while at the same time, avoid giving any indicators that the events transpiring at the front were meeting with less and less success as the war continued. German radio was state run as were several newspapers and periodicals such as the *Völkischer Beobachter, Der Adler* and *Die Wehrmacht*. As actual information concerning these deaths was not as widely disseminated as it might have been in a democratic society, Hitler could manage this information to a certain degree in the timing and description of the deaths in official obituaries. These announcements were normally published in the *Heeres-Verordnungsblatt*, the official periodic newspaper of the German Army High Command. Published on the 5th, 15th and 25th of each

Obituary Publication Dates

Name	Date Killed	Date Obituary Published
GL Braun	Nov. 4, 1941	Dec. 15, 1941
GdI von Briessen	Nov. 20, 1941	Dec. 5, 1941
GM Neumann-Silkow	Dec. 9, 1941	Dec. 25, 1941
GM Koch	Dec. 22, 1942	Jan. 25, 1943
GdI von Hartmann	Jan. 26, 1943	Mar. 15, 1943
GL Kamecke	Oct. 15, 1943	Jan. 25, 1944
GM Roth	Nov. 7, 1943	Mar. 5, 1944
GL Szelinski	Dec. 9, 1943	Mar. 25, 1944
GL von Groddeck	Jan. 10, 1944	Apr. 5, 1944
GdA Stemmermann	Feb. 18, 1944	May 25, 1944
GdA Marcks	June 12, 1944	Aug. 25, 1944
GdI Hauffe	July 22, 1944	Oct. 25, 1944
GL Kraiss	Aug. 2, 1944	Dec. 5, 1944
GdI Laux	Sept. 2, 1944	Nov. 25, 1944

month, it presented not only obituaries, but also lists of award recipients, articles on professional training and equipment and other articles of a military nature.

The Germans masked setbacks by staggering the appearance of many of these obituaries. GdI Wilhelm Wegener, for example, was actually killed September 24, 1944 [the *Heeres-Verordnungsblatt* lists the 23rd], the obituary was dated January 20, 1945, but did not appear in the newspaper until January 25, 1945 – a delay of some four months. The above table shows this delay in publication:

In examining this sample, it appears as though the delay between the actual event and its subsequent publication in the Heeres-Verordnungsblatt increased from one month during 1941, to one or two months in 1942, and to two to three months in 1943 and 1944.

Delay in publication was not the only manipulation of information concerning general officer obituaries. None of them listed a specific unit the general commanded; rather the phrase "commander of an infantry division",

---

OBITUARY

On January 26, 1943, the Commander of an Infantry Division

General der Infanterie
Alexander von Hartmann
Bearer of the Knight's Cross of the Iron Cross 1939

was killed in action in the battle of Stalingrad.

The Army has lost one of its most outstanding officers. Unwavering courage and an unfailing will to win were the marked features of his truly military character.

Already proving himself extraordinarily as a regimental commander during the Western Campaign, this highly meritorious general commanded the division entrusted to him in the fight against the Bolshevist world enemy and, with unsparing personal commitment, led his brave troops to great successes, especially in the battle for Kharkov in May 1942. In the grim fighting for Stalingrad, he set an example and inspired his troops as he fought side by side with his grenadiers. A shining example of manliness and loyalty, he heroically died in the foremost front line amidst his men.

His great merits for the People and the Fatherland shall never be forgotten.
This March 11, 1943.

Der Führer
Adolf Hitler

"commander of a panzer division", or "commanding general of an army corps" were used. Most also did not give any information concerning the location of the unit by which some inferences concerning the fatality could be deduced by the public. Again, most simply stated "in Russia" or "in France". Shown here are six obituaries which break the rule of silence and provide some insights. The underlined text in each is not from the original, but serves to highlight the ever deteriorating military situation faced by the Third Reich as the war continued. The first two, GdI von Hartmann and GL Stempel, concerned the battle for Stalingrad.

Captured German Generals at Stalingrad (Author photos)

Eight generals, three corps commanders and five division commanders were killed in the associated battles in and around Stalingrad. Many others became prisoners of war including GFM Paulus. Perhaps more than any other battle these losses, and the horrendous casualties incurred in the 6th Army, shook German society to the core. For three days following the disaster German state radio played nothing but the solemnest of martial music,

---

OBITUARY

On January 26, 1943, the Commander of an Infantry Division

Generalleutnant
Richard Stempel

Bearer of the German Cross in Gold as well as the
Clasps to the Iron Cross, 1st and 2nd Class of the World War

was killed in action during the fight for Russia.

With gratitude the Army honors the merits of this outstanding officer. Already proving himself extraordinarily as a regimental commander, he led the division entrusted to him to exceptional successes in the fight against the Bolshevist world enemy. Being a man of utmost bravery and stalwart determination, his impetuous, aggressive spirit swept his troops ahead into victorious action. In the heroic battle for Stalingrad he invariably stood in the foremost front lines, and set a lasting example of supreme dedication for the troops under his command, until death amidst his grenadiers became the final purpose of his life, which had been imbued by his courageous and steadfast will to win.

The Army shall never forget his successful work for the People and the Fatherland.

This March 22, 1943.

Der Führer
Adolf Hitler

Bruckner's Seventh Symphony and the "Eroica", a dirge often played at military funerals – and no amount of glossing over details in an obituary could ameliorate this deepest dread and coldest chill.

By the time von Hartmann was killed in action the fighting strength of the division had dwindled to one hundred eighty three men, seven non-commissioned officers and three officers. The general literally was fighting side by side with all of his troops at the bitter end of the battle.

GL Richard Stempel fell in the fight as well. He had commanded the 371st Infantry Division since April 1942; and was awarded the German Cross in Gold that month for his previous exploits as the commander of the 183rd Infantry Division.

GL Stempel's death, described in the obituary as killed in action was mis-represented. The general had actually shot and killed himself in the desperate final days of the encirclement. It is possible though, that the High Command did not actually know his exact fate in early 1943.

OBITUARY

On May 30, 1943, the Commander of a Jaeger Division
Generalleutnant
Ernst Rupp
Bearer of the Knight's Cross of the Iron Cross 1939

was killed in action during the fight for Russia.

An outstanding officer, a man of exemplary courage and steadfast belief in the future of Germany has met with death on the field of honor.

Already proving himself as chief of staff of an army corps and regimental commander, this highly meritorious general led the Jaeger division entrusted to him to ever new successes by unsparing personal commitment. During the heavy Winter's Battle of 1942, in the advance to the Caucasus as well as the <u>grim and severe fighting for the Kuban bridgehead</u>, he stood in the foremost front line side by side with his brave infantrymen, setting a shining example of utmost dedication and loyalty for his troops.

The Army shall never forget his great merits for the People and the Reich.

This June 20, 1943.

Der Führer

Adolf Hitler

The German 17th Army, comprising six corps and 400,000 soldiers, waged a difficult defensive struggle in the Kuban area, opposite the Crimean peninsula, from 1942 to the fall of 1943. During this time, GL Ernst Rupp and five other German generals were killed in action. The Kuban Bridgehead, as it came to be known, was portrayed as an heroic and successful defense – which to some degree it was; but like many other campaigns on the Eastern Front it drained tremendous military assets from being used for offensive operations elsewhere. The mention of the bridgehead in Rupp's obituary highlighted this continual depletion of limited German combat power and the severity of the defensive fighting in this difficult terrain.

The announcement of the death of GL Richard Müller was an important clue as to the failure of the German "Citadel Offensive" at Kursk in July 1943 and the transition of the Soviet Army to the strategic offensive – the momentum of which Stalin would not lose for the remainder of the war. On July 13, Hitler informed his generals that the offensive, which had gained limited objectives, would have to be called off. Simultaneously, Stalin attacked toward Orel with elements of the *West, Bryansk* and *Central Fronts*. Almost immediately the Red Army gained a depth of 16 miles and Müller, with his 211th Infantry Division, were steamrolled in the process. The totality of the destruction of the division was complete; no record of any account of the general's death exists. Undoubtedly, many Germans could detect a serious reversal in the end of their own offensive and the precarious defense that was overrun only three days later – obvious, but not specifically stated in his obituary.

As previously described, the encirclement at Cherkassy, also known as Korsun, was the worst German debacle since Stalingrad. Elements of two corps, with 56,000 men were trapped; and in the ensuing breakout attempt 20,000 troops including GdA Stemmermann, lost their lives. The portion of the obituary concerning "standing side by side" with his troops in the difficult struggle at Cherkassy seems to stretch the credibility the general may have had in Final Victory.

OBITUARY

On February 18, 1944 the Commanding General of an Army Corps

General der Artillerie
Wilhelm Stemmermann
Bearer of the Knight's Cross
of the Iron Cross 1939 with Oak Leaves

was killed in action in Russia.

A true soldier, a personality of utmost dedication and a man of inspiring determination has left us. After proving himself in an outstanding manner as chief of staff of an army corps, this meritorious general led an infantry division in the fight against Bolshevism, setting a shining example of manliness and loyalty for his men. Even as a commanding general of an army corps, he repeatedly stood in the foremost front lines side by side with his grenadiers, inspiring the men under his command by his unconditional personal commitment to ever greater actions during the heavy fights for Cherkassy. Steadfastly believing in final victory, he now died heroically amidst his troops.

His exceptional merits for the People and the Reich shall never be forgotten.

This May 19, 1944.

Der Führer

Adolf Hitler

The benign description of the fighting at Cherkassy cannot begin to describe the sheer terror hundreds and thousands of German soldiers felt as they frantically tried to swim the half-frozen Gniloy Tikich River in their hard-frozen uniforms – as thousands of Soviet troops and hundreds of tanks tried to kill them.

GdI Friedrich Mieth fell in August 1944 in the even more disastrous battles for Rumania. Although listed as killed in action, he may, in fact, have suffered a fatal heart attack.

By the time of GdI Friedrich Mieth's obituary, even more revealing words began to creep into the official death notices. In Mieth's, the retrograde battle in Rumania is described – a far cry from the more offensively toned obituaries of previous years. Additionally, the general is listed as having given his life for his people and his nation, *Volk und Reich*, which is quite a different cry than for Final Victory – as by this time there was no possibility for victory of any sort for Germany.

OBITUARY

On September 2, 1944, the Commanding General of an Army Corps

General der Infanterie
Friedrich Mieth

Bearer of the Knight's Cross
of the Iron Cross 1939 with Oak Leaves

was killed in action.

An outstanding officer, a personality of utmost dedication and rigorous self-discipline has left us.

After successfully completing his assignments as an army chief of staff and member of the Army General Staff; and after particularly proving himself as a division commander, he led the army corps placed under his command with clear and goal-oriented firmness in the fight against Bolshevism. Time and again, his steadfast courage and persistent will to win swept his troops forward, never failing to set an example and to inspire his men both in the attack and during counterattack operations. The brave general, at the furthest front of his combat troops, who – following the shining example of their commander – were successful in their heroic efforts to fight their way through during intense retrograde actions in Rumania, lost his life for the People and the Reich shortly before his forces were able to reach friendly lines.

The Army will always treasure the memory of his great merits.

This December 12, 1944.

Der Führer

Adolf Hitler

For Volk and Reich

FIELD BURIALS

A further affliction which adversely affected the morale of the troops was that in the closing stages it was no longer possible to bury the dead, for the men had by that time become too exhausted to be able to dig graves in the hard, frost-bitten ground.

(GFM Friedrich Paulus) [2]

Many generals never received a proper burial, as their bodies were never recovered from the battlefield. Others were interred in field cemeteries immediately behind the front-lines after a local funeral and honors ceremony within the command. GdSS Eicke, who died in an aircraft shootdown on February 26, 1943, fell into this category. Eicke was buried with full Waffen SS honors on March 1 at the village of Otdochnina in the Ukraine. That Fall, as Soviet troops closed on the area, *Reichsführer-SS* Heinrich Himmler ordered that Eicke's body be dug up and moved to a safer area at the Hegewald Military Cemetery at Zhitomir. This was done, but in the Spring of 1944 the Red Army seized this area of the Ukraine as well, and Eicke's corpse was left behind.[3]

GdSS Theodor Eicke's gravesite

The actual conduct of a general officer's funeral at the front-line areas was well orchestrated – with as much ceremony and dignity that field conditions would permit. An honor guard, often division officers who were Knight's Cross winners, would carry the Battle Flag-draped coffin to its final resting place at a military cemetery. The general's awards and decorations would be displayed at the ceremony before being sent to his next of kin in Germany. Often a military band provided martial music. The grave marker was most often a simple wooden Maltese Cross very similar to the markers of the common foot soldiers who lay nearby. In many cases senior commanders attended the ceremony. For instance, when GM von Hünersdorff was killed in action in 1943 during the Battle of Kursk, GFM von Manstein attended the funeral at Kharkov.

Funeral ceremony in Russia of GM von Hünersdorff (DOW July 17, 1943)

STATE FUNERALS

Other generals received far more elaborate State Funerals. Rommel's funeral occurred October 18, 1944 at Ulm and had many elements typical of these elaborate affairs. GFM Gerd von Rundstedt served as the ranking dignitary and initially served as the reviewing officer of the funeral procession as it approached the Town Hall. Marching this day were two Army infantry companies, a mixed Navy, Luftwaffe and Waffen-SS company, and several Nazi Party formations including a detachment of Hitler Youth.[4]

Once inside the Town Hall, the ceremony began with the Funeral March from the "Eroica" by von Beethoven. Von Rundstedt followed this by presenting a commemorative speech and then laid a wreath near the foot of the coffin. Standing next to the coffin for the duration of the ceremony were former members of the Africa Corps and Knight's Cross winners in dress uniform with officer sabers. At the front of the coffin stood a soldier holding the funeral awards pillow – a black square satin display with the deceased general's Knight's Cross and other military decorations displayed. As the wreath was laid the military band played a stanza of *"Ich hat einen Kameraden"*, a traditional German soldier's song of farewell, while outside a salute battery fired a 19-gun salute. Next, the German National Anthem was played, and von Rundstedt expressed his personal condolences to the family, saluted the deceased and departed the hall.[5]

The coffin, draped with a German Battle Flag, was then carried to a gun carriage which in turn moved with the procession to the city crematorium. At the gravesite more speeches were given and the salute battery fired three salvos, as several more wreathes were placed on the coffin. The ceremony was concluded with an additional playing of *"Ich hat einen Kameraden"*.[6]

GO Hube's State Funeral was held in Berlin with much pomp and circumstance. *Reichsmarshall* Goering delivered the eulogy, and Frau Hube even seemed caught up in the solemnity of the event as she along with Hitler standing beside her gave a crisp Nazi salute to the coffin of her late husband.[7] Later, the coffin was escorted to the Invalids Cemetery by Generals Eberbach, Gollnick, Breith and Nehring. All total three *Generalfeldmarschall*, five *Generaloberst* and nineteen *General der Infanterie/Panzer* attended his elaborate funeral.[8]

Reichsmarshall Göring with a eulogy.

161

The Way to the Invalids Cemetery

Hitler and Frau Hube

GO Eugen Ritter von Schobert had a multi-stage ceremony after his death September 12, 1941 at the head of the 11th Army. First, at the actual site where his death had occurred in a crash of his Fieseler Stork in a Soviet minefield, a small memorial stone was placed. In the nearby city of Nykolayiv, on the Bug River, a large granite memorial was erected in honor of the army commander. Von Schobert was buried at this site September 15,

1941, his coffin draped by a wreath sent by Hitler. An artillery battery fired a final salute and overhead Luftwaffe bombers flew in tribute. On September 23, 1941 Munich hosted the formal State ceremony for von Schobert. Thirteen thousand onlookers packed the square between the Army Museum and the War Memorial and listened to GO Fritz Fromm, the Commander of the Replacement Army, eulogize the fallen leader.[9] Hitler, however, did not attend the ceremony.

GO Eduard Dietl had perhaps the largest State Funeral during the war on July 1, 1944. On that day, the remains of the general were transported from Graz to Schloss (castle) Klessheim near Salzburg, Austria for the ceremony. Hundreds of spectators were in attendance. Adolf Hitler himself delivered the eulogy for the "Hero of Narvik", one of the Führer's favorite generals during the war. The escorting generals were led by GFM Ferdinand Schörner. Dietl was laid to rest the following day in the *Nordfriedhof* (North Cemetery) of Munich where his granite headstone bore a facsimile of the Narvik Shield campaign award representing perhaps Dietl's greatest victory.[10]

Hitler at Dietl's State Funeral

These and many other State Funerals were great spectacles, often attended by thousands of German citizens who lined the funeral routes and filled the funeral halls when this was permitted. Many of these deceased military leaders had also served as larger than life popular figures for the public. Many, in life, were besieged by adoring young people for autographs and handshakes – in much the same way as sports figures are often mobbed in other cultures. In death, at a State Funeral, these admirers had the ability to say a final

The Guard of Honor at Dietl's State Funeral

good-bye to perhaps one of their personal heroes. This almost worship of accomplished military figures could be a boost for Nazi propaganda efforts – until the enormity of their loss finally began to register in mounting numbers to the German people.

State funeral for GFM von Schobert, 1941

State funeral for GO Curt Haase, in Berlin, February 13, 1943.

State funeral of General Brockdorff-Ahlefeldt, May 13, 1943.

State funeral of SS-Obergruppenführer Heydrich, assassinated in Prague, 1942. [11]

CHAPTER NOTES

[1] James Lucas, *War on the Eastern Front*, New York: Stein and Day, 1979, p. 207.

[2] Görlitz, *Paulus*, p. 272.

[3] Sydor, *Soldiers*, p. 273.

[4] Law, *Rommel*, p. 344.

[5] *Ibid.*

[6] *Ibid.*

[7] Frau Hube seems to have continued with her extreme loyalty to the state and to the memory of her late husband. The author has a wartime picture postcard of the late general which Frau Hube has hand-written a dedication on the back of the card – perhaps to an admirerer of the general. Hitler while attending many State funerals, had a very negative view toward many of his generals. While in many arguments with them, his views can best be summed up by several observations of Propaganda Ministry Chief Joseph Göbbels in his diary: "He is absolutely sick of the generals. He can't imagine anything better than having nothing to do with them, His opinions of all generals is devastating. Indeed, at times it is so caustic as to seem prejudiced or unjust, although on the whole it no doubt fits the case … All generals lie, he says. All generals are disloyal." Source: Matthew Cooper, *The German Army 1933-1945*. p. 448.

[8] Hube's grave in the Invalids Cemetery in Berlin had no marker or any other identification when visited in 1990. It was possibly destroyed during the intense Soviet bombardment in 1945 or perhaps left to decay by the Communist regime in power after the war.

[9] Leo Leixner, *Generaloberst Eugen Ritter von Schobert: Lebensbild eines deutschen Armeeführers*, Munich: NSDAP Verlag, 1942, pp. 14-15. (Book provided to the author courtesy of Mr. Robert Sevier.)

[10] Dietl's grave still exists in the Nordfriedhof in Munich. He is buried in section *(Felf)* 114, Row *(Reihe)* 1, Number *(Nummer)* 34. Veterans groups from German mountain units still adorn it with flowers and candles at Christmas.

[11] Heydrich's grave in the Invalids Cemetery could not be found either in 1990.

✠ CHAPTER 13 ✠

CONCLUSION

I won't shoot myself, but I'll let the Russians shoot me. I'll stand alone on the railway embankment, firing at the enemy, and they'll kill me. My wife is a competent woman, she'll surely get on as best she can without me; my son has been killed and my daughter is married. We won't win this war and the man who is in Supreme Command is not the man we took him for.

GL Alexander von Hartmann at Stalingrad, (48 hours before his death) [1]

In the preceding accounts we have seen the magnitude of German general officer commander casualties on all fronts during World War II. Doctrine, from the First World War to the Second, emphasized front-line leadership. Personal bravery, reflected in their World War I service was carried into the next war by all the generals later killed in action.The German World War II awards system recognized bravery, and many senior commanders continued to display personal courage on the battlefield. Many were wounded and returned to command again.

However, their concept of personal battlefield lethality, shaped as it was in World War I, was outdated by the increased lethality of World War II, multiplying the ways a general officer commander could be killed in action. It included enemy artillery, minefields, anti tank fire, small arms fire, grenades, air attacks, tank fire, snipers, aircraft shootdowns, naval gunfire and partisans. Many of these causes, such as air attacks and tank fire, were relatively infrequent occurrences in World War I. Others, such as artillery fire, had far more sophisticated fire control and advanced targeting procedures than twenty years previously.

German Army doctrine traditionally valued front-line leadership. World War I doctrine emphasized the role of senior leaders on the battlefield. Later doctrine, refined in the 1930's, also stressed front-line leadership by senior level leaders. The German Army's views on war, which would be executed in World War II, were outlined in 1936, in the *Truppenführung* reemphasized the importance of front-line senior level leadership, and was followed almost religiously during the war.

Rotation of general officers within the German Army was a case of too few senior grades for too many positions in the expanded army. To meet the requirements, competent staff officers were often sent to the front with inadequate preparation, where many died within a few months of assuming command. The increased battlefield lethality multiplied the ways in which senior leaders could be killed and included air attacks, artillery, partisans, mine-fields, and snipers. Many of the fatal engagements occurred while moving in command vehicles as the commanders traversed the battlefield. Commanders transferring from one front to another had to quickly learn the tactics, techniques and procedures of a new enemy, which were often signifi-cantly different from those displayed by a different enemy, on a different front, only weeks before.

The German medical system soon became overworked in caring for wounded personnel, as evidenced by the high proportion of soldiers who died from their wounds after reaching medical treatment stations. Other gen-eral officer casualties never made it that far; the nature of the World War II mobile battlefield hindering their prompt evacuation. Any medical system that could not provide anesthesia for the amputation of the leg of a corps commander – as happened with GL Karl Eibl – was certainly taxed beyond all limits.

Finally, despite acquiring many critical lessons concerning battlefield lethality during the war, training for division and corps commanders in a pre-command course was inadequate to prepare these men for all the threats they would encounter.

The loss of these senior commanders adversely affected Germany in many ways. First, at the moment of loss the division, corps or army experienced a temporary loss in command and control due to the absence of a commander. Often the loss of the general took several hours to be reported to headquar-ters due to a lack of information or confusion on the battlefield.

Although the German tactical system stressed independent action by subor-dinate commanders, there undoubtedly were decisions that were not made due to the absence of a commander. A look at losses to just corps comman-ders, for instance, shows how disruptive this transition could be.

Twenty-nine times a German corps commander was killed in action, died of wounds or committed suicide. Ten of these commanders led Germany's principal offensive formations – the panzer corps. On five different occasions the XXIV Panzer Corps experienced a commander fatality; in the XXXIX Panzer corps it happened three times.

German Corps Commander Losses

	Name	Unit	Date
GL	von Speck	XVIII AK	15.6.40
GdI	von Briesen, K.	LII AK	20.11.41
GdPz	von Langermann u. Erlencamp	XXIV PzK	3.10.42
GdA	Wandel	XXIV PzK	14.1.42
GL	Jahr	XXIV PzK	20.1.43
GL	Eibl	XXIV PzK	21.1.43
GdI	Zorn, H.	XXXXVI PzK	2.8.43
GdA	Stemmermann, W.	XI AK	18.2.44
GdA	Marks, E.	LXXXIV AK	12.6.44
GdA	Pfeiffer, G.	VI AK	26.6.44
GdA	Martinek	XXXIX PzK	28.6.44
GL	Schünenmann	XXXIX PzK	29.6.44
GdI	Hauffe	XIII AK	22.7.44
GdI	Mieth	IV AK	2.9.44
GdSS	Phleps	V SS	21.9.44
GdI	Wegener	L AK	24.9.44
GdI	Schneckenburger	AK Belgrade	14.10.44
GdI	Priess	XXVII AK	21.10.44
GdI	Recknagel	XXXXII AK	23.1.45
GdI	Block, J.	LVI PzK	26.1.45
GL	Källner	XXIV PzK	18.4.45
GdPz	Decker	XXXIX PzK	21.4.45
GdSS	Kleinheisterkamp	XI SS	2.5.45
GL	Baade	LXXXI AK	8.5.45
GdI	von Erdmannsdorff, W.	LXXXXI AK	8.5.45
GL	von Bodengausen	L AK	9.5.45
GdI	Dostler	LXXV AK	1945
GdSS	Krüger, F.W.	V SS	10.5.45
GdSS	Krüger, W.	VI SS	20.5.45
GdPz	Fehn, G.	XV GebK	5.6.45

The same pattern emerges for the commanders of the panzer divisions – the heart of Germany's offensive capabilities. The following chart shows losses at this command level as well.

Panzer Division Commanders Killed in Action

	Name	Unit	Date	Replacement
GL	von Prittwitz	15 PzD	10.4.41	Oberst
GM	von Weber	17 PzD	20.7.41	Generalmajor
GM	Neumann-Silkow	15 PzD	8.12.41	Oberst
GM	Mack	23 PzD	26.8.42	Generalmajor
GM	von Bismarck	21 PzD	31.8.42	Oberst
GM	von Randow	21 PzD	21.12.42	Oberst
GL	Fischer, W.	10 PzD	1.2.43	Generalmajor
GL	Angern	16 PzD	2.2.43	Oberst
GdSS	Eicke	3 SS	26.2.43	Generalmajor*
GM	von Hünersdorff	6 PzD	17.7.43	Oberst
GL	Schilling, W.	17 PzD	21.7.43	Oberst
GL	Schmidt, G.	19 PzD	7.8.43	Oberst
GM	Sieberg	14 PzD	2.11.43	Oberst
GM	Schulz, A.	7 PzD	28.1.44	Oberst
GMdSS	Witt	12 SS	14.6.44	Oberst*
GM	Schmidhuber	13 PzD	11.2.45	Oberst
GM	von Elverfeldt	9 PzD	6.3.45	Oberst
GLdSS	Ostendorff	2 SS	4.5.45	Oberst*
GM	von Nostitz-Wallwitz	24 PzD	31.5.45	Major

* Waffen-SS rank equivalence

Nineteen panzer division commanders were killed in action. Only four (22%) were replaced by a general officer commander. A full fourteen (74%) were replaced by colonels, and one (4%) was even replaced by a major! Although it may at first appear a flight of historical fancy to say that fate held sway on the life or death of one division commander – in a war of millions of combatants, a further look is in order. During the southern front battles at Kursk in 1943, German hopes centered on the success of the 4th Panzer Army breaking through Soviet defenses, smashing the strategic reserves of the *Steppe Front* and then advancing to the city of Kursk to cut off several enemy armies. The 4th Army in turn was protected along its right flank, which became exposed to the enemy based on the German advance, by the III Panzer Corps advancing parallel to the east. The lead division of the corps was the veteran 6th Panzer and was commanded by GM von Hünersdorff. The division advanced over forty miles in its mission and closed to within fifteen miles of the lead elements of the 4th Panzer Army before encountering the Donets River – which had to be crossed quickly to continue the momentum of the attack. On July 12 the river was crossed at Rzhavets and the advance continued just as the massive tank battle of Prokhorovka just to the north reached its crescendo. Two days later von Hünersdorff fell mortally wounded – the III Panzer Corps never closing the last few miles.

Other panzer division commanders were seriously wounded and also had to be replaced. On May 15, 1940 GM Stever, the commanding general of the 4th Panzer Division, was wounded by artillery shrapnel near Gembloux (near Namur) Belgium. GM Hans von Esebeck, 15th Panzer Division was wounded July 5, 1941. GL Kirchner, the commander of the 1st Panzer Division, was wounded in an enemy air attack by a bomb fragment on July 15, 1941 near Sajanje (east of Lake Peipus) while riding in his command car at night. His replacement was a *Generalmajor*. GM Dietrich von Saucken, 4th Panzer Division, was seriously wounded on January 2, 1942 near Chmelewaja (Oka River). GL Gustav von Vaerst, of the 15th Panzer Division was wounded May 26, 1942. GM Georg von Bismarck, 21st Panzer Division was wounded July 17, 1942. On August 8, 1942 GM von Esebeck, now the commander of the 2nd Panzer Division, was wounded again in action, this time near Rshev. He was replaced by an *Oberst*. GM Traugott Herr, 13th Panzer Division, stepped on a mine on October 31, 1942 and suffered a serious head wound. His replacement was an *Oberst*. On August 20, 1944 GL Heinz von Lüttwitz, was wounded in the throat and the back near St. Lambert near Argentan in Normandy. GL Karl Mauss, commander of the 7th Panzer Division, was seriously wounded March 23, 1945 by artillery fire and lost a leg. He, too, was replaced by an *Oberst*. These were just some of the accounts of panzer division commanders being wounded in action. The continuity, the experience, the tactical agility required by offensive operations and offensive formation commanders – the panzer divisions, simply had to be affected by these losses.

Once the commander's loss became known at headquarters, a temporary commander was appointed to fill the vacant post until a permanent replacement was designated. This presented an additional command and control problem. The temporary commander most often came from within the unit; in the case at division often a senior regimental commander assumed temporary command. While a great many regimental commanders were quality officers, certainly well-versed in on-going combat operations at their own level, they often initially were not completely prepared to assume command at this higher level. It is not inconceivable that many of their initial decisions in the new post were more tentative than those that would have been made by a more comfortable incumbent commander. For example, after the XXIV Panzer Corps lost three commanders in seven days the acting corps commander from January 21 to February 9, 1943 was *Oberst* Otto Heidkämper – an officer whose rank was more appropriate to command of a regiment instead of a corps! The elevation of junior commanders had a domino effect at lower levels. Should a regimental commander be called forward to replace a fallen division commander, his place in turn had to also be temporarily filled – often by a senior battalion commander, and so forth. Thus, junior officers at all levels were often forced to assume command at levels for which they had not been thoroughly prepared. This may have developed leaders in the long run, but certainly caused turmoil in the short.

Finally at the tactical level, the loss of many of these charismatic leaders seriously affected morale of the soldiers and officers in the unit. Many of these senior leaders were viewed in larger-than-life terms. Soldiers often fought alongside these men for several years – and the generals were often thought of as somewhat invincible. The reality of their deaths brought home to the soldier the vulnerability of the German Army in a way no Allied propaganda could eclipse.

At the operational level – corps, army and army group, despite what some post-war historians profess, the German Army did not have an overabundance of far-sighted, operationally proficient commanders from which to draw. Many general officers were forced into retirement not as the result of anti-Nazi activities, but because they were, in reality, not suited to continue to lead forces on the evolving World War II battlefield. Many still thought in terms of the Great War. Many were unable to grasp the complexities of combined arms on the mobile battlefield. Many were extremely branch parochial. A great number were never able to understand how land, sea and air forces could and should work together. In short, not every general was a carbon copy of a Rommel, a Manstein or a Student. Older commanders' performances were sometimes reviewed.

For example, according to Dermot Bradley and Richard Schulze Kossens, *Tätigkeitsbericht des Chefs des Heerespersonalamtes General der Infanterie Rudolf Schmundt: 1.10.42 - 29.10.44.*, as a result of the events of the winter of 1941 42 on the Eastern Front, the High Command ordered a review of all older division and higher troop commanders. This review of performance was code-named *"Winterfestigkeit"* (Winter firmness or solidarity). All commanders who exhibited less than exemplary steadfastness during the bitter winter fighting were to be replaced by more stable commanders. Instructions for implementing this program were issued to all army groups and armies. Commanders who were physically ill were affected by the program as well. As a result some thirty-five corps and division commanders were sent back to Germany in varying degrees of disgrace. When outstanding operational level commanders were killed in action – such as GdA Marcks, GdPZ von Langermann und Erlencamp or GdI Zorn; or died in accidents – such as GO Hube or Dietl, it was simply not possible to replace them without a drop-off in skill. Hitler did not deny the talents of most of these operational thinkers to the German Army – combat did. Such was an implied detriment of waging a two-front war.

At the strategic level, the German populace constantly received reports of general officer casualties; probably undermining, to a degree, their support for the war. As with the case of front-line soldiers, the public had been exposed for many years to the exploits and valorous deeds of many of the more well-known generals; and their loss must have been deeply felt. Many of the more prominent figures such as Dietl and Rommel, furthermore, could influence Hitler, to a degree, to make more sound military decisions, and the loss of men such as these facilitated Hitler's increased meddling with all facets of the war.

One final question remains. In any post-war study concerning the German Army it is pertinent to ask the question of whether the outcome of the war hung in the balance. In this work the question is: If the German Army had been able to significantly reduce their general officer fatalities could they have won the war? The answer is definitely **"No"**. The military and industrial capacity of the Allies overmatched the Third Reich in every facet. To be sure, Germany produced numerous superb weapons throughout the war, but the ultimate weapon – the atomic bomb, was achievable only by the United States and its allies. But reasonable speculation need not end here. An appropriate follow-on question is: If the German Army had been able to significantly reduce general officer casualties could they have substantially altered the course of the war? I believe the answer to this question to be **"Yes"**.

We have already seen that the overall effects of general officer losses hobbled the command and control of the panzer forces, reduced unit morale, and crippled the esprit on the home front. To further support the contention that the course of the war could have indeed been altered let us examine just three individual cases of these losses a bit further.

First, the death of GL Wilhelm Süssmann, the commander of the 7th *Flieger* Division at the very start of the German invasion of Crete significantly disrupted the German plan of action. No one assumed acting command of the division for several hours and a general officer did not arrive on the scene until GL Julius Ringel – a non-airborne officer, came from Greece. The result was confusion and higher German casualties than necessary – some 6,000 in all. The Germans won the battle; but with lower losses Hitler may not have been so reluctant to commit the *Fallschirmjäger* later in the war. German paratroops could have been used to great effect in Africa or an airborne invasion of Malta. But based on the heavy losses at Crete – exacerbated by Süssmann's death, the Führer basically said "never again".

Second, the death of GO Ritter von Schobert, on September 12, 1941 was a double edged blow. Von Schobert was a veteran commander having served for two and one-half years as a corps commander and as the 11th Army commander for almost one year. As previously discussed, upon von Schobert's death, GdI Erich von Manstein was taken out of command of the LVI Panzer Corps and placed in command of the 11th Army. In his new assignment he turned in an outstanding performance in capturing the Crimea and the fortress of Sevastopol the next year. But his loss from the LVI Panzer Corps robbed the pivotal central theater of operations of a key leader. The corps was a key component of GO Hermann Hoth's 3rd Panzer Group during the campaign to take Moscow. Hoth's tanks, minus von Manstein, captured

174

Kalinin on October 14, 1941 – but the remainder of the month featured weather conditions and mud which slowed the advance to a crawl. At the beginning of November Stalin began the transfer of troops and equipment from the Far East to Moscow in earnest. On November 15 Army Group Center kicked off its final offensive against Moscow, but the correlation of forces had significantly changed, and the German Army failed to capture the Soviet capital. Had von Manstein remained with the corps it is quite possible that his leadership could have spurred a quicker seizure of Kalinin and points east before the atrocious Fall weather and Siberian troops hobbled the panzers. A resultant fall of Moscow – or at the least-unfavorable conditions for the Soviets to launch their Winter counteroffensive, could have altered the course of the conflict.

The last fatality that could have significantly altered the course of the war was that of GO Walter von Reichenau in January 1942. He had just assumed command of Army Group South and his place in 6th Army was filled by GdPz Friedrich Paulus – a leader of far less experience and independence. During the later climactic fight at Stalingrad, a less-than-decisive Paulus contributed to the 6th Army's demise. The hard-headed, independent von Reichenau, had he been in command of the Army Group, and therefore the direct superior of Paulus, may well have withdrawn the 6th Army to safety at the beginning of the Soviet encirclement – a move that may well have finished von Reichenau's career but saved a large portion of the 6th Army. Von Reichenau had confronted the Nazi establishment at least three times previously and prior to his death had grown more disenchanted with Hitler. He additionally had the courage to stand up to Hitler and had a sensible military mind; and sensible judgment called for a withdrawal from Stalingrad before the Soviet noose tightened. Stalingrad was the turning point in the war on the Eastern Front. Without a successful Soviet encirclement at Stalingrad, that turning point would have been pushed into 1943 at the earliest.

Other German losses significantly influenced specific tactical situations – but the course of the war can not reasonably be linked to any one of them. Other deaths – Hube, Dietl, Rommel and Model occurred past the point when the pendulum of the conflict swung strongly against the Germans. And that did not bode well for the generals.

The masters of the *Blitzkrieg* had been devoured by the monster they created.

CHAPTER NOTES

[1] Schröter, Stalingrad, p. 231.

✠ EPILOGUE ✠

... ruhig fliesst der Rhein
Quiet flows the Rhine
(words from a German ballad)

Fifty years after World War Two there are not many traces left of either those German generals who fell in combat; or for those who survived the war. The German wartime cemeteries in Russia were bulldozed over after the Red Army retook their lost lands. The Russian people had suffered mightily during the German occupation and millions had perished. No Russian wanted to ever again be reminded of German militarism – and the thousands of wooden Iron Cross tombstones soon became part of the endless steppe.

In Western Europe a more benign fate accompanied the German defeat; and German military cemeteries were allowed to remain intact on foreign soil. Maintained by the *Volksbund Deutsche Kriegsgräberfürsorge*, the national office for war cemeteries, these final resting places dot France, Belgium, Italy and many other nations. They hold the remains of common soldiers and officers alike. GFM Walter Model rests in the German Military Cemetery at Vossenack in the Hürtgen Forest. These are well-maintained but grim graveyards filled with dark brown and green scrub-like heather and dotted with large granite crosses that remind one of the monuments on Easter Island. Often they are located near the large American military cemeteries which seem infinitely brighter with their row on row of white crosses instead of drab plaques, and blooming flowers instead of blossom-less vegetation.

In every German village, town and city there are the civilian cemeteries which often hold a small stone or plaque which remember a fallen general from the war but hold no actual remains. General Otto Lancelle is remembered in such a manner at Garmisch; his bronze marker affixed to the headstone of his wife Elisabeth who died in this mountain town in 1948. In another part of the cemetery stands a wrought iron marker for GL Walter Ritter Stettner von Grabenhofen, who fell in Yugoslavia but whose memory remains in the German Alps. Other markers in other towns commemorate those German generals who became prisoners of war during the conflict, died in captivity and never returned.

The former state military cemetery, the Invalids, in Berlin has been ravaged by time. During the many eras of German military might, it served as the final resting place for such notable figures as von Schlieffen, Scharnhorst, Mölders, Udet, Hube and many others. After the war it lay in what was then East Berlin under Soviet control, and was allowed to deteriorate into an overgrown lot. Many graves were covered with weeds and many headstones went missing. GFM Walter von Reichenau, the commander of the 6th Army who died of a stroke in Russia in 1942 lies here – but his tombstone in 1990 lay in

Memorial plaque to General Lancelle (Author photo)

a clump of bushes, perhaps thrown there by vandals. Even more unkempt is the gravesite of World War One ace Ernst Udet. In 1990, his headstone lay not on his plot, but askew along a wall where lawn mowers and other maintenance equipment was stored. There has been some discussion among veteran's organizations of refurbishing the Invalids to its former state but the political fears of a resurgent right wing nationalist party may prevent this.

Von Reichenau gravestone (Author photo)

In other cemeteries the decay of time is just as certain if somewhat more orderly than at the Invalids. In inquiring as to the last resting places of several notable World War Two generals it became obvious that most city cemetery offices and grounds keepers were unaware of many of the men that rose to high command were buried in their city cemeteries. Their numbers decrease every year. Under the German burial system, plots are leased for up to twenty, thirty and forty years. If the lease is not renewed after that time, the stone is removed and another individual is buried on top of the former occupant – permanently erasing his former presence.

This process has already begun to occur, and many gravesites now remain unknown and unnoticed. GFM Erwin Rommel's remains intact in the small Herrlichen cemetery, outside Ulm and will probably stay a well-preserved memorial. Fresh flowers often adorn the grave, and former enemies who are now NATO allies annually place wreaths at the plot. About a mile distant, the site where the field marshal took poison is memorialized as well with a prominent marker.

Rommel gravesite (Author photo)

However, other high ranking World War Two generals such as Schörner, von Blomberg, Hausser, von Leeb and Dietrich have much more modest surroundings and may fall victim to Father Time as grave space becomes a premium, and budgets to maintain military cemeteries come under more intense scrutiny as governments tighten spending.

History has now traveled fifty years from the high water mark of German military might and territorial expansion. Then, when a military leader fell in combat (or committed suicide as did the Luftwaffe's Ernst Udet) he was given a magnificent state funeral with pomp and ceremony characteristic of one of the most powerful nations on earth.

History moves on and the pomp and ceremony of yesteryear quickly turns to distant memories and overgrown cemeteries as symbolized by Udet's gravestone in 1990. Perhaps that is just as well.

Udet's funeral march 1941. (Author photo)

Udet's gravestone lying in cemetery maintenance area 1990. (Author photo)

Von Brächitsch, Räder, Keitel, Milch and Göring at State Funeral for
GO Werner von Fritsch, 1939. (Author photo)

181

✠ GLOSSARY ✠

Glossary of Frequently Used Abbreviations and Terms
(German equivalent in bold print)

Armeeabteilung – Army Detachment – A uniquely German level of command intermediate between a corps and an army, usually under an enlarged corps headquarters. (**AA**)

Army – **Armee** – military organization usually controlling two to four corps, plus several separate units of army troops, used by the German Army and also the Western Allies. A German army typically had between 200,000 and 250,000 troops. A Soviet army was the size of a Western corps.

Army Group – **Heeresgruppe** – military organization usually controlling two to four armies used by the German Army and also the Western Allies. (**HG**/**AG** = army group)

Corps – **Korps** – military organization usually controlling two to five divisions, plus several separate units of corps troops, used by the German Army and also the Western Allies. A Soviet corps was a smaller organization, just larger than a Western division. (**AK** = army corps, **PzK** = panzer corps, **GebK** = mountain corps, **FlK** = flak corps, **FsK** = airborne corps, **LF** = luftwaffe field corps)

Division – military organization of 10,000 to 16,000 soldiers (depending on type) used by the German Army and also the Western Allies. A Soviet division was significantly smaller. (**ID** = infantry division, **PzD** = panzer division, **JD** = light infantry division, **LwF** = luftwaffe field division, **PGD** = panzer grenadier division, **LLD/FlD/FJD** = airborne division, **Flak** = flak division, **RID** = reserve infantry division, **SD** = security division, **VGD** = volks grenadier division, Ski = ski division)

DOW – Died of Wounds. Deaths from battle wounds and/or battle injuries after admission to some medical installation.

Fallschirmjäger – paratroopers – an airborne unit. (**FSJ**)

Front – a uniquely Soviet military organization roughly equivalent to a western army group.

Führer – Leader. Hitler's title as German chief of state.

Guards – Honorary designation given to elite Soviet units that had distinguished themselves in combat.

Heer – Army.

KIA – Killed in Action. Dead on the field of battle without ever having been admitted to a medical installation alive; may have been seen alive after wounding.

kilometer – 1,000 meters. A measure of distance used by most military forces on maps and for operations. A mile is equal to 1.6 kilometers (100 miles equals 160 kilometers).

Korpsabteilung – Corps Detachment – A uniquely German level of command intermediate between a division and a corps, usually under an enlarged division headquarters. (**KA**)

Kriegsmarine – The German Navy in World War II. Commanded by Admiral Erich Räder and later by Admiral Karl Dönitz)

Luftwaffe – Air Force. The German air arm during the Third Reich. Hermann Göring was head of the Luftwaffe.

MIA – Missing in Action. Battle casualties reported missing from their unit under circumstances indicating that their missing status is a result of enemy action. Many of those reported MIA were subsequently reported to be captured or declared dead.

mm – millimeters. Frequently used measurement concerning weapons' caliber. One inch is equal to 25.4 millimeters. A 50mm anti-tank gun, for example, fired a round roughly two inches in diameter.

OKH – **Oberkommando des Heeres** – High Command of the Army. The Supreme Command of the Army.

OKW – **Oberkommando der Wehrmacht** – High Command of the Armed Forces. The top command set up by Hitler on February 4, 1938 to replace the old War Ministry (**Reichskriegsministerium**). The OKW was divided into four departments; Operations, Foreign Intelligence, Supply and General Purpose. GFM Wilhelm Keitel was head of OKW operations.

Panzer – Armor – an armored or tank unit, or a specific armored vehicle. (Pz)

Reichswehr – Defensive Land Forces. Name of the standing Army, 100,000 man strong, during the era of the Weimar Republic 1918-1933 and continued to 1935.

S - Suicide

SS – **Schützstaffel** – Originally the black-shirted personal Guard of Hitler, but later transformed into the political police, dedicated to maintaining the principles of National Socialism. The **Waffen-SS** was the military arm and largest of the major branches of the SS. Heinrich Himmler was the head of the SS.

Shock Army – A Soviet Army reinforced to lead breakthrough operations.

STAVKA – Stavka Verhovnogo Glavnokommandovaniya – Staff of the Supreme High Command. The top-level Soviet military executive committee.

Wehrmacht – Armed Forces. The official name of the combined Army, Navy (**Kriegsmarine**), and Air Force in the Third Reich. The term replaced the former **Reichswehr**.

ALPHABETICAL CASUALTY LIST
GERMAN GENERAL OFFICER COMMANDERS
KILLED IN ACTION

	Name	Unit	Location Killed	Date	Cause of Death
GL	Angern	16 PzD	Stalingrad/USSR	2.2.43	Small Arms Fire
GL	Arndt, E	708 ID	Groghy/Aube.France	24.8.44	
GMdSS	Augsberger	20 SS	Grottkau/Silesia	17.3.45	
GL	Baade	LXXXI AK	Segeberg/Schleswig	8.5.45	Air Attack
GM	Bader	97 JD	Prosnitz/Czechoslovakia	9.5.45	
GL	Bäntsch	82 ID	Voronezh/USSR	31.1.43	
GL	Bässler, J.	242 ID	Vienna/Austria	8.11.44	
GL	Baltzer	182 ID	Prague/Czechoslovakia	10.5.45	
GL	Bergmann	137 ID	Sjawki/Kaluga/USSR	21.12.41	Small Arms Fire
GM	Berthold	31 ID	Juchnow/USSR	24.1.42	Unknown
GM	Betzel	539 ID	Danzig/Poland	21.3.45	Artillery Fire
GM	Beutler	340 ID	Brody/Poland	21.7.44	
GM	von Bismarck, G.	21 PzD	El Alamein/Africa	31.8.42	Artillery Fire
GdI	Block, J.	LVI PzK	Kielce/Vistula/Poland	26.1.45	
GM	Blümke	257 ID	Tiraspol/Tighina/USSR	4.9.44	Air Attack
GL	von Bodenhausen	L AK	Frauenberg/Courland	9.5.45	Suicide
GM	Braun	68 ID	Kharkov/USSR	14.11.41	Mine
GdI	von Briesen	LII AK	Andrejewka/USSR	20.11.41	Air Attack
GM	Buck	198 ID	Kljutschewaja/USSR	6.9.42	AT Grenade
GM	von Bülow, W.	111 ID	Obronoje/USSR	30.8.43	
GM	Crisolli	20 LwF	Bologna/Italy	12.9.44	Partisans
GdPz	Decker	XXXIX PzK	Wendhausen/Germany	21.4.45	Suicide
GM	Domansky	50 ID	Pillau/East Prussia	26.4.45	
GL	von Drabich-Wächter	326 ID	Normandy/France	2.8.44	
GL	Drescher	267 ID	Niemen River/USSR	13.8.44	
GM	Dürking	96 ID	Sanok/Poland	11.9.44	Anti-Tank Fire
GL	Eibl	XXIV PzK	Podgornoje/USSR	21.1.43	Grenade
GdSS	Eicke	3 SS	Kharkov/USSR	26.2.43	Downed Aircraft
GM	von Eichstedt	294 ID	Guragalbina/Rumania	26.8.44	Unknown
GM	von Elverfeldt	9 PzD	Cologne/Germany	6.3.45	Small Arms Fire
GdI	von Erdmannsdorff, W.	LXXXXI AK	Laibach/Yugoslavia	8.5.45	Partisans
GM	Erhard	7 Flak	Düsseldorf/Germany	17.4.45	Suicide
GL	Falley	91 LLD	Normandy/France	6.6.44	Small Arms Fire
GdPz	Fehn, G.	XV GebK	Yugoslavia	5.6.45	Partisans
GM	Finger	291 ID	Czestochowa/Poland	27.1.45	Tank Fire
GM	Fisher, K.	267 ID	Uljewo/Vyasma/USSR	31.3.42	
GL	Fischer, W.	10 PzD	Mareth/Africa	5.2.43	Minefield
GMdSS	Freitag	14 SS	Andra/Austria	10.5.45	Suicide
GL	Gabcke	294 ID	Kharkov/USSR	22.3.42	
GL	Geitner	295 ID	Artemowsk/USSR	22.1.42	
GM	von Groddeck	161 ID	Breslau/Silesia	10.1.44	Air Attack
GM	Gruner	111 ID	Sevastopol/Crimea/USSR	12.5.44	Tank Fire
GM	Gurran	23 ID	Opotscka/USSR	22.2.44	

GL	Haccius	46 ID	Taman/Caucasus/USSR	14.2.43	Air Attack
GM	Hahne	197 ID	Vitebsk/USSR	24.6.44	
GL	von Hartmann	71 ID	Stalingrad/USSR	26.1.43	Small Arms Fire
GdI	Hauffe	XIII AK	Lvov (Lemberg)/Poland	22.7.44	Artillery Fire
GM	Haus	50 ID	Pillau/East Prussia	16.4.45	
GL	Heinrichs	89 ID	Liege/Belgium	8.9.44	
GL	Hellmich	243 ID	Cherbourg/Normandy	17.6.44	Air Attack
GM	Henke, K.	290 ID	Pillau/East Prussia	27.4.45	
GM	Herold	10 PGD	Bochnia/Poland	28.11.44	Partisans
GL	Hewelke	339 ID	Vitebsk/Bobruisk/USSR	?.1.42	Partisans
GL	Himer	46 ID	Crimea/USSR	23.3.42	Naval Gunfire
GM	Hippler	329 ID	Lake Ilmen/USSR	23.3.42	Minefield
GM	von Hirschfeld	78 ID	Tarnow/Poland	18.1.45	Air Attack
GM	von Hünersdorff	6 PzD	Kharkov/USSR	17.7.43	Sniper
GL	Hundt	1 SKI D	Troppau/Czechoslavakia	21.4.45	
GL	Jahr	XXIV PzK	Podgornoje/USSR	20.1.45	Suicide
GL	Jost	42 JD	Villadosa/Italy	22.4.45	
GL	Källner	XXIV PzK	Sokolniza/Bohemia	18.4.45	Unknown
GM	Kalmukoff	31 ID	Swoncz/USSR	13.8.41	Minefield
GL	Kamecke	137 ID	Kolpen/Dnjepr/USSR	16.10.43	Air Attack
GM	Kirschner	320 ID	Saybusch/Poland	11.2.45	
GdSS	Kleinheisterkamp	XI SS	Halbe/Berlin/Germany	2.5.45	Suicide
SFdSS	Klingenberg	17 SS	Herxheim/Germany	22.3.45	
GM	Koch, V.	323 ID	Voronezh/USSR	22.12.42	
GM	Kossmala	344 ID	Oberglogau/Silesia	5.3.45	
GM	Krämer	11 Flak	Rattaj/Czechoslovakia	11.5.45	
GL	Kraiss	352 ID	St-Lo/France	2.8.44	Tank Fire
GM	Krech	41 ID	Molei/Greece	27.4.44	
GL	Kress	4 GebD	Novorossijsk/USSR	11.8.43	Sniper
GdI	von Krosigk	16 Army	Kanden/Courland	16.3.45	Air Attack
GdSS	Krüger, F. W.	V SS	Austria	10.5.45	Suicide
GdSS	Krüger, W.	VI SS	Courland	20.5.45	Suicide
GM	Kühme	SD	Hallschlag/Germany	25.12.44	
GM	Lancelle	121 ID	Kraslawa/Duna/USSR	3.7.41	Small Arms Fire
GM	Lang, J.	95 ID	Pillau/East Prussia	16.4.45	
GdPz	von Langermann und Erlencamp	XXIV PzK	Storoshewoje/USSR	3.10.42	
GdI	Laux	16 Army	Riga/Latvia	2.9.44	Downed Aircraft
GL	Lechner, A.	377 ID	Voronezh/USSR	29.1.43	
GL	Löweneck	39 ID	Petschenegi/USSR	14.5.43	Minefield
GL	Löwrick, K.	542 ID	Pillau/East Prussia	8.4.45	
GM	Mack	23 PzD	Terek/Caucasus/USSR	26.8.42	Artillery Fire
GdA	Marcks, E.	LXXXIV AK	St-Lo/Perriers/France	12.6.44	Air Attack
GdA	Martinek	XXXIX PzK	Beresinow/USSR	28.6.44	Air Attack
GL	Mickl	392 ID	Fiume/Italy	10.4.45	Partisans
GdI	Mieth	IV AK	Vutcani/Rumania	2.9.44	Unknown
GFM	Model	Army Group B	Duisburg/Germany	21.4.45	Suicide
GM	Möckel	16 ID	Karlsruhe/Germany	24.3.45	
GM	Möhring	276 ID	Belfort/France	18.12.44	
GL	Müller, R.	211 ID	Orel/USSR	16.7.43	

GLdSS	Mülverstedt	4 SS	Luga/USSR	10.8.41	Artillery Fire
GM	Neumann-Silkow	15 PzD	Derna/Africa	8.12.41	Artillery Fire
GM	von Nostitz-Wallwitz	24 PzD	Eckenförde/Germany	31.5.45	Artillery Fire
GM	Obenaus	545 VGD	Jaslo/Poland	15.1.45	
GM	Oschmann	338 ID	Fraunbe/France	14.11.44	
GLdSS	Ostendorff	2 SS	Bad Aussee/Austria	4.5.45	Artillery Fire
GL	Peschel	6 LwF	Vitebsk/USSR	30.6.44	
SFdSS	Petersen	18 SS	Pilsen/Czechoslovakia	9.5.45	Suicide
GL	Pfeifer, H.	65 ID	Fonale/Italy	22.4.45	Air Attack
GdA	Pfeiffer, G.	VI AK	Beresina/USSR	26.6.44	Air Attack
GL	Philipp	134 ID	Bobruisk/USSR	27.6.44	Suicide
GdSS	Phleps	V SS K	Arad/Rumania	21.9.44	Small Arms Fire
GL	Pistorious	4 LwF	Gankowitsch/Rwesh/USSR	27.6.44	
GdI	Priess	XXVII AK	Hasenrode/East Prussia	21.10.44	
GL	von Prittwitz	15 PzD	Tobruk/Africa	10.4.41	Anti-Tank Fire
GM	von Randow	21 PzD	Tripoli/Africa	21.12.42	Minefield
GM	Recke	161 ID	Panskaje/Kharkov/USSR	15.8.43	Small Arms Fire
GdI	Recknagel	XXXXII AK	Petrikau/Lodz/Poland	23.1.45	Partisans
GL	Rein	69 ID	Schloßberg/East Prussia	18.1.45	
GL	Renner	174 RID	Ozarow/USSR	26.8.43	Partisans
GM	von Reuss	62 ID	Bokovskaya/Chir/USSR	22.12.42	Small Arms Fire
GL	Richter, W.	263 ID	Riga/Latvia	3.6.44	Minefield
GL	Rittau	129 ID	Martinowo/Rshev/USSR	22.8.42	Artillery Fire
GM	von Roden	286 SD	Berlin/Germany	3.5.45	
GL	von Rost	44 ID	Stuhlweissenburg/Hungary	23.3.45	Anti-Tank Fire
GL	Roth	88 ID	Zhitomir/USSR	6.11.43	Unknown
GL	Ruebel	163 ID	Schievelbein/Pomerania	8.3.45	
GMdSS	Rumohr	8 SS	Budapest/Hungary	11.2.45	Suicide?
GL	Rupp, E.	97 JD	Kuban/USSR	30.5.43	Air Attack
GL	de Salengre Drabbe	384 ID	Tiraspol/Bessarabia	25.8.44	
GM	Scheidies	61 ID	Gluschitza/USSR	7.4.42	Sniper
GL	Scherbening	406 ID	Urft/Germany	18.12.44	
GL	Schilling, W.	17 PzD	Doljenhaja/Isjum/USSR	21.7.43	
GM	Schmidhuber	13 PzD	Budapest/Hungary	11.2.45	Suicide?
GM	Schmidt, A.	159 ID	Besancon/France	8.9.44	
GL	Schmidt, F.	50 ID	Kuban/USSR	26.6.43	Minefield
GL	Schmidt, G.	19 PzD	Kharkov/USSR	7.8.43	Suicide?
GL	Schmidt, K.	526 ID	Aalsmeer/Holland	3.3.45	
GdI	Schneckenburger	AK Belgrade	Belgrade/Yugoslavia	14.10.44	
GO	von Schobert	11 Army	Nykolayiv/USSR	12.9.41	Minefield
GLdSS	von Scholz, F.	11 SS	Narva/Estonia	28.7.44	Artillery Fire
GM	Scholze	20 PGD	Potsdam/Berlin/Germany	28.4.45	Suicide
GL	Schroeck	192 ID	Lüneberg/Germany	1945	
GL	Schünenmann	XXXIX PzK	Pagost/Beresina/USSR	29.6.44	Air Attack
GMdSS	Schuldt	19 SS	Velikaya/USSR	15.3.44	Anti-Tank Fire
GM	Schulz, A.	7 PzD	Schepetowka/USSR	28.1.44	Artillery Fire
GM	von Schwerin, B.	207 SD	Dorpat/Estonia	17.9.44	Small Arms Fire
GM	Seidel, E.	257 ID	Dobel-Wildbach/Germany	11.4.45	
GM	Sieberg	14 PzD	Kirovograd/USSR	2.11.43	Anti-Tank Fire
GM	Sieckenius	391 SD	Markish-Buchholz	28.4.45	Suicide

GM	von Siegroth	712 ID	Halbe/Berlin/Germany	2.5.45	
GL	von Speck	XVIII AK	Pont sur Yonne/France	15.6.40	Small Arms Fire
GM	Stegmann	77 ID	Briebeque/France	18.6.44	Air Attack
GdA	Stemmermann, W.	XI AK	Khil'ki/Cherkassy/USSR	18.2.44	Anti-Tank Fire
GL	Stempel	371 ID	Stalingrad/USSR	26.1.43	Suicide
GL	Stephan, F.	104 JD	Carinthia/Austria	8.5.45	
GL	Stettner von Grabenhofen	1 GebD	Belgrade/Yugoslavia	18.10.44	Suicide?
GM	Strahammer	114 JD	Italy	2.5.45	
GM	Sudau	548 ID	Königsberg/East Prussia	9.4.45	Artillery Fire
GM	Sümmermann	90 ID	Mamali/Africa	10.12.41	Air Attack
GL	Süssmann	7 FID	Aegina/Mediterranean	20.5.41	Glider Crash
GL	Szelinski	376 ID	Krementschug/USSR	9.12.43	
GL	von Thadden	1 ID	Vordingborg/Denmark	?.5.45	
GM	Thomas	999 ID	Mediterranean Sea	1.4.43	Downed Aircraft
GdA	Wandel	XXIV PzK	Chilino/USSR	14.1.43	
GM	von Weber	17 PzD	Krassnyj/USSR	20.7.41	
GM	von Wedel	10 LwF	Dorpat/Estonia	5.2.44	
GdI	Wegener	L AK	Wolmar/Latvia	24.9.44	Air Attack
GM	Wengler	83 ID	Pillau/East Prussia	25.4.45	Air Attack
GMdSS	Witt	12 SS	Venoix/Normandy/France	14.6.44	Naval Gunfire
GM	Wüstenhagen	256 ID	Vitebsk/USSR	26.6.44	Tank Fire
GMdSS	Zehender	22 SS	Budapest/Hungary	11.2.45	Suicide?
GL	Zickwolff	343 ID	Brittany/France	17.9.43	
GdI	Zorn, H.	XXXXVI PzK	Krassnaja/Orel/USSR	2.8.43	Air Attack
GL	Zutavern	18 PGD	Minsk/USSR	6.7.44	Suicide

CHRONOLOGICAL CASUALTY LIST
GERMAN GENERAL OFFICER DEATHS BY DATE

	Name	Unit/Higher HQ	Location Killed	Date
GL	von Speck	XVIII AK/9 Army/AG B	Pont sur Yonne/France	15.6.40
GL	von Prittwitz	15 PzD/Africa Corps	Tobruk/Africa	10.4.41
GL	Süssmann	7FlD/XI FlK	Aegina/Mediterranean	20.5.41
GM	Lancelle	121 ID/II AK/16 Army	Kraslawa/Duna/USSR	3.7.41
GM	von Weber	17 PzD/XXXXVII AK/2 PzGp	Krassnyj/USSR	20.7.41
GLdSS	Mülverstedt	4 SS/LI AK/18 Army	Luga/USSR	10.8.41
GM	Kalmukoff	31 ID/XII AK/2 Army	Swoncz/USSR	13.8.41
GO	von Schobert	11 Army/AG South	Nykolayiv/USSR	12.9.41
GM	Braun	68 ID/LV AK/6 Army	Kharkov/USSR	14.11.41
GdI	von Briesen, K.	LII AK/17 Army/AG South	Andrejewka/USSR	20.11.41
GM	Neumann-Silkow	15 PzD/Africa Corps	Derna/Africa	8.12.41
GM	Sümmermann	90 ID/Pz Army Africa	Mamali/Africa	10.12.41
GL	Bergmann	137 ID/XXXXIII AK/2 Pz Army	Sjawki/Kaluga/USSR	21.12.41
GL	Geitner	295 ID/XXXXIV AK/17 Army	Artemowsk/USSR	22.1.42
GL	Hewelke	339 ID/Army Group Center	Vitebsk/Bobruisk/USSR	1.42
GM	Berthold	31 ID/XXXXIII AK/4 Army	Juchnow/USSR	24.1.42
GL	Gabcke	294 ID/XVII AK/6 Army	Kharkov/USSR	22.3.42
GL	Himer	46 ID/XXXXII AK/11 Army	Crimea/USSR	23.3.42
GM	Hippler	329 ID/X AK/16 Army	Lake Ilmen/USSR	23.3.42
GM	Fisher, K.	267 ID/XX AK/4 Pz Army	Uljewo/Vyasma/USSR	31.3.42
GM	Scheidies	61 ID/I AK/18 Army	Gluschitza/USSR	7.4.42
GL	Rittau	129 ID/XXIII AK/9 Army	Martinowo/Rshev/USSR	22.8.42
GM	Mack	23 PzD/XXXX AK/1 Pz Army	Terek/Caucasus/USSR	26.8.42
GM	von Bismarck, G.	21 PzD/Africa Corps	El Alamein/Africa	31.8.42
GM	Buck	198 ID/LVII AK/17 Army	Kljutschewaja/USSR	6.9.42
GdPz	von Langermann und Erlencamp	XXIV PzK/2 Hung. Army/AG B	Storoshewoje/USSR	3.10.42
GM	von Randow	21 PzD/Africa Corps	Tripoli/Africa	21.12.42
GM	Koch, V.	323 ID/VII AK/2 Army	Voronezh/USSR	22.12.42
GM	von Reuss	62 ID/Army Det. Hollidt	Bokovskaya/Chir/USSR	22.12.42
GdA	Wandel	XXIV PzK/8 Ital. Army/AG B	Chilino/USSR	14.1.43
GL	Jahr	XXIV PzK/8 Ital. Army/AG B	Podgornoje/USSR	20.1.43
GL	Eibl	XXIV PzK/8 Ital. Army/AG B	Podgornoje/USSR	21.1.43
GL	von Hartmann	71 ID/LI AK/6 Army	Stalingrad/USSR	26.1.43
GL	Stempel	371 ID/IV AK/6 Army	Stalingrad/USSR	26.1.43
GL	Lechner, A.	377 ID/XIII AK/2 Army	Voronezh/USSR	29.1.43
GL	Bäntsch	82 ID/XIII AK/2 Army	Voronezh/USSR	31.1.43
GL	Angern	16 PzD/XI AK/6 Army	Stalingrad/USSR	2.2.43
GL	Fischer, W.	10 PzD/5 Pz Army	Mareth/Africa	5.2.43
GL	Haccius	46 ID/XXXXIX AK/17 Army	Taman/Caucasus/USSR	14.2.43
GdSS	Eicke	3 SS/SS PzK/4 Pz Army	Kharkov/USSR	26.2.43
GM	Thomas	999 ID/AG Africa	Mediterranean Sea	1.4.43
GL	Löweneck	39 ID/XXXXII AK	Petschenegi/USSR	14.5.43
GL	Rupp, E	97 JD/XXXXIV/17 Army	Kuban/USSR	30.5.43

GL	Schmidt, F	50 ID/XXXXIX AK/17 Army	Kuban/USSR	26.6.43
GL	Müller, R.	211 ID/LIII AK/2 Pz Army	Orel/USSR	16.7.43
GM	von Hünersdorff	6 PzD/III PzK/Army Det Kempf	Kharkov/USSR	17.7.43
GL	Schilling, W.	17 PzD/1 Pz Army	Doljenhaja/Isjum/USSR	21.7.43
GdI	Zorn, H.	XXXXVI PzK/9 Army/AG Center	Krassnaja/Orel/USSR	2.8.43
GL	Schmidt, G.	19 PzD/LII AK/4 Pz Army	Kharkov/USSR	7.8.43
GL	Kress	4 GebD/V AK/17 Army	Novorossijsk/USSR	11.8.43
GM	Recke	161 ID/XXXXII AK	Panskaje/Kharkov/USSR	15.8.43
GL	Renner	174 RID/Rear Area	Ozarow/USSR	26.8.43
GM	von Bülow, W.	111 ID/XXIX AK/6 Army	Obronoje/USSR	30.8.43
GL	Zickwolff	343 ID/XXV AK/7 Army	Brittany/France	17.9.43
GL	Kamecke	137 ID/XXXXVI AK/2 Pz Army	Kolpen/Dnjepr/USSR	16.10.43
GM	Sieberg	14 PzD/LVII AK/1 Pz Army	Kirovograd/USSR	2.11.43
GL	Roth	88 ID/VII AK/4 Pz Army	Zhitomir/USSR	6.11.43
GL	Szelinski	376 ID/XI AK/8 Army	Krementschug/USSR	9.12.43
GM	von Groddeck	161 ID/XXXXII AK	Breslau/Silesia	10.1.44
GM	Schulz, A.	7 PzD/XIII AK/4 Pz Army	Schepetowka/USSR	28.1.44
GM	von Wedel	10 LwF/III SS/18 Army	Dorpat/Estonia	5.2.44
GdA	Stemmermann, W.	XI AK/8 Army/AG South	Khil'ki/Cherkassy/USSR	18.2.44
GM	Gurran	23 ID/XXXXIII AK/16 Army	Opotschka/USSR	22.2.44
GMdSS	Schuldt	19 SS/VI SS/16 Army	Velikaya/USSR	15.3.44
GM	Krech	41 ID/LXVIII AK/AG E	Molei/Greece	27.4.44
GM	Gruner	111 ID/V AK/17 Army	Sevastopol/Crimea/USSR	12.5.44
GL	Richter, W.	263 ID/X AK/16 Army	Riga/Latvia	3.6.44
GL	Falley	91 LLD/LXXXIV AK/7 Army	Normandy/France	6.6.44
GdA	Marcks, E.	LXXXIV AK/7 Army/AG D	St Lo/Perriers/France	12.6.44
GMdSS	Witt	12 SS/I SS/7 Army	Venoix/Normandy/France	14.6.44
GL	Hellmich	243 ID/LXXXIV AK/7 Army	Cherbourg/Normandy	17.6.44
GM	Stegmann	77 ID/LXXXIV AK/7 Army	Briebeque/France	18.6.44
GM	Hahne	197 ID/VI AK/3 Pz Army	Vitebsk/USSR	24.6.44
GdA	Pfeiffer, G.	VI AK/3 Pz Army/AG Center	Beresina/USSR	6.6.44
GM	Wüstenhagen	256 ID/VI AK/3 Pz Army	Vitebsk/USSR	26.6.44
GL	Pistorious	4 LwF/LIII AK/3 Pz Army	Gankowitsch/Rwesh/USSR	27.6.44
GL	Philipp	134 ID/XXXV AK/9 Army	Bobruisk/USSR	27.6.44
GdA	Martinek	XXXIX PzK/4 Army/AG Center	Beresinow/USSR	28.6.44
GL	Schünemann	XXXIX PzK/4 Army/AG Center	Pagost/Beresina/USSR	29.6.44
GL	Peschel	6 LwF/LIII AK/3 Pz Army	Vitebsk/USSR	30.6.44
GL	Zutavern	18 PGD/XII AK/4 Army	Minsk/USSR	6.7.44
GM	Beutler	340 ID/XIII AK/4 Pz Army	Brody/Poland	21.7.44
GdI	Hauffe	XIII AK/1 Pz Army	L'vov/Poland	22.7.44
GLdSS	von Scholz, F.	11 SS/III SS/Army Det. Narva	Narva/Estonia	28.7.44
GL	von Drabich-Wächter	326 ID/II FsK/7 Army	Normandy/France	2.8.44
GL	Kraiss	352 ID/II FsK/7 Army	St-Lo/France	2.8.44
GL	Drescher	267 ID/XII AK/4 Army	Niemen River/USSR	13.8.44
GL	Arndt, E.	708 ID/II FsK/7 Army	Groghy/Aube/France	24.8.44
GL	de Salengre Drabbe	384 ID/XXX AK/6 Army	Tiraspol/Bessarabia	25.8.44
GM	von Eichstedt	294 ID/LII AK/6 Army	Guragalbina/Rumania	26.8.44
GdI	Mieth	IV AK/8 Army/AG S. Ukraine	Vutcani/Rumania	2.9.44

GdI	Laux	16 Army/AG North	Riga/Latvia	2.9.44
GM	Blümke	257 ID/XXX AK/6 Army	Tiraspol/Tighina	4.9.44
GM	Schmidt, A.	159 ID/IV LF/19 Army	Besancon/France	8.9.44
GL	Heinrichs	89 ID/LXXXVIII AK/1 Fs Army	Liege/Belgium	8.9.44
GM	Dürking	96 ID/XI SS/1 Pz Army	Sanok/Poland	11.9.44
GM	Crisolli	20 LwF/XIV AK/14 Army	Bologna/Italy	12.9.44
GM	von Schwerin, B.	207 SD/II AK/ Army Det. Narva	Dorpat/Estonia	17.9.44
GdSS	Phleps	V SS K/2 Pz Army/AG F	Arad/Rumania	21.9.44
GdI	Wegener	L AK/18 Army/AG North	Wolmar/Latvia	24.9.44
GdI	Schneckenburger	AK Belgrade	Belgrade/Yugoslavia	14.10.44
GL	Stettner von Grabenhofen	1 GebD/AK Belgrade	Belgrade/Yugoslavia	18.10.44
GdI	Priess	XXVII AK/4 Army/AG Center	Hasenrode/East Prussia	21.10.44
GL	Bässler, J.	242 ID/LXII AK/19 Army	Vienna/Austria	8.11.44
GM	Oschmann	338 ID/LXXXV AK/19 Army	Fraunbe/France	14.11.44
GM	Herold	10 PGD/AG A	Bochnia/Poland	28.11.44
GM	Möhring	276 ID/7 Army	Belfort/France	18.12.44
GL	Scherbening	406 ID/II FsK/1 Fs Army	Urft/Germany	18.12.44
GM	Kühme	Security Division	Hallschlag/Eifel	25.12.44
GM	Obenaus	545 ID/XI SS/17 Army	Jaslo/Poland	15.1.45
GM	von Hirschfeld	78 ID/XI SS/17 Army	Tarnow/Poland	18.1.45
GL	Rein	69 ID/XXVI AK/3 Pz Army	Schloßberg/East Prussia	18.1.45
GdI	Recknagel	XXXXII AK/4 Pz Army/AG A	Petrikau/Lodz/Poland	23.1.45
GdI	Block, J.	LVI PzK/9 Army/AG A	Kielce/Vistula/Poland	26.1.45
GM	Finger	291 ID/XXXXII AK/4 Pz Army	Czestochowa/Poland	27.1.45
GM	Kirschner	320 ID/XXXXIX AK/1 Pz Army	Saybusch/Poland	11.2.45
GMdSS	Rumohr	8 SS/IX SS/6 Army	Budapest/Hungary	11.2.45
GMdSS	Zehender	22 SS/IX SS/6 Army	Budapest/Hungary	11.2.45
GM	Schmidhuber	13 PzD/IX SS/6 Army	Budapest/Hungary	11.2.45
GL	Schmidt, K.	526 ID/1 Army	Aalsmeer/Holland	3.3.45
GM	Kossmala	344 ID/XI AK/1 Pz Army	Oberglogau/Silesia	5.3.45
GM	von Elverfeldt	9 PzD/LXXXI AK/15 Army	Cologne/Germany	6.3.45
GL	Rübel	163 ID/X SS/3 Pz Army	Schievelbein/Pommerania	8.3.45
GdI	von Krosigk	16 Army/AG Courland	Kanden/Courland	16.3.45
GMdSS	Augsberger	20 SS/1 Pz Army/AG Center	Grottkau/Silesia	17.3.45
SFdSS	Klingenberg	17 SS/XIII SS/1 Army	Herxheim/Germany	22.3.45
GL	von Rost	44 ID/IV AK/8 Army	Stuhlweissenburg/Hungary	23.3.45
GM	Möckel	16 ID/LXXXX AK/1 Army	Karlsruhe/Germany	24.3.45
GL	Betzel	4 PzD/XXXXVI AK/2 Army	Danzig	27.3.45
GL	Löwrick, K.	542 VGD/XXIII AK/2 Army	Pillau/East Prussia	8.4.45
GM	Sudau	548 ID/IX AK	Königsberg/East Prussia	9.4.45
GL	Mickl	392 ID/LXXXXVII AK	Vratnik Pass/Yugoslavia	10.4.45
GM	Seidel, E.	257 VGD/LXIV AK/19 Army	Dobel Wildbach/Germany	11.4.45
GM	Haus	50 ID/LV AK	Pillau/East Prussia	16.4.45
GM	Lang, J.	95 ID/IX AK	Pillau/East Prussia	16.4.45
GM	Erhard	7 Flak/III Flak Corps	Düsseldorf/Germany	17.4.45
GL	Hundt	1 Ski/XI AK	Troppau/Czechoslovakia	17.4.45
GL	Källner	XXIV PzK/1 Pz Army/AG Center	Sokolniza/Bohemia	18.4.45
GdPz	Decker	XXXIX PzK/12 Army	Wendhausen/Germany	21.4.45
GFM	Model	Army Group B/OB West	Duisburg/Germany	21.4.45

GL	Jost	42 JD/LXXVI AK/10 Army	Villadosa/Italy	22.4.45
GL	Pfeifer, H.	65 ID/XIV AK/14 Army	Finale/Italy	22.4.45
GM	Wengler	83 ID/AK Hela	Pillau/East Prussia	25.4.45
GM	Domansky	50 ID/LV AK	Pillau/East Prussia	26.4.45
GM	Henke, K.	290 ID/II AK/18 Army	Pillau/East Prussia	27.4.45
GM	Scholze	20 PGD/XI SS/9 Army	Potsdam/Berlin/Germany	28.4.45
GM	Sieckenius	391 SD/V SS/9 Army	Markish-Buchholz/Germany	28.4.45
GM	Strahammer	114 JD/LI AK/14 Army	Italy	2.5.45
GM	von Siegroth	712 ID/XI SS/9 Army	Halbe/Berlin/Germany	2.5.45
GdSS	Kleinheisterkamp	XI SS/9 Army	Halbe/Berlin/Germany	2.5.45
GM	von Roden	286 SD/9 Army	Berlin/Germany	3.5.45
GLdSS	Ostendorff	2 SS/II SS	Bad Aussee/Austria	4.5.45
GL	Baade	LXXXI AK/15 Army/AG B	Segeberg/Schleswig	8.5.45
Gdl	von Erdmannsdorff, W.	LXXXXI AK/AG E	Laibach/Yugoslavia	8.5.45
GL	Stephan, F.	104 JD/LXXXXI AK	Carinthia/Austria	8.5.45
SFdSS	Petersen	18 SS/VIII AK/17 Army	Pilsen/Czechoslovakia	9.5.45
GL	von Bodenhausen	L AK/16 Army/AG Courland	Frauenberg/Courland	9.5.45
GM	Bader	97 JD/XXXXIX AK/1 Pz Army	Prosnitz/Czechoslovakia	9.5.45
GMdSS	Freitag	14 SS/I Kav/2 Pz Army	Andra/Austria	10.5.45
GdSS	Krüger, F.W.	V SS/9 Army/AG Vistula	Austria	10.5.45
GL	Baltzer	182 ID/LXXII/8 Army	Prague/Czechoslovakia	10.5.45
GM	Krämer	11 Flak/I Flak Corps	Rattaj/Czechoslovakia	11.5.45
GdSS	Krüger, W.	VI SS/16 Army/AG Courland	Courland/Latvia	20.5.45
GM	von Nostitz-Wallwitz	24 PzD/XXVI AK/4 Army	Eckernförde/Germany	31.5.45
GdPz	Fehn, G	XV GebK/AG E	Yugoslavia	5.6.45
GL	Schröck	192 ID	Lüneberg/Germany	1945
GL	von Thadden	1 ID/XXVI AK	Vordingborg/Denmark	5.45

SOURCES AND REFERENCES

Achlasov, V.I. and Pavlovich, N.B., *Soviet Naval Operations in the Great Patriotic War 1941-1945*, Annapolis, Maryland: Naval Institute Press, 1973.

After The Battle, Volume 72, London: After The Battle Magazine, 1989.

Angolia, LTC John R., *For Führer and Fatherland, Military, Political and Civil Awards of the Third Reich, Volumes 1 & 2*. San Jose, CA: R. James Bender Publishing, 1976.

Angolia, LTC John R., *On the Field of Honor; A History of the Knight's Cross Bearers, Volumes 1 & 2,* San Jose, CA: R. James Bender Publishing, 1979.

Barnett, Correlli, *Hitler's Generals*, New York: Grove Weidenfeld, 1989.

Beebe, Gilbert and DeBakey, Michael E., *Battle Casualties: Incidence, Mortality, and Logistic Considerations*, Springfield, IL: Charles C. Thomas, 1952.

Beekman, Frans & Kurowski, Franz, *Der Kampf um die Festung Holland*, Herford, FRG: E.S. Mittler Verlag, 1981.

Bender, Roger James, and Law, Richard D., *Uniforms, Organization and History of the Afrikakorps*, San Jose, CA: R. James Bender Publishing, 1986.

Bender, Roger James, and Odegard, Warren W., *Uniforms, Organization and History of the Panzertruppe*, San Jose, CA: R. James Bender Publishing, 1980.

Bennett, Ralph, *ULTRA in the West*, New York: Scribner's, 1979.

Blumentritt, Günther, "The German Armies of 1914 and 1939", U.S. Army Historical Division Study MS# B-296, Washington, D.C.: Office of the Chief of Military History, 1947.

Böhm, Erwin, *Geschichte der 25. Division*, Stuttgart, FRG: Kameradenhilfswerk 25 e.V.

Bradley, Dermot, Hildebrand, Karl-Friedrich and Rövekamp, Markus, *Die Generale des Heeres 1921-1945, Band 2*, Osnabrück, Germany: Biblio Verlag, 1993.

Bradley, Dermot & Schulze-Kossens, Richard, *Tätigkeitsbericht des Chefs des Heerespersonalamtes General der Infanterie Rudolf Schmundt*, Osnabrück, FRG: Biblio Verlag, 1984.

Brett-Smith, Richard, *Hitler's Generals*, San Rafael, CA: Presidio Press, 1977.

Breuer, William B., *Hitler's Fortress Cherbourg: The Conquest of a Bastion*, New York: Stein and Day, 1984.

Buchner, Alex, *Ostfront 1944: The German Defensive Battles on the Russian Front 1944*, West Chester, PA: Schiffer Publishing, 1988.

Buchner, Alex, *Ostfront 1944: Tscherkassy, Tarnopol, Krim, Witebsk, Bobruisk, Brody, Jassy, Kischinew*, Friedberg, FRG: Podzun-Pallas-Verlag, 1988.

Carell, Paul, *Hitler Moves East, 1941-1943*, Boston: Little, Brown and Company, 1968.

Carell, Paul, *Der Russlandkrieg: Fotografiert von Soldaten*, Frankfurt, FRG: Ullstein, 1968.

Carell, Paul, *Scorched Earth*, London: George G. Harrap & Co, 1970.

Carell, Paul, *The Foxes of the Desert*, New York: E.P. Dutton, 1961.

Conze, Dr. Werner, *Die Geschichte der 291. Infanterie Division 1940-1945*, Bad Nauheim, FRG: Hans-Henning Podzun Verlag, 1953.

Cooper, Matthew, *The German Army 1933 - 1945*, New York: Stein and Day, 1978.

Cooper, Matthew, *The Nazi War Against Soviet Partisans*, New York: Stein and Day, 1979.

Craig, William, *Enemy at the Gates: The Battle for Stalingrad*, New York: E.P. Dutton, 1973.

Creveld, Martin van, *Command in War*, Cambridge, Massachusetts: Harvard University Press, 1985.

Creveld, Martin van, *Fighting Power: German and U.S. Army Performance, 1939-1945*, London: Arms and Armour Press, 1983.

Crow, Duncan, *Armored Fighting Vehicles of Germany*, New York: ARCO Publishing, 1978.

Der Schicksalsweg der 13. Panzer-Division, 1939-1945, Friedberg, FRG: Podzun-Pallas-Verlag, 1986.

Dettmer, Friedrich, Jaus, Otto & Tolkmitt, Helmut, *Die 44. Infanterie-Division, Reichs-Grenadier-Division Hoch-und Deutschmeister 1938-1945*, Friedberg, FRG: Podzun-Pallas-Verlag.

Dupuy, T.N., *A Genius for War: The German Army and General Staff, 1807-1945*, Fairfax, Virginia: Hero Books, 1984.

Dupuy, R. Ernest and Trevor N., *The Encyclopedia of Military History*, New York: Harper & Row, 1970.

Engelmann, Joachim, *Zitadelle: Die grösste Panzerschlacht im Osten 1943*, Friedberg, FRG: Podzun-Pallas-verlag.

English, John A., *A Perspective on Infantry*, New York: Praeger, 1981.

Erickson, John, *The Road to Berlin*, Boulder, Colorado: Westview Press, 1983.

Fellgiebel, Walther-Peer, *Die Träger des Ritterkreuzes des Eisernen Kreuzes 1939-1945*, Friedberg, FRG: Podzun-Pallas-Verlag, 1986. (& Ergänzungsband)

Fischer, Hubert, *Der deutsche Sanitätsdienst 1921-1945*, Band 4. Osnabrueck, FRG: Biblio Verlag, 1985.

Folttmann, Josef and Hanns Möller-Witten, *Opfergang der Generale*, Berlin: Bernard & Gräfe, 1959.

Geyer, Hermann, *Das IX. Armeekorps im Ostfeldzug 1941*, Neckargemünd, FRG: Scharnhorst Buchkameradschaft, 1969.

Geyer, Michael, *"The Transformation of the German Officer Corps"*, Ann Arbor, MI: University of Michigan.

Görlitz, Walter, *History of the German General staff 1657-1945*, New York: Praeger, 1953.

Görlitz, Walter, *Paulus and Stalingrad*, New York: The Citadel Press, 1963.

Gräser, Gerhard, *Zwischen Kattegat und Kaukasus, Weg und Kämpfe der 198. Infanterie-Division 1939-1945*, Tuebingen, FRG: Traditionsverband ehemaligen 198. Infanterie-Division, 1961.

Grams, Rolf, *Die 14. Panzer-Division, 1940-1945*, Friedberg, FRG: Podzun-Pallas-Verlag, 1986.

Guderian, Heinz and Kurt Zeitzler, "Comments on P-41a to P-041hh", U.S. Army Historical Division Study MS# P-041ll, Washington, D.C: Office of the Chief of Military History, 1953.

Hästrup, *Jörgen, European Resistance Movements, 1939-1945: A Complete History*, Westport, Conneticutt: Meckler Publishing, 1981.

Halder, Franz, "Control of the German Army General Staff", U.S. Army Historical Division Study MS# P 041d, (Washington, D.C.: Office of the Chief of Military History), 1952.

Handbook on German Military Forces, Gaithersburg, Maryland: The Military Press, 1970.

Hardesty, Von, *Red Phoenix, The Rise of Soviet Air Power, 1941-1945*, Washington, D.C: Smithsonian Institution Press, 1982.

Hastings, Max, *Overlord: D-Day and the Battle for Normandy*, New York: Simon and Schuster, 1984.

Haupt, Werner, *Das War Kurland*, Friedberg, FRG: Podzun-Pallas-Verlag, 1987.

Haupt, Werner, *Geschichte der 134. Infanterie Division*, Bad Kreuznach, FRG: Kameradenkreis der 134. Infanterie Division, 1971.

Haupt, Werner, *Heeresgruppe Nord*, 1941-1945, Dorheim, FRG: Verlag Hans-Henning Podzun, 1966.

Haupt, Werner, *Kriegsschauplatz Italien, 1943-1945*, Stuttgart, FRG: Motorbuch Verlag, 1977.

Healy, Mark, *Kursk 1943: The Tide Turns in the East*, London: Osprey, 1992.

Heckmann, Wolf, *Rommel's War in Africa*, Garden City, NY: Doubleday & Company, 1981.

Held, Walter, *Verbände und Truppen der deutschen Wehrmacht und Waffen-SS im Zweiten Weltkrieg*, Eine Bibliographie der deutschsprachigen Nachkriegsliteratur, Band 1-3, Osnabrück, Germany: Biblio Verlag, 1989.

Hinze, Rolf, *Das Ostfront-Drama 1944*, Stuttgart, FRG: Motorbuch Verlag, 1988.

Hinze, Rolf, *Der Zusammenbruch der Heeresgruppe Mitte im Osten 1944*, Stuttgart, FRG: Motorbuch Verlag, 1980.

Hinze, Rolf, *Die 19. Panzer-Division, 1939-1945*, Friedberg, FRG: Podzun-Pallas-Verlag.

Hnilicka, Karl, *Das Ende auf dem Balkan 1944/45*, Göttingen, FRG: Musterschmidt Verlag, 1970.

Hoffmann, Joachim, *Kaukasien 1942/43*, Freiburg, Germany: Rombach Verlag, 1991.

Hoffmann, Peter, *Hitler's Personal Security*, Cambridge, Massachusetts: The MIT Press, 1979.

Hofmann, Rudolf, "German Efficiency Report System", U.S. Army Historical Division Study MS# P-134. Washington, D.C: Office of the Chief of Military History, 1952.

Hossbach, Friedrich, *Infanterie im Ostfeldzug 1941/42*, Osterode, Germany: Giebel & Oehlschlaegel, 1951.

Husemann, Friedrich, *Die guten Glaubens waren; Geschichte der SS-Polizei-Division, Band I - III*, Osnabrueck, FRG: Munin Verlag, 1984.

Kaltenegger, Roland, *Deutsche Gebirgsjäger im Zweiten Weltkrieg*, Stuttgart, FRG: Motorbuch Verlag, 1977.

Kaltenegger, Roland, *Die Deutsche Gebirgsjäger 1935-1945*, Muenchen, FRG: Universitas Verlag, 1989.

Kaltenegger, Roland, *Gebirgssoldaten unter dem Zeichen des "Enzian", Schicksalsweg und Kampf der 4. Gebirgs-Division 1940-1945*, Graz, Austria: Leopold Stocker Verlag, 1983.

Kaltenegger, Roland, *Operationszone "Adriatisches Küstenland"*, Graz, Austria: Leopold Stocker Verlag, 1993.

Keilig, Wolf, *Das Deutsche Heer, 1939-1945, Band I-III*, Bad Nauheim, FRG: Podzun-Verlag, 1956.

Keilig, Wolf, *Die Generale des Heeres*, Friedberg, FRG: Podzun-Pallas-Verlag, 1983.

Keilig, Wolf, *Rangliste des Deutschen Heeres, 1944/45*, Friedberg, FRG: Podzun-Pallas-Verlag.

Kemp, Anthony, *German Commanders of World War II*, London: Osprey, 1982.

Kielmansegg, Graf, *Der Fritschprozess 1938*, Hamburg, FRG: Hoffmann und Campe Verlag, 1949.

Kiriakopoulos, G.C., *Ten Days to Destiny: The Battle for Crete*, New York: Franklin Watts, 1985.

Kleikamp, Helmut, "German Army High Command, The Army Personnel Office", U.S. Army Historical Division Study MS# P 041hh, (Washington, D.C.: Office of the Chief of Military History), 1952.

Knobelsdorff, Otto von, *Geschichte der niedersächischen 19. Panzer-Division, 1939-1945*, Friedberg, FRG: Podzun-Pallas-Verlag, 1958.

Köhl, Robert Lewis, *The Black Corps*, Madison, WI: University of Wisconsin Press, 1983.

Krätschmer, Ernst-Günther, *Die Ritterkreuzträger der Waffen-SS*, Oldendorf, FRG: K.W. Schuetz Verlag, 1982.

Kuhn, Volkmar, *Rommel in the Desert*, West Chester, PA: Schiffer Publishing, 1991.

Landwehr, Richard, *Narva 1944: The Waffen-SS and the Battle for Europe*, Silver Spring, Maryland: Bibliophile Legion Books, 1981.

Lasch, Otto, *So Fiel Königsberg*, Stuttgart, FRG: Motorbuch Verlag, 1976.

Law, Richard D. & Luther, Craig W.H., *Rommel: A Narrative & Pictorial History*,

San Jose, CA: R. James Bender Publishing, 1980.

Leixner, Leo, *Generaloberst Eugen Ritter von Schobert: Lebensbild eines deutschen Armeeführers*, München: Zentralverlag der NSDAP, 1942.

Lenfeld, Erwin & Thomas, Franz, *Die Eichenlaub-träger, 1940-1945*, Wiener Neustadt, Austria: Weilburg Verlag, 1983.

Lewin, Ronald, *The Life and Death of the Afrika Korps*, New York: Quadrangle, 1977.

Liddel Hart, B.H., *The Rommel Papers*, New York: Da Capo, 1953.

Lucas, James, *Last Days of the Third Reich*, New York: William Morrow and Company, 1986.

Lucas, James & Cooper, Matthew, *Panzer Grenadiers*, London: MacDonald and Jane's, 1977.

Lucas, James, *War on the Eastern Front*, New York: Stein and Day, 1979.

Luther, Craig W.H., *Blood and Honor: The History of the 12th SS Panzer Division "Hitler Youth," 1943-1945*, San Jose, CA: R. James Bender Publishing, 1987.

MacDonald, Callum, *The Killing of SS Obergruppenführer Reinhard Heydrich*, New York: The Free Press, 1989.

Macksey, Kenneth, *Kesselring: The Making of the Luftwaffe*, New York: David McKay Company, 1978.

Madej, W. Victor, *German Army Order of Battle, 1939-1945, Volumes I, II, & III*, Allentown, PA: Game Marketing Company, 1981.

Maier, Georg, *Drama zwischen Budapest und Wien*, Osnabrueck, FRG: Munin Verlag, 1985.

Majdalany, Fred, *The Fall of Fortress Europe*, Garden City, NY: Doubleday & Company, 1968.

Manteufel, Hasso von, *Die 7. Panzer Division im Zweiten Weltkrieg*, Friedberg, FRG: Podzun-Pallas-Verlag, 1986.

Manteuffel, Hasso von, "Fast Mobile and Armored Troops." U.S. Army Historical Division Study MS# B-036, Washington, D.C: Office of the Chief of Military History, 1945.

Mehner, Kurt, *Die Geheimentagesberichte der Deutschenwehrmachtführung im Zweiten Weltkrieg 1939-1945, Band 2-12*, Osnabrueck, Germany: Biblio Verlag, 1992.

Meyer, Hubert, *Kriegsgeschichte der 12. SS-Panzerdivision "Hitlerjugend", Band I & II*, Osnabrueck, FRG: Munin Verlag, 1982.

Meyer-Detring, Wilhelm, Die 137. *Infanteriedivision im Mittelabschnitt der Ostfront*, Nördlingen, FRG: C.H. Beck'schen, 1966.

Mitcham, Samuel W., Hitler's Legions, *The German Army Order of Battle, World War II*, New York: Stein and Day, 1985.

Mitcham, Samuel and Friedrich von Stauffenberg, *The Battle of Sicily*, New York: Orion Books, 1991.

Model, Hansgeorg, Der deutsche Generalstabsoffizier, Frankfurt, FRG: Bernard & Graefe Verlag, 1968.

Möller-Witten, Hanns, *Mit dem Eichenlaub zum Ritterkreuz*, Rastatt, FRG: Erich Pabel Verlag, 1962.

Müller, G. und F.W., Guttmann, *Geschichte der 207. und 281. Infanterie Division*, Kiel, FRG: 1958.

Müller-Hillebrand, Burkhart, *Das Heer 1933-1945, Band II & Band III*, Frankfurt: E.S. Mittler & Sohn, 1956.

Munson, Kenneth, *German Aircraft of World War 2 in Colour*, Poole, England: Blandford Press, 1978.

Neumann, Joachim, *Die 4. Panzer-Division 1938-1943, Band 1*, Bonn, FRG: Selbstverlag, 1985.

Niepold, Gerd, *Battle for White Russia*, London: Brassey's, 1987.

Orgill, Douglas, *The Gothic Line*, New York: W.W. Norton & Company, 1967.

Ott, Ernst-Ludwig, *Die Spielhahnjäger 1940-1945, Bilddokumentation der 97. Jäger-Division*, Friedberg, FRG: Podzun-Pallas-Verlag, 1982.

Ott, Ernst, *Jäger am Feind*, München, FRG: Selbstverlag, 1966.

Paul, Wolfgang, *Brennpunkte, Die Geschichte der 6. Panzerdivision (1. leichte), 1937-1945*, Krefeld, FRG: Hoentges-Verlag, 1977.

Pohlmann, Hartwig, *Geschichte der 96. Infanterie-Division 1939-1945*, Bad Nauheim, FRG: Hans-Henning Podzun Verlag, 1959.

Rangliste des Deutschen Reichsheeres, *Nach dem Stande vom 1. Mai 1929*, Berlin: E.S. Mittler & Sohn, 1929.

Rebentisch, Ernst, *Zum Kaukasus und zu den Tauern, die Geschichte der 23. Panzer-Division, 1939-1945*, Forchheim, FRG: Sperl, 1982.

Ryan, Cornelius, *The Last Battle*, New York: Simon and Schuster, 1966.

Ryan, Cornelius, *The Longest Day, June 6, 1944*, New York: Simon and Schuster, 1959.

Saft, Ulrich, *Krieg in der Heimat; Das bittere Ende zwischen Weser und Elbe*, Langenhagen, FRG: Verlag-Saft.

Scheurig, Bodo, *Free Germany; The National Committee and the League of German Officers.*, Middleton, Connecticutt: Wesleyan University Press, 1969.

Schimak, Anton, Lamprecht, Karl & Dettmer, Friedrich, *Die 44. Infanterie Division*, Wien, Austria: Austria Press, 1969.

Schmidt, August, *Geschichte der 10. Division, 1933-1945*, Bad Nauheim, FRG: Podzun-Verlag, 1963.

Schneider, Jost W., *Their Honor was Loyalty!*, San Jose, CA: R. James Bender Publishing, 1977.

Schröter, Heinz, *Stalingrad*, New York: E.P. Hutton, 1958.

Seemen, Gerhard von, *Die Ritterkreuzträger, 1939-1945*, Friedberg, FRG: Podzun-Verlag, 1976.

Selz, Barbara, *Das Grüne Regiment*, Freiburg, FRG: Otto Kehrer Verlag, 1970.

Senger und Etterlin, Jr., Dr. F.M. von, *Die 24. Panzer-Division, 1939-1945*, Neckargemünd, FRG: Kurt Vowinckel Verlag, 1962.

Shores, Christopher, Ring, Hans & Hess, William, *Tunesien 42/43, Luftkämpfe uber Fels und Wüste*, Stuttgart, FRG: Motorbuch Verlag, 1981.

Sigailis, Arthur, *Latvian Legion*, San Jose, CA: R. James Bender Publishing, 1986.

Sorge, Martin K., *The Other Price of Hitler's War*, New York: Greenwood Press, 1986.

Spires, David Nelson, "The Career of the Reichswehr Officer", (Doctor of Philosophy Dissertation: University of Washington), 1979.

Stahl, Generalleutnant Friedrich, *Heereseinteilung 1939*, Friedberg, FRG: Podzun-Pallas-Verlag.

Stöber, Hans, *Die Eiserne Faust: Bildband und Chronik der 17. SS-Panzergrenadierdivision Götz von Berlichingen*, Neckargemünd, FRG: Kurt Vowinkel Verlag, 1966.

Stöber, Hans, *Die lettischen Divisionen im VI. SS-Armeekorps*, Osnabrück, FRG: Munin-Verlag, 1981.

Stumpf, Reinhard, *Die Wehrmacht Elite: Rang- und Herkunftßtruktur der deutschen Generale und Admirale 1933-1945*, Boppard am Rhein, FRG: Harald Boldt Verlag, 1982.

Sydnor, Charles W. Jr., *Soldiers of Destruction: The SS Death's Head Division, 1933-1945*, Princeton, NJ: Princeton University Press, 1977.

Taylor, Telford, *The March of Conquest: The German Victories in Western Europe - 1940*, New York: Simon and Schuster, 1958.

Tessin, Georg, *Verbände und Truppen der deutschen Wehrmacht und Waffen-SS im Zweiten Weltkrieg 1939-1945, Band I - XIV*, Osnabrück, FRG: Biblio Verlag, 1979.

Thomas, Franz & Wegmann, Günter, *Die Ritterkreuzträger der Deutschen Wehrmacht 1939-1945, Teil III: Infanterie, Band 1: A-Be, Band 2: Bi-Bo*, Osnabrück, FRG: Biblio Verlag, 1987.

Thomas, Franz & Wegmann, Günter, *Die Ritterkreuzträger der Deutschen Wehrmacht 1939-1945, Teil VI: Die Gebirgstruppe, Band 1: A-K*, Osnabrück, FRG: Biblio Verlag, 1993.

Tieke, Wilhelm, *Das Ende Zwischen Oder und Elbe: Der Kampf um Berlin 1945*, Stuttgart, FRG: Motorbuch Verlag, 1981.

Tieke, Wilhelm, *Im Feürsturm letzter Kriegsjahre*, Osnabrück, FRG: Munin Verlag, 1975.

Tieke, Wilhelm, *Tragödie um die Treü: Kampf und Untergang des III. (germ) SS-Panzer-Korps*, Osnabrück, FRG: Munin Verlag, 1971.

Tiemann, Reinhard, *Geschichte der 83. Infanterie-Division 1939-1945*, Friedberg, FRG: Podzun-Pallas-Verlag, 1986.

Tys-Krokhmaliuk, Yuriy, *UPA Warfare in Ukraine*, New York: Vantage Press, 1972.

Velten, Wilhelm, *Vom Kugelbaum zur Handgranate, der Weg der 65. Infanterie Division*, Neckargemünd, FRG: Kurt Vorwinkel Verlag, 1974.

Wagner, Ray, *The Soviet Air Force in World War II*, Garden City, New York: Doubleday & Company, 1973.

Werthen, Wolfgang, *Geschichte der 16. Panzer-Division*, Friedberg, FRG: Podzun-Pallas-Verlag, 1958.

Whitaker, W. Denis, *Rhineland*, New York: St. Martin's Press, 1989.

Ziemke, Earl F, *Battle for Berlin: End of the Third Reich*, New York: Ballantine Books, 1968.

Ziemke, Earl F. and Bauer, Magna E., *Moscow to Stalingrad: Decision in the East*, Washington, D.C.: U.S. Government Printing Office, 1987.

Ziemke, Earl F., *Stalingrad to Berlin: The German Defeat in the East*, Washington, D.C.: U.S. Government Printing Office, 1966.

Ziemke, Earl F., *The German Northern Theater of Operations, 1940-1945*, Washington, D.C.: U.S. Government Printing Office, 1959.

Zivkovic, Georg, *Heer- und Flottenführer der Welt*, Osnabrück, FRG: Biblio Verlag, 1971.

Zhukov, G.K., *The Memoirs of Marshal Zhukov*, New York: Delacorte Press, 1971.

Zydowitz, Kurt von, *Die Geschichte der 58. Infanterie-Division 1939-1945*. Kiel, FRG: Hans-Henning Verlag, 1952.

329. (Hammer) Infanterie Division Erinnerungen aus dem Kampfgeschen 1942-1945, Traditionsband der Ehemaligen 329. Infanterie Division. Düsseldorf, FRG: 1968.

Microfilm:

XXXXVI Panzerkorps, Ia, "Kriegstagebuch", 2.8.43, National Archives Microfilm Publication T-314, Roll 1086, Washington, D.C.: The National Archives and Records Service, General Services Administration, 1970.

L Armeekorps, Ia, "Kriegstagebuch", 24.9.44, National Archives Microfilm Publication T-314, Roll 1249, Washington, D.C.: The National Archives and Records Service, General Services Administration, 1970.

LII Armeekorps, Ia, "Kriegstagebuch", 20.11.41, National Archives Microfilm Publication T-314, Roll 1276, Washington, D.C.: The National Archives and Records Service, General Services Administration, 1970.

39 Infanterie Division, Ia, "Kriegstagebuch", 14.5.43, National Archives Microfilm Publication T-315, Roll 907, Washington, D.C.: The National Archives and Records Service, General Services Administration, 1970.

50 Infanterie Division, Ia, "Kriegstagebuch", 26.6.43, National Archives Microfilm Publication T-315, Roll 948, Washington, D.C.: The National Archives and Records Service, General Services Administration, 1970.

61 Infanterie Division, Ia, "Kriegstagebuch", 7.4.42, National Archives Microfilm Publication T-315, Roll 1016, Washington, D.C.: The National Archives and

Records Service, General Services Administration, 1970.

129 Infanterie Division, Ia, "Kriegstagebuch", 22.8.42, National Archives Microfilm Publication T-315, Roll 1376, Washington, D.C.: The National Archives and Records Service, General Services Administration, 1970.

174 Reserve Infanterie Division, Ia, "Kriegstagebuch", 26.8.43, National Archives Microfilm Publication T-315, Roll 1536, Washington, D.C.: The National Archives and Records Service, General Services Administration, 1970.

PERSONNEL INDEX

W

Z

Eric von Manstein at a field funeral.

Hitler speaking at the funeral of Heydrich.

Hermann Göring speaking at the funeral of Ernst Udet.

The gravesite of Ernst Udet.

State funeral of Ritter von Schobert, 23 September, 1941.

Werner Mölders funeral.

PHOTOGRAPHIC CREDITS

All the photographs in this book have been provided by the Bundesarchiv except for the following:

The Author – pages; vi, 23, 24, 26, 38, 153, 177, 178, 179, 180, 181.

ECPA – page 158.